OMNIBUS

OMNIBUS

Coming of Age Out West in the Early 20th Century

ELIZABETH CHAMBERS

1966

Two Friends
Sebastopol, CA, USA

Library of Congress Control Number: 2022902770

ISBN 978-0-578-35878-9

Editing by Heather Ross
Cover and interior design by Jazmin Welch

ELIZABETH CHAMBERS AT
PACIFIC GROVE | *1913*

CONTENTS

BOOK *of* ROY

ELIZABETH WAS MY MATERNAL GRANDMOTHER, and *Omnibus*, which she wrote when she was in her sixties, is her memoir of her life, an offering to her three children: Laurie, Arnold and Beva. More accurately, it is a memoir of roughly the first half of her life, as she ends this work at the death of her first husband, Roy, my grandfather, who died when she was still in her thirties and my mother, Beva, was nine.

Elizabeth wrote *Omnibus* so her children, and descendants, would know about the family into which we were born, and be aware of the experiences, attitudes and history that may shape us.

This reminds me of something that tree and soil scientists have recently discovered about underground networks of mycelium, which attach to tree roots, feed water and nutrients to trees and receive tree sap sugars in return. We now know that these mycelium networks connect groves of trees and can sense when certain trees need more resources, which they then divert from other trees to the struggling one. This knowledge begs the question: is a tree a separate being, or is a networked grove of trees, linked together through mycelium strands, a larger organism? It's a different way of looking at the world, of defining identity. Elizabeth's memoir includes the mycelium strands that connect her to her family.

She also was reflecting on how much change there is in a lifetime. She used to say that she couldn't imagine a life with more changes than she experienced, going from horse and buggies to a man on the moon. Although her descriptions of the San Francisco Bay Area and Montana in the early days of the twentieth century seem like a different world, change was just getting warmed up.

There are a few references in this work that reflect the prejudices and attitudes toward people of other races that were prevalent during Elizabeth's lifetime. I have left them in, as they reflect that era and help us see how attitudes have changed over time. For me, they make me wonder what attitudes and prejudices I carry that will seem startling to my descendants. You may also notice unusual spellings or, in some cases, spelling errors in transcribed correspondence; these have also been retained to keep the original voices intact.

I'm publishing this edition of *Omnibus* in memory of my mother, Beva, who died at age 92 in September 2020. She was another strong woman in this family.

Mark Farmer
Sebastopol, California, March 2022

OMNIBUS!

"Why *that* title?" you ask.

"What *better* title?" I ask.

After stating the primary use of the word "omnibus," which is to signify a capacious and, usually, a public conveyance, *Webster's Seventh Collegiate Dictionary* (1965) defines the word's secondary meaning as "a book containing reprints of a number of works."

"This book a 'reprint'?" you question.

"Yes, a reprint," say I.

This book is but the "reprint" of the writings of lives, originally printed in years of living by Irene, Arthur, Roy and

ELIZABETH.

San Luis Obispo,
California.

October 1966

FOREWORD
***

LAURIE'S NUDGE DID IT!—To be sure, I had thought of the project. I had even *intended* to get at it. In actuality, though, I had not lifted a finger—Laurie's letter arrived at The Rogue saying, in essence, "I do wish you would make some notes on the stories Grannie used to tell of her youth. I can't quite remember them." It was 1964 and Laurie, my firstborn, was deliberating offering me an agreeable chore to compensate for my lack of vigor in fishing the river for salmon ten hours EACH day.

"Grannie" was Irene—Irene Laurie. Irene was excitement, Irene was drama. Irene was fabulous. Little wonder that I had worshiped her. Even less wonder that I had been almost out of my teens before I became aware of anything not in Irene's immediate orbit. Irene most assuredly would be the star of my drama—the principal character of the story I would compile for my children about their forebears. Of course, there would necessarily be ramifications—many ramifications.

Some of the marvelous tales of the Gay Nineties that Irene used to spin, like any broken web, were but tattered fragments hanging in my memory. Others I knew so well—had known so long—that they seemed a part of my very being. With a shock I realized that Beva knew none of these. Arnold probably did not know them either. Yet oddly enough my initial impetus to put memories on paper—long, long before Laurie's prodding—had come indirectly from Arnold.

Writing the routine mandatory high school senior English autobiography, under six or seven assigned chapter headings, Arnold had put more than half his literary effort in the first chapter, "Family Background." He had remembered incidents that Irene had told him which I either had never heard or had blankly forgotten. He had devoted page after page to great-grandparents on whom he

iv

had never cast an eye. He had divulged a depth of knowledge of Pilling family events a generation or two removed. Finally, thousands upon thousands of words farther on, he had worked down to his mother. Just eight words had sufficed him to deal with me, "My mother had a short and uneventful childhood."

At the time I had thought my history and accomplishments as portrayed by my son simply hilarious. How *could* one childhood be shorter or longer than another? Perhaps even then, amidst my hilarity, had been conceived the embryonic idea that if I, myself, were to set down some remembered incidents of my "short" childhood they would *not* be "uneventful" because, perforce, they would mark the great flow of history. How different from his childhood, how *infinitely* different from the childhood of *his children*, would be the social, the cultural, the economic, the material surroundings and incidents of the days of my childhood!

In truth I did agree with Arnold about the importance of family history. My story would reach far back for its beginnings. But there again Arnold gave me pause. With his remarkable memory, with his habit of jotting down documentary historic data, accurate as I would try to make my story, he would be liable to disprove my every date—plus a salient fact or two. No matter! MY version of the family's past would I write.

"Someone[1] has said, 'EVERY PERSON IS
AN OMNIBUS IN WHICH ALL HIS ANCES-
TORS ARE RIDING'."

From *Serendipity*

by J. Wallace Hamilton

ELIZABETH AND IRENE
CHAMBERS | *1915*

1 The "someone" was Oliver Wendell Holmes in 1867. In Chapter III of his novel, *The Guardian Angel*, a rather long passage (not directly quoted) is often summarized as "We are omnibuses
in which our ancestors ride." *The Guardian Angel* and Holmes' other two novels, unsuccessful at
the time of publication (1861 to 1885), recently have been called the first American psychological
novels.

BOOK
of
IRENE

TO HEAR IRENE TELL THE STORY one sensed that the *Mayflower* had barely put out her shallop to discover Plymouth Rock so that the hardy Pilgrim Fathers aboard her could handily step ashore when in sailed another English ship bearing the Remington brothers three! Be that as it may, much of the genealogy of Irene's mother, Laura Remington, is well documented, for tracing her own ancestral line was the latter-life hobby of Carrie Dieterich Manny. To be sure our branch of the family was not endowed with the mechanical, inventive and financial skills that produced Remington guns, Remington typewriters and Remington fortunes but Carrie did come up with some ancestors to warrant a show of dignified pride.

The only one she found who tangled with the law didn't even go to jail but had only to pay a fine of twenty shillings and, to my mind, adds spice to the whole ancestral line. The fine was imposed on John Remington for frequenting the company of Elizabeth Osgood of Andover, Massachusetts. He was bound to "good behavior and not to frequent her company unreasonably." At all events—reasonably or unreasonably—John married Elizabeth in 1657 thereby concluding the incident with an honorable note for posterity.

Remington implies a family from the town of Rheims, France. (Rem=Rheims, ing=a family, ton=town.) In Yorkshire, England, in 1372 Rimington (a spelling variation) was a local name and Richard Rimington was Gentleman of the Horse to Henry Fitzroy, natural son of Henry VIII. In 1500 a Remington was Lord Mayor of London and again in 1615.

The first American ancestor, John, came to Newbury, Massachusetts, from England in 1637. He was made a freeman which term implies that he was a church member and owner of a hundred acres of land. Down the American line we find five

1

Remingtons graduated from Harvard by 1798 (one of them in 1696). Remingtons in colonial times served as Judge of Probate, on the Governor's Council in Massachusetts, in the Assembly, as Judge of the Supreme Court—and in the Revolutionary War.

Laura's father, Isreal Remington, of the eighth generation in America, was born September 17, 1799, in Providence, Rhode Island. His father, Samuel (1764-1841) later moved from New England to Manlius, New York, where he engaged first in farming, then cotton manufacturing and subsequently in the making of paper. In 1822 Isreal, who was with his father in Manlius, wrote his brother Arnold in New England to "come West" to avail himself of the better business opportunities. So Isreal's was one of the hundreds of thousands of letters posted "back East" which over the years have stimulated the westward migration that has peopled our vast country from coast to coast.

ON OCTOBER 9, 1825, at Orville, New York, Isreal married Laura Hickox, whose ancestor William Hickok (or Hickox) came from London on the ship *Hector*, arriving in Boston in 1637. He took land in New Haven, Connecticut. His American-born son settled in Waterbury, Connecticut in 1680. Laura Hickox Remington, of the seventh American generation, was born in Cazenovia, New York, May 7, 1806, and died in Galesburg, Illinois, in 1881—Isreal had died in Manlius in 1845.

Six children were born of this Hickox-Remington marriage—the first three girls in quick succession to be followed more than six years later by the first of three boys.

Frances Helen (Helen)	born August 20, 1826
Laura (Loll)	born November 21, 1828
Sarah Adeline (Add)	born December 9, 1830
Reginald Heber (Hebe)	born April 21, 1837
Henry Harrison (Hat)	born April 13, 1841
Francis Albert (Frank)	born July 15, 1844

All were born in Manlius except Hebe, whose birthplace is noted as Oswega, New York.

*   *   *   *   *   *   *

Laura Remington Laurie recounted few incidents of her childhood but few as they were they carried the tingling thrill of America's westward conquest of the wilderness. One winter her father, tongue in cheek, coming in from the woods propped a strangely twisted walking stick in a corner of the hearth. Before long, in the glowing warmth, the "stick" began to move a bit, then slithered to the floor—a harmless winter-stiff snake had reacted to the thaw of

REMINGTON WOMEN | Left to right: Laura Remington, Laura Hickox Remington (mother of the girls), Adeline Remington, Helen Remington. *Probably 1850s, from a daguerreotype.*

an "early spring"! The Indians would noiselessly appear and stare in the kitchen window. They would beg for food, for sweets—cookies and molasses. A pie cooling on the sill might disappear as by magic! Except for their innocent demands on a meager larder they did no harm and were not feared. The Erie Canal linking the waters of the Hudson River to Lake Erie was completed in 1825. This great engineering accomplishment shortened the Remington's trek from Manlius, New York, when the family pushed further west to settle in Akron, Ohio. Laura's description of the patient mules that trod the towpath to pull their boat along the canal never failed to fascinate me.

*   *   *   *   *   *   *

The Remington girls were endowed with a special spirit of silly fun and gaiety that all shared. That very sharing together contributed the more to the good time and laughter. This merriment prevailed even in their letters. If the Remington family ran true to form, letter writing in the mid-nineteenth century, for unmarried women at least, was a type of recreation—a hobby. In these letters they prattled on with a sort of gay nonsense rather than actual humor but handled their words expertly to produce pleasing epistles that more than a century later still sparkle with life.

The family circle in the surviving letters enlarges to include a few who need to be identified.

CARRIE POWERS was a cousin of the Remington girls—for whom Helen subsequently named her own daughter.

CHARLOTTE HICKOX GRANGER, "Aunt Lotte," born in 1790, was a sister of Joseph Hickox, Laura Remington's father. She married

Amos Granger (1789-1866) who was a successful businessman and was a congressman serving from New York in the House of Representatives 1855-1859. Because of Amos Granger's outstanding position and greater wealth than others in the family Aunt Granger was looked upon with a certain respect. Respected she was but not a companion in the hilarity the others so artlessly conjured into being. Aunt Granger lived to a hearty ninety-three.

CHARLOTTE HICKOX, "Lotte," her niece and namesake, was a sister of Laura Hickox Remington, so much younger that she was only two years the senior of Laura's eldest daughter, Helen. A rollicking spinster, Lotte seems to have enjoyed each moment of the forty-seven years of her life.

Laura Remington Laurie used to tell of the blackface escapade in which she indulged with Lotte. The Isreal Remingtons were to have a dinner party. The girls, then in their midteens, were not to be present. This ultimatum did not set well with Lotte and Loll— so to the burned cork! Disguised as negro maids they waited on table and enjoyed all the fun and frivolity of their elders without their deception being discovered.

Though full of hilarity Lotte had a more serious side. Endowed with a good mind she worked her way through a year or two at Knox College in Galesburg, Illinois. Few financial opportunities were open to unmarried women of her era. With little or no money she apparently "lived around" among her relatives and friends making herself useful in a household by sewing or helping with other tasks. Her gaiety and sense of humor would have made her an asset in any family group.

In January 1851 Helen's letter to Carrie Powers told of a New Year's Eve dance in Akron. She came from Uniontown to attend it and returned there after dancing until two in the morning. "The room was most brilliantly lighted not by gas but by tallow candles which were all *neatly arranged* in tin candle sticks in niches in the wall. - Ode was there with Add Thompson and they danced the polka as usual. - He started on last Thursday for California. Mr. Wheeler Netty's father died there a short time since and it was necessary for someone to go to settle his business—So Ode undertook the journey."

Lotte who went from Middlebury, Ohio, to visit Dan Hickox at Genesee, Waukesha County, Wisconsin, in 1853 noted that "when you travel now days you are carried through so quickly, you have no opportunity of observing anything or enjoying anything so I can not give you very glowing descriptions." In the early 1850s the United States could not boast of an "affluent society." Lotte described Dan's family, "six little towheads that congregate around the social hearth, happy and contented in their humble home, a little bread and molasses soothing all their sorrows, and a cold potato the sweetener of their joys. - You never went to a *raising* as I did yesterday, and then rode on an Ox team up to the village." She further wrote of "the bloomers" who are "all spiritualists and have their circles."

*   *   *   *   *   *

The strong bond that held the three Remington sisters lasted their lives through. Though Laura had previously lost two daughters, each sister raised to maturity a single daughter and each was past thirty when the daughter was born.

Helen started her married life in Hoboken, New Jersey, though Galesburg, Illinois, soon became the permanent home of the John

Dieterichs. John was well enough established financially when they were married to give Helen more than she had been used to having. In a sedate way she enjoyed being better dressed though she seemed to feel it was not quite as exciting as twisting, turning and retrimming hand-me-down bonnets. In latter years Helen may have understood John who became so stern and penurious, but surely he and his daughter had difficulty finding any common ground or understanding. As a child Irene disliked and feared her Uncle John. Though in later years he told her he always *knew* she put the toast crusts, she so disliked, in a semicircle under the far side of her plate, at the time he made no issue of it. In contrast Carrie's deceit in hiding candy and other sweets in her bureau drawers for between meal consumption drew no mercy from her father. Throughout the melee of Dieterich home life Helen composed beautiful poetry. In that era of Victorian culture her works were ever in demand for various community and family events. Many newspaper clippings of her charming poems remain. She died December 17, 1900.

ALL THREE REMINGTON BOYS served in the Union Army during the Civil War. Frank, the baby, enlisted at fourteen. After the war, as a result of army life at this immature age, he became the black sheep of the family, floating from job to job plagued by a war-acquired proclivity to drink. However, Irene remembered her Uncle Frank with great affection. For a period he lived in Peoria with the Lauries. Each day returning from work he would bring home, in his lunch basket, some tiny thoughtful gift for Irene—a pretty leaf, a piece of candy, a smooth pebble. One evening he put his lunch basket on the edge of the table and told Irene to open it herself to see what he had brought her that day. With small fingers trembling with anticipation Irene unfastened the basket and found a precious Black and Tan puppy. How she loved that little dog! (To her dying day she insisted that Black and Tans were the most intelligent, faithful and affectionate of all canine breeds.) No matter how the world may have appraised Frank Remington, Irene adored and idolized him. Though he subsequently was married, divorced and married again he never had a child of his own. Death came to him in Chicago on the first day of February in 1887.

Heber, the oldest of the boys, the war over, married Lina Gurnea. They had a son, Frank, and a daughter, Laura, who became Mrs. Howard Ruggles. Lina, during the long years of her widowhood, made her home with the Ruggleses in Norwalk, Ohio. A kindly, considerate woman loved by all, she lived into her nineties. In 1935 shortly after her death, which followed a prolonged period of invalidism, Irene gave Laura and Howard Ruggles a trip to California. They visited us in Berkeley. (Their daughter Gertene is Mrs. Leonard White of Norwalk.)

After the war Hat also married and had two children—in his case both daughters. Hat is the only brother with any record of his war experiences extant—some letters to his mother and sisters. He served in the Nineteenth Ohio Battery, Twenty-Third Army Corps, First Brigade, Second Division in Tennessee and Kentucky and under General Sherman in Georgia.

December 12, 1862, Camp near Richmond, Kentucky. The things "came through all right. I would of got them before now, but we moved the same night that Mr. Scott got to Lexington, he went to General Granger and he gave him a four horse team, so Scott put the boxes all on together and brought them through with the brigade. -We all thought we would stay and winter in Lexington, but the order came last Thursday night to strike tents and be ready to move by daylight, we marched twelve miles that day, and camped on Daniel Boone's place - there is nothing left but four tall chimneys and they are partly blown down it is the prettiest site that I ever saw." The artillery was ferried across but Hat wrote, "The infantry all had to ford the Kentuck River—it was mighty cold, the river was froze but not hard enough to hold them." Later they "were sitting round the fires drying their feet and clothes."

Christmas day in 1862, foraging in Kentucky, "I went into the back yard and I found knowbody at home but two or three little black boys—John commenced talking to them and they said their folks had all gone to town, he keep attracting their attention while I was looking for something to eat, I looked into a little house that was in the backyard and there I found all I wanted and more to. I took a cake as big as a half bushel, six peach pies, one big turkey all dressed and all the sweet milk I could drink."

And always their pay was behind. Hat commented on that again and again. When he did get paid, he sent money home to his mother or to be saved for himself. From Lexington, Kentucky, March 22, 1863, a news item: "I suppose you have heard of Charlie

Smith's being taken prisoner by the guerrillas." The term guerrilla then was in common use more than a century ago! On July 31, 1863, they held off Morgan's men and saved McConnelsville from rebel capture and burning by the rebels. They were treated royally by the appreciative townspeople. At Knoxville, Tennessee, December 12, 1863, Hat stated that Major General Foster, their new commander, was not liked by the soldiers as well as Bursides. They were on half rations for the winter. "Everything is so high here. Potatoes two dollars a bush. Butter was one dollar and a half per pound, eggs seventy-five cents per dozen. Apples ten cents a piece. Pork twenty-cents per pound, candles ten cents a piece and everything else in proportion, it is awful, worse than confederate prices, we manage though to live, what we can't buy we steal."

From Wilmington, North Carolina, on February 2, 1864, he wrote on United States Sanitary Commission (forerunner of the Red Cross) stationery. Of the town he said, "It is a beautiful place and as it was easily captured and quickly so citizens and negros did not leave, and destroy it as they fled."

March 15, 1864, from Lexington, Kentucky, again, "I can not help but think of our poor prisoners that came into our lines at Wilmington some of them had their feet rotted off, a good many could not speak others had lost their senses and a great many could not walk at all I never saw such a sight in my life, some of them had been confined eighteen months."

"2nd Div. 23rd AC—Atlanta, Georgia, Sept. 16, 1864—

"We are six miles from Atlanta, I went down there yesterday for a ride and to see the city, it is about as large as Akron and I think it was once a very pretty place but now it (is) all tore to pieces by our shell(s). I never saw such a looking lot of houses in my life, some of them have got so many shots through them that they are all most ready to fall over the familys there all had holes dug in the ground and I suppose they had to occupy them most all the time for some parts of our army was shelling the city all of the time. There was a great many women and children killed during the siege, that was all old Hood's fault, for he had plenty of time to send them out of town. General Sherman is sending all noncombatants out of the city. They have the privilege of going north or south."

In the field near Columbia, Tennessee, December 22, 1864, "the surgeon in charge said that he had sixteen hundred wounded rebels—all of their wounded there had to have their wounds dressed without takin(g) any chloroform, they said they suffered awfully, and begged of us to give them some coffee but we had none, some of the boys gave them tobacco, they are all ragged and dirty—some have got no shoes."

From Raleigh, North Carolina, April 20, 1865. "It seames like a dream that we will return to our happy homes in a few weeks—it does not seam possible that this cruel war is coming to an end.

"Addie, the death of the President has cast a sad and gloomy appearance over this army and I suppose over the whole Nation. What an awful thing it is. The South has lost their best friend, I think, President Lincoln has been more lenient with the leaders of this rebellion than Andy Johnson will be."

Laura Laurie, herself, was no hero-worshiper of Lincoln's. She had seen him at least once and the sight had not convinced her of his personal cleanliness. The fact that he was not an aristocrat but was an untidy yokel seemed to outweigh all that she grudgingly admitted he had accomplished for his country.

IN THE YEAR 1867, on the third day of November, Irene Laurie was born to George and Laura Remington Laurie. The Laurie genealogy is scant and fraught with legend. George Laurie was born in Edinburgh, Scotland, about 1818. His was the Laurie clan of "Annie Laurie" fame. As a small boy he had played in the grounds of the royal summer residence which his home adjoined with the royal child who was to become Queen Victoria. Irene telling of this youthful association of her father's in later years before her son-in-law won no credence from Roy. To be sure her stories *were* noted more for vivacity than veracity, however my experience, longer than Roy's, with her interpretations led me to believe that through her overlay of exaggeration some underlying truths were involved. So often, and always somewhat to my surprise, proof *was* found when facts of one of her stories were checked. Queen Victoria and George were the same age and somewhere I once read that Victoria did make childhood visits to Scotland.

What did George Laurie look like? The only picture of him that I ever saw is in the bulky old photo album, the cover marked in gold letters with his name. His features were regular, were good but he was a gentle looking rather than a handsome man. From hearsay I know he had red-auburn hair and beard. He was short (so short that I once heard Laura Laurie say he was ineligible for military service in the Civil War, but as he would have been forty-three at the outbreak of the war his age was reason enough for his absence from the ranks). As Laura, herself, was barely five feet they must have been a petit couple indeed. (Irene, five feet, two and a half inches, considered *herself* short.)

Just where and how did George and Laura meet? The first documented proof is a letter from George, which is contained in a two by four inch envelope printed in ornate fine-lined scrolls and curlicues

"MY OWN BABY, OF COURSE!"

***

13

with but little space left for the address. This letter, an invitation to the Misses Helen and Laura Remington for an evening sleigh ride, breathes fun and gaiety—though the letter is interrupted by serious business, "a customer with 4 or 5 pounds of 'paper rags' to trade out in molasses, pins, needles, etc." The second "s" of the double "s" is written as an "f" in the fashion of the period. This epistle is not dated but must have been the avant-garde that gave George courage to write to Laura alone on a four by six inch sheet printed with a three-quarter-inch border of dainty conventionalized flower design in fine black-line-drawing.

Miss Remington,
        If it is not presuming too much on your good nature I would be happy to have you accompany me to an Oyster Supper interspersed with some dancing; in Middlebury this evening.

Remaining Yours,
G. Laurie

Akron
Feby 27/49
        P.S. Please answer by return mail.

                                                L.

Probably by the end of that year George and Laura were married. Exactly when and where is undocumented.

Before Irene was born to them, comparatively late in life, (Laura was almost forty) they had lost two daughters. No one of these sisters saw any other sister. Ida their first child probably was born in 1850. Laura's sister, Helen, in a letter of October 1851, wrote of Ida, "she runs all about now and is so cunning." By 1852 she is "talking baby talk." However she was not living when in 1857 Annie was born to live but six years herself.

There remains a tiny old-fashioned envelope, addressed, "Mrs. I Remington, Syracuse, N.Y., c/o Mr. A. Granger." (Mrs. Granger was an aunt of Grandma Remington's.) The envelope contains a thick lock of red, red hair. There is no date. Did a fond grandmother receive a lock of Ida's or of Annie's hair? We wonder.

At Galesburg in 1867 Helen Remington Dieterich was expecting her sisters for Christmas. Charlie and Add Gladding would come from Chicago bringing their Flora, who would be past fourteen months. George and Laura Laurie would arrive from Peoria. When Helen and her eleven-year-old, Carrie, saw the Lauries coming up their front walk Laura was carrying a baby in her arms. Helen's first startled and confused thought was that Laura must be carrying little Flora but almost immediately she could see the babe was a tiny one. In consternation she said, "Why Laura, whose baby do you have?" With a toss of her head and a flounce of her skirts Laura answered, "Why, my own, of course!" This was the first that Helen knew anything about this late advent in the Laurie family—Irene.

There is no definite record of where the Lauries spent the fifties or the Civil War years. In the post-war period they lived in Peoria for Irene was born there. They may have lived there all their married life. In Peoria, George was a clerk in the law firm of Ingersoll and Puterbaugh at 210 Main Street. He was a trusted and faithful employee. All the Laurie family worshiped Robert G. Ingersoll and apparently had a fairly intimate contact with the whole close-knit Ingersoll family. The following excerpt from a letter written in longhand by Mr. Ingersoll shows his warm attitude toward the Lauries.

London Sept. 24/75

Dear Laurie,

We were all delighted to receive
yours of the 6th inst. It was just such a
letter as we wanted to read on a real old
fashioned foggy drizzly London day. The
sunshine from home came with your letter,
and the weather—at least while your letter
was read—was beautiful, and the skylark,
of which you spoke, seemed singing with all
his might=======Remember me to little Irene
and thank her for the compliment she paid me
when she said that I always spoke to children
=======With a hundred thanks for your kind
good letter.

I remain

Yrs always

H. G. Ingersoll

It was Ingersoll at the 1878 National Republican Convention in Cincinnati, Ohio, who placed James G. Blaine in nomination for the presidency. Irene used to tell of a train trip the Lauries took with the Ingersolls, I think to meet Blaine at some whistle stop where he was to speak during electioneering. Irene would have been almost nine. On the train Mr. Ingersoll was holding her on his knee as he puffed at a big cigar. Irene asked him to let her smoke his cigar for awhile and he accommodatingly complied. As *she* told the story she smoked away at the cigar for some time, suffering no ill effects and quite enjoying the experience to the surprise and delight of H.G.I.

In a letter to her Cousin Carrie, Irene wrote from Peoria on November 15, 1876, "Mr. Ingersoll says Hays is going to be elected. Mr. Blaine and Mrs. were here. Mrs. Ingersoll introduced me to Mr. Blaine and Mr. Ingersoll to Mrs. Blaine." Many times I heard Irene recount her recollection of Mr. Ingersoll, referring to Blaine, telling her, "Now, you must remember that kiss so later you can say, 'The president of the United States kissed me!'" But by the time of the introductions Mr. Ingersoll knew Hays, not Blaine, would be president.

If the kiss occurred earlier then why all the careful introductions described? Could this have been an instance of how the power of dramatic exaggeration with the leaven of the passing years worked on Irene? Roy's answer would have been in the affirmative. One thing is certain, back in 1876 the final concession to Hays must have been bitter fare for the Peoria clan. All through my childhood, a photograph of Bob Ingersoll, "the great agnostic," the internationally renowned lecturer, graced the mantel shelf in its handsome, ornate, gilt easel-frame.

Carrie Dieterich's diary traces events from 1871 to 1875. In the early fall of 1872 came a telegram, generally a harbinger of bad news in those years, from George Laurie to Carrie's mother, Helen Remington Dieterich, in Galesburg. "Come at once Laura very sick." Helen packed and left on the 5 p.m. train for Peoria. In a few days she wrote Carrie that the "crisis is past" and that Laura would probably live though she was so weak she could not turn in bed without help.[2] The letter bore further comment. "Irene runs wild from morning till night." When Laura was definitely recovering sister Add, who had also come to help with the nursing,

2 Typhoid was Laura's ailment.

left for home. She had wanted to take Irene as far as Galesburg to leave her at Dieterich's "and so did the rest want her to but Uncle George would not let her come." Carrie was crushed. (Carrie, the reserved, the restrained, the unemotional, adored her little cousin Irene with a passion. Everyone else in the Remington family considered Irene "very spoiled as a child"—but not Carrie!) When Laura was well enough to travel Helen brought her with Irene and Grandma Remington to Galesburg for the several weeks of Laura's convalescence. In 1872 one's family stood by in illness, in fact *had* to stand by, for the use of hospitals and registered nurses was for future generations.

In February 1873 Irene with Laura again visited Galesburg and Carrie found "Irene was the same little cut up as before and just as fond of her Cousin Carrie." An invitation printed on a two by five inch card in its tiny envelope remains to tell that Irene had a birthday party when she reached the six-year mark.

1867   1873

IRENE LAURIE

Will receive her young friends from

4-7 o'clock

MONDAY, Nov. 3d.

No 277 Bluff Street.

In 1874 George, while on a business trip, left Irene in Galesburg as Carrie's guest for two nights. "The first evening she was quite homesick and cried almost an hour." In November that same year when Carrie's father was on a trip Carrie and her mother, returning from town, saw Laura who "had been to the house, stuck on a little hat frame Ma had purchased and started out to meet us. When she heard Pa was away, she just held up her dress and kicked out her heels, and we all nearly died laughing." Carrie writes that her Aunt Laura is "such a jolly visitor." (John Dieterich, Carrie's father, a severe, penny-pinching, authoritative man was not blessed with the spirit of fun and foolishness the Remington sisters reveled in.) Friday that week Laura with Irene and Grandma Remington, who had come to Galesburg with her, started for Chicago so Laura "could visit the Exposition—Saturday she went to a Women's Convention and witnessed the proceedings of that and a Woman's Congress."

In June 1875 Laura and Irene attended the Knox College commencement when Carrie graduated. Add and Flora brought Carrie a graduation gift of a "lovely fan," white with an edge of peacock feathers." Surveying the audience from the stage Carrie wrote that "the fans swaying to and fro, all over the house, gave the impression of the whole audience being in motion." Grandma Remington, writing about the Christmas holidays that year, told that Irene "had her tree lighted up with wax candles. It looked quite grand.-George and Laura attended the New Year's Ball the grandest that ever come of(f) in Peoria so the papers say."

By her ninth birthday in 1876 Irene was in the third reader, doing well in school, going to singing and to dancing school. That year there were twenty at her birthday party and Irene wrote her Cousin Carrie, "Mama has a girl, Anna Duffee." Having a hired girl was indeed news for George Laurie made no material success. He was generous to a fault. So often with money in his pocket he would find someone who he felt needed it more than he.

Irene adored her father. With practical Laura busy at household tasks it was George who took long walks through the woods with his little daughter. Irene remembered that he knew the names of birds, where to look for their nests and how to hold her up so she could peek at tiny blue eggs. He knew where baby bunnies lived, at least his stories of small forest creatures convinced her he did. He knew stories too of ages past told by the rocks he picked up along their path. Before they started on a woods ramble he might slip into his pocket a peach for her to feast on as they rested beside the hurrying brook, then George might carve a tiny basket with handle from the peach pit. It is little wonder that Irene often said her father was really a naturalist who worked as a law clerk only to provide bread and butter. Irene thought of her father and the glory and mystery of the out-of-doors simultaneously. Surely he awakened in her a lifelong and passionate love of beauty in nature.

Irene often remarked that her father was "very musical" but just how his talent was demonstrated I never thought to ask. George Laurie was credited, by Irene at least, with having started Emma Abbott on her musical career. (*Who's Who in America* documents the debut of Emma Abbott, 1850-1891, operatic soprano of the seventies and eighties, as having been made in Peoria, Illinois, as a singer and guitar player in 1859.) I have the impression that George Laurie read a great deal. I know that, quite naturally, Scot that he was, "Bobbie" Burns was his favorite poet though he was also especially fond of William Cullen Bryant's works.

I was told George Laurie died of apoplexy. There was something about his working out in the field—the sun was hot. Laura nursed her husband through a long difficult illness till his death early in 1878. There is a receipt of sale to her of the cemetery plot: Page 65, Springdale Cemetery Association—Laura Laurie owner of Lot #979—$20.00 with perpetual care guarantee—the date March 23, 1878.

Shortly after George's death Laura and Irene came to California. Add insisted upon the move. Laura wanted to stay in Peoria. Peoria had been home for so many years. Her life with George had been woven in Peoria. George had left little financially but she had many friends. She knew she could manage. By doing simple sewing, by making preserves and cooking specialties for sale she could support herself and Irene modestly. But Add would not hear of such a plan. Peoria friends urged Laura to stay; they would see that she got enough work to take care of her needs. California had no appeal to Laura but Add would not take no for an answer. Laura and Irene were to live in the Gladding ménage in elite (in 1878) West Oakland. Flora and Irene were only a year apart in age. It would be a good life for them all, living together in California, Add insisted.

Some nine years before, transcontinental rail travel had become a reality. So across the broad land in 1878 Laura and Irene traveled in their lower Pullman berth—but not without incident.

The train was held up by bandits! Two of them there were, a tall man and a short. They had planned well. It was night when they boarded the train. The tall bandit was to rob the occupants of the upper berths, the short one to deal with the lowers. A note of comedy developed when the plan became confused and found the one stretching on tiptoe, the other stooping double. Laura held tight the heavy green curtains of their berth against the intruders. Little deterrent this, the tall robber jerked the curtains wide, muttered in disgust, "Only a woman and child," and molested them no more. Not so lucky was a woman fellow passenger who lay terrified, face down on her pillow with covers tight around her neck. In the dim light, as her dark hair clung to her head, the robber thought her to be a man. When she made no response to his command "Hand over!" he clubbed her over the head. So even in the late 1870s the overland trip to California was fraught with adventure!

Just when the few Laurie possessions (walnut dining table with matching marble-topped sideboard, steel-caned rocker, small sewing table) that ultimately reached California made their journey I have no idea. Perhaps Laura, with a premonition that Add's California idyll might not develop into reality, stored with Peoria friends a few beloved lares and penates.

IN OAKLAND the reconstructed Gladding household from the very beginning must have had stresses and strains for every member. Surely Charles Gladding, though he had sanctioned the arrangement, would have had a dim view of intruders on his domestic bliss. Add, the spoiled one, the determined one, must have been put to it to make her generously conceived plan work into the glowing future for all concerned that she had pictured. Flora at that miserable between-age, around twelve years, must have suffered aplenty from having pretty, attractive, spoiled Irene, her junior by only one year, invade her kingdom. These feelings I *deduce* only. All that I *heard* was the tragic "other side of the story."

The living arrangement did not work out—period. Flora was mean to Irene. I am sure this was not only true but almost inevitable and when it comes to downright meanness, who can do a better job than a twelve-year-old girl to an eleven-year-old girl of whom she is jealous? One reason Add had insisted on the Laurie's move was her own loneliness; she missed the frequent visits that had been customary among the sisters in Illinois. There was always genuine love and affection between Add and Laura but before long the Lauries were living by themselves in meager housekeeping rooms in some large old house not far from the Gladding mansion. Add still felt responsibility, still kept a protective eye on them, for Add had assured Laura if she and Irene would leave Peoria and come to California they would always have a home—would always be taken care of.

It was Laura who took a definite stand and made the move to separate quarters. She could not see Irene—the only person in the world who *really* mattered to her now—mistreated and unhappy. In late years Irene insisted that Laura and she would have had a good life in Peoria if only Add had left them alone. Never did

Irene seem to sense that Peoria without George would have been a struggle—far more of a struggle even than California with Add *and* Flora. To say that Irene felt that the Gladdings owed Laura and herself a living is a suave understatement.

No doubt it was when the Lauries first moved to their own rooms that Add started the twenty-dollar monthly remittance which as long as she lived she sent to Laura (and which Flora faithfully continued to send not only to Laura but to Irene even after Laura's death). To Laura and Irene in those days this twenty dollars was as important as a life preserver to a floundering swimmer in mid-ocean—twenty dollars in that era would support the major burden of existence.

If it had not been for Carrie Dieterich all the details of family history and family life from 1850 to 1880 would have been lost. Carrie, like her own mother, preserved many letters and among them were some of Irene's childhood epistles and poetry. (Late in 1878 Carrie wrote a letter to her beau, George Prince, whom Irene had met in Illinois and liked and very much wanted Carrie to marry. In the letter one of Irene's poems is mentioned. Also Carrie tells George, "The Deed is done. My hair is shingled short." She had had it cut at the barber's. Documentary proof that styles come and go and come again!) Irene's precious little poems are touched with her love of the beauty of Nature (she would have spelled it with a capital "N"—the avant-garde of her day tended to substitute the word Nature for God) but touched too with a certain pathos. Indeed why wouldn't they be? Here were Laura, an almost destitute widow, and her little daughter in a new and strange locale eking out a precarious livelihood. A livelihood however that Laura would see to it, as the years marched on, would enable Irene to move in approved social circles.

Irene missed Carrie. Irene was in fact Illinois homesick. Perhaps it was only to Carrie that she admitted it. By the fall of 1878 Irene was in the fourth grade of Oakland's La Fayette School and proclaiming her dislike of arithmetic (a lifelong attitude). Flora, however, was in the Irving School. Could this school separation of the girls have been an attempt to smooth life in the Gladding-Laurie ménage? We do not know, nor do we know just when Laura and Irene moved to their own quarters at 970 West Sixteenth Street but only that they were there by 1880.

Irene was wont to frequently mention that at twelve years of age she was supplementing the Laurie's meager income by giving painting lessons. Nevertheless it was with a mild feeling of surprise that I found the fact documented in an 1879 letter to Carrie. Apparently no exaggeration warped that story. By 1880 she tells Carrie that she wants to be an artist.

Irene's playmates, she wrote Carrie, were Nellie Grow, Alice McChesney and Mamie Crouch. Nellie Grow is just a name that I often heard Irene mention when speaking of her early California years but Miss McChesney was rediscovered and we had some pleasant outings with her in Pacific Grove, our mutual summer retreat, when I was about the age she and Irene had been at La Fayette School in 1878. She was a charming spinster, very attuned to the beauty of the out-of-doors, and little wonder, as John Muir had been a close McChesney family friend. In fact he had had a room in their home which he made his Bay Region headquarters.

Mr. McChesney, Alice's father, was principal of Oakland High School in 1878, when Alice and Irene met, and for many subsequent years. When Irene fought her losing battle with algebra in her second high school year he was the sympathetic principal. I knew Irene did not finish high school, in fact I have the impression she may have been a drop-out before the end of her sophomore year—that algebra, you know!

Mamie Crouch, Miss Mary Crete Crouch, was our Crete, who with her older sister, Bessie, had a part in our lives till their deaths in about 1938 and 1941. Their mother, Eleanor Crouch, (Aunt Nellie to Irene, Flora and me) had lived in Akron where Laura and Add had known her slightly. When the families met again in California a warm friendship quickly developed.

In my early years Christian Science was a new and radical enough movement to evoke the derision and antagonism of non-believers—our family attitude was no exception to the general rule. Aunt Nellie and the Crouch girls (Crete and Bessie) were, by my youth, devout Christian Scientists. In fact Aunt Nellie was reader in the church at Sacramento where they were living by that time. Aunt Nellie was a sister of Mrs. H. B. Crocker whose former Sacramento residence is now the Crocker Art Gallery.

Aimée Crocker, daughter of the E. B. Crockers, was, to put it mildly, quite a gal! Not until the days of the Hollywood stars was there such publicity of gay partying and ski-jumping in and out of marital ties as was accorded Aimée by the accommodating press. (Aimée, herself, wrote a book about it all titled, *And I'd Do It Again*)

Crete, a vibrant petite blonde, rode Aimée's coattails (or to put it more aptly, her ball gown's flowing train) to many a gay adventure. The one most often recounted was a trip to Hawaii on the Crocker's sea-going yacht. The Hawaiian royal family still held sway in Honolulu. King Kalakaua was entranced with Crete's blonde beauty and the Crocker party was in reality entertained royally.

I never did master the sequence of Aimée's marriages but one detail concerning her first has always intrigued me. The story runs that, playing poker in a Pullman car as they were traveling overland from New York, two young socialite San Francisco bachelors decided one of them should marry Aimée. They met the stakes of the poker game as the right to court Aimée unmolested by any advances made to her by the other. I think but again am not positive, that it was Harry Houghton who lost. I am SURE Porter Ashe won. It must have been well in the 1920s that I remember the last full-page Sunday supplement story complete with photographs telling of Aimée's latest escapades. She ended, quite logically, it seems to me, with a French husband, much younger than herself—the name Gouraud.

Crete Crouch was a quite accomplished watercolorist. She studied under Paul Latimer, famous for his method of color underlay for watercolors as well as for his lovely paintings of California redwoods. Irene was a pupil in Mr. Latimer's outdoor classes on several occasions, for short periods during my childhood. Of course Irene always worked in oil. Could it have been the green-eyed monster? Irene and Laura were wont to say how egotistical Crete and her family were about Crete's art accomplishments. I got the impression that Crete's work in reality was nothing of which to be too proud. Yet we have a very lovely watercolor, for its era, which won Crete the first prize at a state Fair art exhibit. Crete could never have been termed an outstanding artist, but some of her work *was* charming.

If Irene was not jealous of the art Crete produced she was most certainly envious of the art school training Crete had had. Crete's drawing was perfect. Irene's drawing, like her algebra, left much to be desired. Irene knew if art school had been financially possible for her that she could have mastered drawing. Irene had longed for art school. The Gladdings, unlike the Crockers in Crete's case, had not been financially sympathetic.

I BELIEVE Irene gained more from her short period of study under Eugen Neuhaus (1879-1963) than from her longer tutelage under Paul Latimer. Neuhaus, later, was longtime professor of art at the University of California at Berkeley. His wife was a younger sister of Irene's theosophist friend, Carrie York, whose pleasing personality and brilliant mind offset the handicap of her misshapen, hunchbacked body. While Carrie's sister, Lulu, was studying piano in Germany under Leopold Godowsky she met this handsome, strapping, young German artist. He followed her to the United States and they were married.

Not long after, in 1906, the York-Neuhaus family were living in Pacific Grove. Irene was possessed to have Eugen take her as a private pupil in outdoor sketching in oil, which at that period was his medium too. Eugen, who was doing no teaching at the time, was not eager but finally agreed to accept Irene as a private pupil at ten dollars a lesson (big money that, in 1906!). Eugen was enthralled with the current tonal school, reveled in the local fog that would produce what he rapturously referred to as a "gry dy." (Irene thought Neuhaus' pronunciation of "gry dy" to be an accent peculiarly his own but in his book, *Drawn from Memory*, published posthumously, Neuhaus attributes the phrase to Francis McComas, another artist, with his Australian, or more accurately, Tasmanian accent.)

To get the full effect of such a gray day he sought the dunes and beaches. Lacking the penetrating roads of our much later day, sketching on the dunes meant trampling miles carrying heavy artist's paraphernalia. Eugen trudged ahead carrying only his own materials, never offering to lighten Irene's load. Finding a pleasing subject he settled down to painting his own picture, paying little or no attention to Irene's efforts. Hours passed. Furious, Irene strode over, stood behind him and began to tell him what was wrong with *his* picture. Her criticism was well based. He turned and glared at her—then began to change his painting to conform to her suggestions. In afteryears he would comment to Irene on that painting of his, which he sold for a very tidy sum. He always referred to it as "your picture." I do not think Irene's series of Neuhaus lessons exceeded three. Both welcomed their termination, no doubt, yet both brought from the experience a healthy respect for one another in the world of art.

* * * * * * *

Irene was marvelously proficient in various arts and crafts; perhaps a better draftsman than artist though she had a fine color sense. She was original in her concepts but could be a good copyist too. She was highly creative and this creativity stood her in good stead. A few of her inspired touches turned drab housekeeping rooms to cozy attractive living quarters; for by the time Irene first knew Crete, she and Laura had embarked on their long voyage of frugal living in various improvised quarters. In that era the gracious word "apartment" was not in general use to dignify such living arrangements.

One very practical manifestation of Irene's creativity was her ability to turn and twist and utterly disguise hand-me-downs so that her finished creation was far more glamorous than the original garment. (In later years this talent of Irene's both delighted and infuriated Flora who was the source of the large majority of these hand-me-downs.) Laura was determined that Irene move in highly approved social circles and this proclivity of Irene's let her do it and look simply ravishing all the while. With her beauty, her flashing eyes, her vivacity added to the dashing style with which she wore her stunning clothes she seldom failed to be the most attractive woman at any social gathering. Laura's pride knew no bounds!

Such a life took a bit of doing beside the legerdemain with clothes. There loomed the return of social indebtedness. A few letters from Laura to Irene remain to show Laura's deep concern that Irene "keep up her end"—show her appreciation. This was usually accomplished by Irene's painting a picture or writing a clever rhyme for the one to whom she was indebted.

* * * * * * *

The documentarily vague decade of the eighties—Irene's teens and early twenties—must have been a series of stepping stones to Irene's Gay Nineties. We have to reconstruct Irene's life in this mistily veiled period from a few well remembered stories. Somewhat of a tomboy in her early teens she liked to roller-skate around the block with a neighbor boy, George McNear Jr. (I danced sedately with his son, George III at Piedmont parties in my teens.)

Irene did not grow rapidly to sophistication. She and Crete Crouch both loved to play with paper dolls (the figures cut from fashion magazines). They would lock themselves in Irene's room to follow this childish pursuit when they were well into their teens and ashamed to admit that such make-believe still enthralled them. However, simultaneously Irene was augmenting the Laurie income by making and painting various knick-knacks for sale. One highly saleable item, many of which she painted with graceful scrolls and sprays of bright orange California poppies, were miniature wooden wash tubs. Fortunately it was an era of mish-mash interior ornamentation!

Irene concluded her academic endeavors in this decade, still holding to her goal to become an artist. By scrimping and scraping Laura and she saved enough for her to attend classes of a San Francisco artist, named Rogers, well known for his animal studies. This instruction necessitated Irene's crossing on the ferry each morning. It so happened that a young man, unknown to her, took this same ferry frequently. Irene was exquisite at this age but strictly followed at all times the rule which she felt to be infallible, "A young woman who tends quietly to her own business can go alone anywhere, at any time, unmolested." Irene always took a book to read (or at least appear to be reading) on the ferry but out of the corner of her eye she knew what went on around her. The young man would walk hopefully by several times on each ferry trip but never would Irene raise her eyes. Finally one day as she was seating herself and opening her book she said good morning to some Oakland youth of her acquaintance. As she started to read she saw the pacing young man of other ferry crossings quickly go up to her acknowledged acquaintance. It was obvious that he asked to be introduced to that gorgeous gal (or the 1880s equivalent of that term). Almost immediately the two young men strolled over to Irene. Her acquaintance said, "Miss Laurie, may I present William Randolph Hearst? He tells me he has been very eager to meet you for some time!"

KING
RAILROAD
* * *

AS EARLY AS THE 1850S IN WATERTOWN, New York, members of the Remington family knew the Porters. A son, William Porter, left Watertown and made a name for himself out in California, eventually becoming auditor of the Central Pacific Railroad (which later became the Southern Pacific). In 1888 Alfred D. Remington ("A.D.") came West looking for a paper mill site (the Remingtons had been in that business in New York). He went to Oakland not only to call on his widowed cousin, Laura, and her daughter but to look up his old Watertown friend, Will Porter.

A.D. found Will and his family living in Will's widowed mother-in-law's home at 660 Fourteenth Street. Will had married Mary Haskins whose father had been a promoter. ("Promoter," a calling without a specific name in his lifetime, that was eventually to reach a pinnacle in California. Mr. Haskins had indeed been a pioneer!)

From Sam Brannan, Haskins had bought the Calistoga-Napa Railroad which he extended to Vallejo. An attempt to further extend the line to reach Marysville was fought by the mighty Central Pacific Railroad. The story goes that as fast as Haskins' Chinese laborers laid the ties during the days, just so fast did the Central Pacific's Orientals tear them up at night! Eventually Mr. Haskins found it expedient to sell his railroad holdings which were absorbed into the powerful Central Pacific system.

In May 1869 Mary Haskins, a railroad daughter on the brink of her teens, saw the ceremonial golden spike driven to join the Central Pacific from the west to the Union Pacific coming from the east to form the first overland transcontinental railroad to the West Coast. Mary used to point out for me in the famous painting of that occasion (*The Golden Spike* by Thomas Hill which is now in the California State Railroad Museum in Sacramento) just where she and her parents had stood—behind the more notable dignitaries—to witness this colorful bit of the conquering of the West.

Mary had attended the select Napa Seminary for Young Ladies which was quite THE boarding school of the area. Now, in 1888 Mary and Will had two daughters—Adelyn, eight, and Mary, not quite seven, who attended Oakland's elite Miss Horton's School nearby. Alfred saw to it that the Lauries and the Porters met!

When A.D. saw Will he may have noticed that Will did not seem quite himself, seemed tired, not as alert as he used to be. By this time Will's illness had begun. Central Pacific kept him in office as long as possible but soon he had to be at home all the time. His malady was termed "softening of the brain." Later Mary placed him in the King's Daughters Home in Oakland where he remained until his death.

The Porters' friends could not forget that before his illness Will had been an indulgent and adoring husband and father. When Mary put him in the home, then later divorced him, she was severely criticized. What those rendering judgment did not know was that doctors had told Mary that Will would get progressively worse, that, though he had always been gentle, his impaired brain might cause him to turn on the one he loved most, that they considered Mary's life in danger. Even then Mary continued to keep Will in the family home but as times went on and he was less and less himself she lived in mortal fear. It was then (in 1891) that she put him in the home and moved the family to Chicago.

After their 1888 meeting Mary and Irene almost immediately became fast friends. Irene fitted neatly into the Porter family—ten years Mary's junior, ten years Adelyn's senior. Mary was always a very sweet, a very good wife to Will but she was a butterfly and Will, sick or well, knew it and never objected to her fluttering.

Conveniently in these years (1888-1891) a cousin of Mary's, Charlie Hickok (no kin of Laura Hickox Remington), lived in the Haskin-Porter household. Charlie, who was about Mary's age, made not only a strong protector in case Will should become violent but a ready escort for Mary. He was present on most of the escapades Irene shared with her.

One evening partying in San Francisco Mary, Irene, Charlie and one or two others missed the 2 a.m. ferry to Oakland—the last ferry. It was times like this that Mary suddenly became acutely aware of her girls! So it was that the group crossed the Bay in so unconventional a manner that all their lives Mary and Irene were wont to recall it. They were passengers on the newspaper tug which at 4 a.m. carried the San Francisco papers to Oakland for early morning distribution.

Still another jaunt those two loved to recall was their trip with General Shafter from Sausalito to Angel Island in a rowboat! The exact why and when of this voyage are lost in time but the how remains. Stalwart buck privates rowed but the Bay was choppy. Time and again the little craft rose perilously high on a wave crest, then thudded down, shipping a slop of the briny deep. Irene the yachtswoman, the good sailor, took it calmly enough—not Mary. Mary was terrified! At not too infrequent intervals, as she sat facing General Shafter in the tiny boat, she would scream then fling her arms around the General's knees imploring him, "General Shafter! General Shafter, remember I have two daughters at home!"

*   *   *   *   *   *   *

By 1890 railroad had become king in California. Railroad executives frequently traveled in their private cars from their New York offices to San Francisco for business conferences. In the Gay Nineties such a day of office work would be topped off by a sumptuous dinner at The Palace—the old Palace around its courtyard. (Irene never lost her nostalgic love of that magnificent hotel which burned in the 1906 fire.) Even in the nineties the tired businessman IF he was Japanese had the geisha house. Now he has his Playboy Club but in the Gay Nineties, if he dined at The Palace, sheltered Victorian ladies had to fill the void caused by a dual system of morals. Expressed in railroad terminology the rule was that the girls across the tracks stayed across the tracks. There were no compromise-girls; no geishas, no bunnies. But our Gay Nineties brain-weary executives needed the stimulation of female company and who could better offer it than the proper wife of a fellow official who was unfortunately(?) too physically incapacitated to take part in these late-into-the-night revels.

Mary Porter was the essence of ideal Victorian womanhood of her economic class. She was pretty. She was well-dressed. She was gay. She was almost completely useless but that, too, was part of the era. Her house was staffed by capable, devoted servants. She was the 1890s geisha and bunny and proper wife in one pretty package. She loved her daughters but she was careful that they did not interfere with those fabulous dinner parties at The Palace. However the parties needed the leaven of more than *one* woman. Mary, in the role of chaperone, saw the solution in Irene with her beauty and vivacity.

The railroad barons adored Irene! E. H. Harriman, president of the Southern Pacific, Irene did not like, but his administrative assistant, J. C. Stubbs, known to his business associates and friends as "J.C.," soon became Jack to Irene. J.C. frequently came to San Francisco. With him always was his private secretary, Billy Martin of the troublesome crippled leg. Billy, a charming bachelor bubbling with witty humor, was ever faithful to J.C.

The fact that J.C. had a wife in the East seems to have been a footnote in Irene's railroad saga. I don't think they ever met. Once Irene showed me—and it seemed to me even then, as a child, that it was to specially impress it on my youthful mind—a very sweet letter from Mrs. Stubbs thanking Irene for a souvenir spoon she had sent to add to Mrs. Stubbs' collection. Surely J.C. had been impressed on my mind, for from my birth till the bare-walled style of the 1920s his sensitive, aristocratic face had looked down on us from an eight by ten framed photo on Irene's bedroom wall—be it connubial chamber or no.

Manager of the Southern Pacific Company's Pacific System, J. A. Filmore, Irene termed a rather coarse person though well-meaning and generous. (His brother, J. Millard Filmore—they were distant kin of the U.S. president—was manager of the narrow-gauge line, the Pacific Coast Railway Company, which connected Port Hartford—now Avila Beach—to San Luis Obispo and later to the fertile Santa Ynez Valley.)

About 1892 William Vance Dinsmore and his bride, Elizabeth Snell Dinsmore—Adeline Chapman's parents—on their wedding trip came down the coast by steamer. Their ship docked for a couple of days at Port Hartford to load the barley being hauled from the Santa Ynez Valley in wagons drawn by four-horse teams as the southern section of the railroad was not then completed. The Dinsmores took the train on Sunday to San Luis Obispo to find it like a foreign village. Spanish was the only language they heard and people on the streets were in the gay fiesta garb of Mexico or Spain.

The zenith of Irene's conquest of the railroad kingdom came with the naming of a station for her on the Arizona line. She always laughed about this dividend of her railroad contacts for her station, only a flag stop, failed to develop in the fast-growing tradition of the West into a Tucson or a Phoenix. An undated office memo survives to confirm the fact that honor was bestowed on Irene by King Railroad. The memo from Filmore's office reads, "Irene, a new station has been established on the Tucson Div. Located bet. Vail and Pantano—Approved by J. Kruttschnitt. Gen. Man."

From the time of her first dinner at The Palace Irene traveled on a railroad pass. During my early childhood I remember that, though the new ruling rather irked her, Irene had to submit to the nuisance of dropping into the Southern Pacific Company head office in San Francisco annually to have her pass renewed. In this way I met Billy Martin whom Irene adored as one would a faithful spirited dog that had been at one's side during many of life's most thrilling moments. Once Kruttschnitt, as I recall, rather grimly handed the pass across his desk to Irene. She didn't care for him; felt they had no rapport. He had been no part of evenings at The Palace yet as general manager he was important to Irene now. Railroads in general were tightening on passes. It is my recollection that the 1906 earthquake not only shook all California adjacent to the San Andreas Fault but shook a railroad pass out of Irene's hand forever! Railroad's kingdom was not so secure; largess could no longer be thrown wantonly to its sycophants. The nadir of King Railroad's reign had been glimpsed.

*   *   *   *   *   *   *

Finally the Gladdings shook the dust of Oakland and Lincoln from their feet for all time and moved over San Francisco's cobble-stoned streets to their stylish new cupolaed house at 1611 Franklin Street. The Lauries probably made their cross-the-Bay move soon after. At all events in 1893 when Irene set off on the most thrilling adventure of her life, her trip to the World's Columbian Exposition at Chicago, her diary confirms their San Francisco residence.

The diary flows on, its plethora of enthusiasm outweighing its paucity of punctuation. "Sept. 12th So I did manage to forget something the dear mother was good enough to remember it Uncle John crossed the bay with us and Jessie and Lew went as far as the 16th St was not Mr. Meehan good could not have been nicer to his own wife. Harry Houghton spent the evening in my section I have a section and orders that the upper berth is to be kept vacant as long as possible and then some—" Not only did Irene travel on a pass but quite naturally the upper in her section did remain vacant so the porter was able to keep it closed to give comfortable head space in her lower berth.

Two of Irene's escorts could almost be termed "chaperones"; older married men whose wives Irene knew well. Uncle John Pew's wife (whose nephew, Charles Caldwell Dobie, became a well-known San Francisco author) was my "Auntie Pew." Clara and John Pew owned the *Truant*. Irene's happiest sailing days on the Bay were spent aboard this graceful craft. Except for Clara, Irene was the only female crew member on this *Truant*, Sunday after gorgeous Sunday. (Lacking modern cosmetics to protect her sensitive skin from wind-burn on these cruises, Irene always wore a skirted domino mask!)

Jesse Meehan was six feet two, enough to give him fame in those days of not-so-tall men. He was co-owner and manager of the Pullman laundry in Oakland. In this era when rail travel was the fastest, pleasantest mode of overland transportation the amount of Pullman car laundry (bed linens, towels, table linens) must have been prodigious at this Western terminal. The laundry adequately supported the Meehan's great gray-green cupolaed house on the north side of Fourteenth Street, near Seventh Avenue in East Oakland. It was here that I spent my first night away from home. I have no memory of homesickness. I was with Aunt Elizabeth, Irene's bosom friend, after whom, as Irene said, her half of me had been named. (Arthur's half was credited to his mother, Elizabeth Chambers.)

The Meehan household was typical of the era. The house was big with many bedrooms on the second floor. Uncle Jesse and Aunt Katherine occupied the big sunny front bedroom. In a sense this was their home, their castle. The remainder of the household was not without tension but no one ever conceived of any other living arrangement. Jesse, at sixteen and oldest of the several Meehan children, had become head of the family when his father died. It was Jesse, whose conscientious hard work and drive had nurtured his siblings to adulthood, who continued to make a home for his sweet frail mother and only unmarried sister. But Katie Meehan also had a spinster sister. Aunt Pauline Kelly in the west bedroom had the first chaise longue I ever saw. There she would recline reading the latest Victorian novel, a box of chocolate creams at her elbow. Though she looked very stout and robust to me, she was said to be "rather delicate." Aunt Elizabeth was the workhorse of the family, at least in her own estimation. Surely she pampered "Grandma Meehan," never letting her raise a finger. Katie Meehan's frayed nerves showed even on the surface. Administering that household could not have been easy. Uncle Jesse sat above the strife—kind and loving—and picked up the tab financially, in toto, for all under his sheltering roof.

Lew Corwin, a very handsome man about Irene's age, was, I think, a relative of Cousin Alfred Remington's wife. I remember

Lew even in Piedmont days but he was never as ubiquitous as Irene's other bachelors for some unknown reason. Harry Houghton, an acquaintance of Irene's only, was one of San Francisco's socialite bachelors of the nineties.

Back to the diary—second day's entry, "M. Ray Wilson is the sensation of the train everyone is talking of her and I am sorry to say she has discovered me and her gushing way is quite embarrassing. Eliza H. (Harry's sister) seemed very shocked at my speaking to her but I said I had been taught to be polite to everyone." Of the second night out Irene writes, "Went to bed at 9:30 and slept soundly until I felt a hand on my chest which wakened me out the sound sleep to see a man half in my berth could not see his face as the light was behind him but suppose mine was plain to him. I was dazed for a moment then waited to see what he would do. He said, "Well how's this" I said You have made a mistake in your berth. Still he did not seem inclined to depart And said "What's that" I again informed him he was in the wrong berth and he turned around and walked off" Next day Irene confided in Harry Hoghton and was "glad I did as Mr. Fuller (Will Fuller of the firm of W. F. Fuller and Company, a fellow passenger) had just told him he did something last night he had not done in years—walked in his sleep." Irene adds, "Am glad it was explained or I could not have slept well tonight."

These diary entries were Irene in summary; adoring her devoted mother, basking in the attention of attractive men, preferring unconventional independence to prim tradition and BELIEVING —credulous to the point of naivete. A sleepwalker! She would sleep peacefully. Everything was explained!!

On the third day she records, "the Tasheiras are on the train." The previous day they had "come calling" on Irene in Nol. 3, her section, on the Santa Ysabella, a proud new Pullman sleeper. But the following morning it was "Tashie" alone with whom she breakfasted. It plagues the imagination to figure how he disposed of Mrs. Tasheira to make possible this breakfast "a deux." I remember Tashie, Dr. Tasheira, short and rather broad, with thick white hair, white sideburns, white mustache. Actually Irene did not like him too well but other ladies—Clara Pew, Mary Porter—swooned at his charm.

To welcome Irene to Chicago Elizabeth Meehan (who must have been visiting her married sister there) waited at the station the three hours for Irene's late train. In Chicago Irene roomed in a boarding house with a handsome, tuberculous widow from San Francisco, Mrs. Johnson, whom I met once about 1912. Very stately and pretty she was even then. Irene covered the Fair quite seriously. The diary makes one feel she must have seen everything. She mentions with enthusiasm the nightly pyrotechnical displays, but it was the Art Palace—the paintings—that transcended all else for Irene. Again and again the major part of the time within the fairgrounds was spent in the Palace of Fine Arts. However the diary relates other activities as well as the often inspiring, always educational and unfailingly bone-tiring days at the Fair.

She went to hear the noted Dr. Swing, "he is not a sectarian is that not sufficient to say he is smart. The hall was packed—poor delivery ungraceful gestures and poses am sure if he stepped from behind the altar that I should discovered he was bowlegged—a man of at least 65—inflection very peculiar, articulation slow." However Irene *did* approve his ecumenical theme! This time her description was thoroughly accurate. No exaggeration here, for the *Dictionary of American Biography* tells us of David Swing that, though he had been controversial as a sectarian, he preached each week until his death in October 1894 to crowds of three or four thousand in Chicago's Central Music Hall and that he was "Homely, awkward without oratorical gifts."

By September twentieth Irene was confined to bed with "Russian influenza," the doctor calling daily. Old Dr. Myers told her she "not only had R. I. but just missed having Typhoid Fever." She was back at the Fair, against his orders, by the twenty-second—a wonder she survived!

October fourth Mr. Bacheldor entertained Mrs. Johnson and Irene at dinner with his several men guests who included "old C.J. Stow." Irene saw Henry Irving and Ellen Terry in *Merchant of Venice*. She went to Carrie Dieterich's. "Carrie's children are very nice, bright children but you talk about order and dirt." By October tenth Mary arrived from Ashtabula, Ohio, where the Porters were visiting. At one time or another everyone else seems to have gotten to Chicago, too—Elizabeth, Flo, Alfred (Remington), Lizzie (McCarthy), Mrs. Kit (I wonder if this was Mary Porter's friend, whom I knew in the 1920s? Mrs. Kittredge, whose daughter, Ethel, was the wife of one of the Baldwins of Hawaiian fame). At dinner on October thirtieth Irene even had the good fortune to meet R. G. Ingersoll and his daughter, Maude.

At the end of one day's entry, "Mary has had word from three men in one hour." But shortly Mary, who now was rooming with Irene at a small hotel near the Fair, was taken ill. "It makes me so mad here I have been nursing Mary combing her hair and dressing her—on my return from town today I found her flying around dressed and curled and combed and as chipper as you please, a man waiting for her in the parlor." Irene had been to town to shop "for her for four hours for a birthday party for Adeline." (Mary Goddard remembers that these party favors were tiny Chinese slippers filled with candy.)

Constantly Irene was getting letters from New York from J. G. Stubbs. There is no doubt that Jack was very important in her life at this period. One of the letters she termed "a glorious one." About November first Jack, with the ever-present Billy Martin, came to Chicago and Irene. Immediately J.C. was introduced to Aunt Add who would act as Irene's chaperone on the trip to California in J.C.'s private car. Add and Flora lacked Irene's contacts with King Railroad. That she, through Mr. Stubbs, was able to play grande dame and make private car travel available to them gave Irene inestimable satisfaction. Such a gay group as it was on that journey; Flora and Billy Martin were a jolly pair. Add was not too prim to enjoy and join in the gaiety. Mary Porter "saw them off" by going with them as far as Minneapolis where they stopped for an afternoon of sightseeing.

All in all it was a marvelous trip. How Irene did love Nature's beauty! Her diary rings with descriptions of the lovely country along the route. On the next to last page she writes, "my birthday J. made as a present of buffalo horns (for many of my childhood years they formed a hanging hat tree in our front hall); bought at Medicine Hat. Day closed with a glorious sunset over Satchtchwan (sic) River. Received such a pretty toast at dinner from J. that my life might be as bright and glorious as the day, and as that sunset proved to be pleasant so might everything be so in the future." On a table decorated with fern leaves and roses brought on ice, was served her birthday dinner of "soup, oysters, fish, turkey, salad, pudding, pie—later nuts and raisins." Their car came through the Northwest on the Canadian Pacific. Irene mentions glaciers on Mt. Macdonald and the great Douglas firs as they follow the Frasier

River. The diary ends, "Snow storm at North Bend big flakes." In that swirl of snowflakes Irene's Cinderella journey vanishes.

* * * * * * *

Stimulated by King Railroad, California commercialized on the fair-going proclivity that Chicago's 1893 Exposition had developed in the American public by producing the Midwinter Fair in San Francisco in 1894. Irene had some minor position in the Fair's administrative offices that year. Tom Vivian was a newspaperman—editor of some special department on a San Francisco daily paper. I think he covered the Midwinter Fair. He was not only an utterly delightful companion, full of brilliant humor and bubbly but was constantly the possessor of press passes which assured the very best seats in San Francisco's theaters. During this period Irene saw all the stage greats of that era. Tom made a charming escort but he was, nevertheless, the typical newspaperman—no Horatio Alger hero, he, but rather an intermittent devotee to John Barleycorn.

Tom and Irene no doubt attended the old Tivoli (of which Irene often spoke with affection) which had opened as a legitimate theater in 1879 on Eddy Street between Powell and Mason. Irene knew well and enjoyed dining at San Francisco's famous restaurants of the nineties—Marchand's, Zinkand's, Maison Riche, Elanco's, and The Poodle Dog, which later Irene always felt was rated too high on the list of fine eating places.

It may have been this year, too, that Irene visited Dr. Jordan's Museum at Sixth and Market—an adventure she always felt had been rather daring even though she was well chaperoned. She just had to see the much-talked-of, famous exhibits—the pickled head, complete with beard, of Joaquin Murietta in the jar and in a second jar the hand, missing two fingers, purported to be that of Murietta's trusted lieutenant in banditry, "Three-fingered Jack."

*   *   *   *   *   *   *

Early in 1894 the Porters with Mrs. Haskins were back in California. They bought a house on Post Street in San Francisco not far from the Lauries' rooms at 1904 Laguna Street. In partial answer to my request for details of our mothers' early years of friendship Mary Porter Goddard in 1964 wrote, "That summer of 1894 Irene was very important to us. Mama was visiting in Sacramento when Grandmother came down with a severe case of pneumonia. I hastened to your mother a few blocks away and she called the Doctor, got word to Mama, etc. Grandma pulled through." Following this illness of Mrs. Haskins, so that in such an emergency a doctor could be summoned, Mary had a telephone installed in the Post Street house. It was one of the earliest phones in a private residence in all the Bay Area. Another time when Mrs. Haskins was ill Mary and Irene were both off on some jaunt (possibly their Castle Crags-Shasta Springs trip on which Irene caught the largest Dolly Varden trout of the season on the McCloud River—her only fishing venture, too). This time it was Laura who solicitously called on Mrs. Haskins then next day took her some nourishing soup.

In 1894 an old Vallejo friend of Mr. Haskins', a Mr. Wilson lived at the Grand Hotel in San Francisco. Like many California men he owned a vast collection of gems—finely set and of various sizes. Among the many nice things he did for Mrs. Haskins and more especially for Mary and Irene was to present each with a diamond. Irene's, in a Tiffany setting, was her first ring of value. She had a passion for rings! In her mind Mr. Wilson's gift to her was made in sympathy because he saw Flora showered with much largess—jewels and furs—while poor Irene was given nothing to delight a young woman's heart.

*   *   *   *   *   *

The Lauries lived on at 1904 Laguna. The Porters had sold the Post Street house and moved to 4144 Grand Boulevard in Chicago. Irene's visit there in the fall of '96 marked the beginning of the strong bond between her and the Porter girls who by that time were in their midteens and were highly companionable. Adelyn, the nonconformist, was in minor rebellion at having to acquire all the niceties of a super-nice era. At table, to better instill manners, there was a "kitty." Any infraction of the social code called for a penny from the offender. Adelyn supplied most of the pennies for the kitty. Stubbornly she insisted, among other things, that as long as a spoon came to a convenient point she would sip from that point. Younger sister Mary was growing up less rebelliously. Either she was made for this Victorian era or the era for her. She aspired to art. Irene helped her with her painting, which led, a little later, to Mary's having a winter at Chicago's Art Institute.

Mary Porter's divorce was in an embryonic state. Meanwhile she was quite carried away by the charms of one Frank Knox. He, possibly, was the "why" of this last Chicago move of Mary's. Most surely she expected to eventually marry Frank. Irene, visiting at 4144, developed a severe case of tonsillitis, followed by inflammatory rheumatism. She was very ill. Mary, admittedly, was no nurse but Frank proved to be a natural at nursing. It was he who waited on and cared for Irene. Tonsils or no, the old propinquity angle; Frank asked the convalescing Irene to marry him. Not to Mary's liking, that! I am not sure just how Irene's trip ended. She never for a moment considered Frank's proposal but not unnaturally it caused a rift between Mary and Irene for awhile—the only rift in their half century of devoted friendship.

Meanwhile Mama Laurie's letters to Irene during this Chicago sojourn were doubly precious. Some of them remain and the people Laura mentions seeing in Irene's absence tell much the story of Irene's life in the Gay Nineties. Of course Laura saw Add and Flora and therefore Mabel Love, for at this time she and Flora were almost inseparable. Once Laura mentions George James, an ardent suitor of Flora's, however the time that Flora was to be at all interested in men admirers was pretty much at a close. At various times members of the Meehan family, Clara Pew and Evie Titus called at Laguna Street to assuage Laura's loneliness. Jesse and Evis Titus (friends of Flora's, too) were originally Sacramento residents for Jesse was proprietor of a hotel there. Later, during my San Jose childhood, we often drove out to see them on their fruit ranch in Mountain View where, hotel days passed, they lived quietly, Evie's mother with them. Grandma Gordon, I called her. She had white hair parted in the middle and drawn into a tight bun at the back. She wore a black alpaca skirt and black silk bodice with white ruching at her neck. She carried a white handkerchief tucked in her belt. She was the prototype of all grandmothers in 1900.

Even in Irene's absence the Go Easy Club kept in touch. Laura had calls from May DuBois, Nellie Zeile and George Burdick. Vic and May DuBois, Ed and Nellie Zeile with George and Irene *were* the Go Easy Club—a cycling group who of a Sunday might load their bicycles aboard some local train to reach beautiful and far remote country through which to enjoy their rides. Vic, as a National Guard general, became a Spanish-American War hero. San Francisco honors his memory by DuBois Street and DuBois Tunnel. Kay DuBois was often Irene's guest in the late '20s when these two last survivors of the Club rediscovered one another. The Edward Zeitles, a hearty German couple, had three children. In my teens, their children grown, they lived in a wonderful old country home in North Berkeley in the area of the present Hopkins and Peralta Avenues, near the stately old Samuel C. Posen castle. Colonel George Burdick (also of the Guard) was a bachelor. Working conscientiously in the Anglo Bank in San Francisco he would remain a bachelor to his death, for after his widowed mother's death he continued to be the sole support of two spinster sisters.

ONE OF LAURA'S LETTERS mentions that Lizzie called. That would be Irene's close friend, Lizzie McCarthy. I have no neat dates to fasten on incidents in the story of the fabulous McCarthy-Chamot family in San Francisco. However Lizzie's part in China's Boxer Rebellion of 1900 is documented in two fairly recent books—Walter Lord's *The Good Years* (1960) and Peter Fleming's *The Siege at Peking* (1959). In Fleming's book most of the information about the Chamots is contained in a long footnote credited to Dr. P. Campiche: "Notes sur la Carrière d'Auguste Chamot" in the *Revue Historique Vaudoise*, March 1955.

Lizzie McCarthy with her mother, traveling in the Orient, made a stopover at the internationally elite Hotel de Pekin, which proved of long enough duration to bud a romance that in due time brought the hotel's attractive French-Swiss proprietor, F. Auguste Chamot, to San Francisco to claim Lizzie as his bride. As to dates involved I know only that by the spring of 1900 Mme Chamot was installed in the Hotel de Pekin next to the French Legation in that compact area, within Peking's inner walled city, bounded on the north by the Imperial Palace and on the south by the Great Tartar Wall and occupied by the foreigners, their legations and their few places of business. Fleming states that "a resourceful Swiss, named Chamot, managed with the help of his American wife, the Peking Hotel." At this time Auguste was thirty-three; Lizzie about thirty-two. During the siege Auguste's contacts with the Chinese proved invaluable. Campiche says he "played a major part in victualling first the besieged and after, the relieving forces." Like Fleming, Lizzie mentioned the odor of decaying mule meat during the siege, as animals devoid of feed and forage died of starvation. Lizzie indicated that, though the people in the legations were not near to starvation, that as their food supplies dwindled they were

MME AUGUSTE CHAMOT

***

not above eating meat that had quite an aroma. Auguste and Lizzie at the hotel did much to feed the hungry besieged at the legations. Lord states, "-they ground flour and ran a sort of catering service for discriminating refugees."

During the siege Campiche tells us, though, the hotel formed "part of a dangerous sector of the outer defences." Mme Chamot "never left it to join the other ladies in comparative safety in the British Legation." Lizzie was quick to tell us that listening to the petty gossip of the women in the British Legation would have been more deadly to her than the position she eventually took beside the men on the wall. She said that she did not know how many Chinese Boxers she may have shot. She actually saw only seven fall that she *knew* she, herself, had killed.

On May 29 the Chamots headed a small, unofficial armed rescue party (mounted on ponies) that escorted twenty-nine Belgians (engineers and their families) to the relatively safe besieged legation area from a town sixteen miles out of Peking just before the frenzied Boxers entered the village, looting and burning all in sight. Later bands of Boxers broke into Peking's outer city and began burning the churches. The diplomats made no attempt to help but the Chamots rescued the padre and twenty-five nuns (twenty of them Chinese) from the blazing South Cathedral. Campiche mentions that "the Chamots throughout the siege behaved with gallantry and resource," and adds that Mme Chamot was "certainly a plucky woman."

When reading Fleming's *The Siege at Peking* certain passages brought to mind memories of isolated bits that, as a child of four or five, I had heard Lizzie tell Irene of the China she so loved and of its savage Boxer War. So many names of places, things and people rang with a familiar sound. I recall two incidents which Lizzie said were not generally known. One was that a messenger (an ignorant but faithful Chinese) was sent out and got through because when the poor ragged fellow, hastening to his destination, was stopped and searched by Boxers the finely written message he carried was not found. It had been tightly rolled and placed inside a section of quill which had then been inserted in the messenger's rectum.

The other story had to do with blowing up gates of the city. I do not know which gates or just when except that I understood the dynamiting to be important in breaking the siege. Two Japanese volunteered to swaddle their bodies in gun powdered wadding and dynamite. Making human bombs of themselves they squirmed, unseen, under the gates and blew themselves to bits to effect relief of the besieged. Lizzie's admiration of these men and their deed knew no bounds.

Four hundred eighty men, of whom almost half had been killed or wounded by the end of the fifty-five days the siege at Peking lasted, held off a force of at least twenty thousand savage Boxer rebels. On the night of victory, the siege broken, there was general rejoicing. Walter Lord writes of that historic night: "-at the battered Hotel in Pekin, M. Chamot sensed the mood perfectly. Like the good innkeeper he was, he magically produced champagne for everybody."

Lizzie understood and loved the Chinese people, holding them in high esteem. Eugene Burdick, coauthor of *The Ugly American*, would have approved of Lizzie Chamot as an American citizen abroad. She learned the language of the Chinese with whom she came in contact. Years later in San Francisco she acted as court interpreter when occasionally a litigant was from northern China. San Francisco's Chinatown spoke the commoners' dialect of Cantonese while Lizzie spoke the Pekinese of the northern and higher-ranking Chinese. For a period after Auguste's death she was the only English-speaking person in the area who could translate that dialect.

Many of the things Lizzie told about China were deeply impressing to a child. I can almost see the hand carts piled high with refuse from which extended the moving foot or hand of a new-born baby girl. This phenomenon Lizzie had often seen in China which prized boy babies but whose poor people often did not keep girl babies. Lizzie told, too, of the deforming binding of feet of the healthy and high-class Chinese girls. But as a child I occasionally saw such ladies, even in San Francisco's Chinese quarter, able to walk only because of an attendant on either side giving support. This physical foible was an assertion of wealth; there could be no doubt these women had always had servants!

A family story asserts that Auguste with his infinite respect for the Chinese people during the loot of Peking refused to loot. But knowing, as he did, the true value of Chinese articles he was not above giving a soldier the price of a drink for some article Auguste knew to be of value and which the soldier had taken from no one knew where. According to Campiche such rationalizing was the order of the day and he refers to Auguste as being "pre-eminent among the serious looters." All in all the Chamots did return to the United States with much treasure.

Entering at the San Francisco customs port Auguste was asked by an official, "What's this thing?" Auguste answered, "Oh, my wife was in a lot of private theatricals. Guess it's part of a costume." The customs official said, "Well, nothing on that then," and flung to the corner of the room the somewhat bedraggled object with a soiled ribbon or two dangling. Auguste held his breath, hoping no damage would be done, for it had been a headdress of the Dowager

Empress and the wiggly spirals all terminated in real pearls or precious stones. (Lizzie gave Irene one of the Empress' hairpins. Irene had it set in a ring, the ruby surrounded by the pearls, which are relatively valueless because they are pierced in the Chinese mode to be mounted, as they were, on spiral prongs. The ring is now Beva's.)

In the Chamot "collection" were several juis. Historically, juis are first known in ancient Chinese paintings which show a priest carrying one resting on his arm in a procession, indicating that juis were kept in temples in ancient times. The Chamots referred to them as family luck symbols which graced the homes of the distinguished wealthy and passed down the family line as an omen of good health, longevity and prosperity for the family home. A jui might originally have been awarded to honor a war hero or a leading citizen outstanding for his good deeds.

The Chamots gave a jui to Mother McCarthy and one to Lizzie's bachelor brother Gene. Calling his "a soup ladle" that he did not know what to do with, Gene promptly presented it to Irene. It is made of one solid piece of opaque green jade. Sixteen inches long, its greatest width is four inches and maximum height two inches. The jade itself is carved with Chinese good luck symbols and characters and undoubtedly was originally otherwise unornamented. As generations rolled on and the family, whose symbol of good fortune it was, became more affluent some wealthy lord of the house ordered the jui encased in a band of intricately wrought pure and unalloyed gold which would meet in several places across its top in a delicate tracery sparkling with gems. Though the looting soldier Auguste gave the *pour bière* for it did not realize the value of the jui as a whole he did recognize the more precious stones set in the gold filigree. By the time Auguste rescued the jui most of the gems had been pried out; only the semi-precious turquoise and moonstones with one lone ruby remained. The greater part of the Chamot's valuable loot, including several other juis, was bought, through an agent, by J. Pierpont Morgan for his collection.

Over the years Mrs. McCarthy and Lizzie had brought Irene many gorgeous gifts from the Orient. The hundreds of ermine skins Irene at one time had made into a below-waist-length cape of voluminous lines with a high collar which stood out almost like a ruff. There were various pieces of silk brocade and one lovely corn-colored embroidered silk so pure it has withstood the years. A gray silk crepe kimono, pink-silk lined, with padded roll of pink silk at the bottom, had an eighteen-inch border embroidered in delicate pink flowers. Only its obi survives. A round ivory box—a single piece of ivory—carved with many, many faces was another gift.

Because the Chamots had so continuously helped the people of the various legations, as well as for their brave acts of rescue, Auguste was honored by several foreign powers with decorations and financial rewards. It must have been on these funds, coupled with Morgan's money, that the Chamots lived "high on the hog" for a time. In my own mind much of this living was done on McCarthy money which I believe may also have built the Inverness house and certainly did provide the *Ramona* which undoubtedly is the yacht referred to by Campiche. The *Ramona* was a palatial craft for the era and Irene enjoyed many a sail on her but the *Ramona* never won Irene from her first love, Uncle John Pew's *Truant*.

Because of the Chamot's international acclaim they were often entertained by representatives of foreign governments who came to San Francisco. One fabulous dinner, at which Irene was present, was occasioned by the presence of a French man-of-war in port.

The Chamots had been entertained aboard her. Reciprocating, they invited the ship's officers, a gallant group of dashing young Frenchmen, to this sumptuous dinner. Irene's vivacious charm captivated these discriminating young gentlemen. Language proved no barrier to the compliments they paid her, her dinner partner drinking a champagne toast to her from her own dainty satin slipper.

*   *   *   *   *   *   *

One of my early memories is of the red velvet and mahogany splendor of the McCarthy-Chamot residence in San Francisco. Here their French butler, Paul, always presided at table with courtly manner and immobile face—save for the time I broke my usual children-should-be-seen-and-not-heard behavior to rise in my high chair and gesture down the long table shouting, "Gene, Gene, don't play with your spoon, it isn't polite!" The resultant specially hearty roar of laughter was occasioned because no one in the family ever dared to suggest to austere Eugene that he vary his independent way of life even in the minutest detail. The laughter was impressed on MY memory only because Paul, too, laughed—an unheard-of thing.

I remember also going to the stables, far back of the house, where Lizzie's beloved Chinese pony, Pepper, was tended by a trusted groom. (It was Pepper that Lizzie had ridden on that daring rescue of the Belgian families.) There was also another sorrel horse and hounds, Schwartz, a black (naturally) male and Gretchen, an adorable brown velvet female that I first met as a tiny pup. We both fell asleep together on the porch of the Inverness house. This summer home had just been completed and Irene was there to help with the interior decoration. I recall some delightful small oriental masks on the stairway wall. It was on the landing of the stairway that I best remember Belinda. Her dinner had not set well and up it had come. At such times a young mind is duly impressed with a Saint Bernard's size and capacity for food!

The Inverness house was named Tăchūsă. So it sounded at least. I do not know the spelling but I do know it is a Chinese word and that accenting the first syllable is important. Like many Chinese words with a change of accent comes a change of meaning and one possible accent arrangement of Tachusa is a word never spoken in polite society. One's tongue had to be well trained if the name of the house was to be mentioned to a Chinese!

To be sure Lizzie loved animals but I remember nothing of the "menagerie" mentioned by Campiche. In San Francisco some time before her marriage Lizzie rescued a gopher snake that boys had been stoning and did take it home where it quickly adjusted to domestic life. When Lizzie sat down the snake would glide up in front of her chair and wave its head from side to side till she took it up in her lap. Its presence was not welcomed by her brothers; returning from a night out on the town they didn't know WHAT they were seeing!

In later years at Inverness Lizzie had a pet raccoon. (In the 1920s when we visited the deserted shell of lovely Tachusa we saw the raccoon house in a tree beside an upper bedroom window. That and the handsome marble wash basins are all I clearly remember of that, my second visit to Inverness). Once when Lizzie, leaving Inverness, took the ferry for San Francisco she was wearing a voluminous tweed coat with a great inner pocket where she had tucked her raccoon. The mischievous raccoon slipped out and with his clever paws relieved the man passenger sitting next Lizzie of his wallet. Quite a rumpus ensued when the man discovered his loss, called an officer of the boat and accused Lizzie, the only person who had been near him. She had been quietly reading all the while. Even in her anger at the unjust charge she thought to investigate the inner pocket and found both the coon and the missing wallet. Nothing could convince the man that she had not trained her raccoon to be a pickpocket!

Lizzie was one of the first women to drive an automobile in San Francisco. Once when brakes failed on a hill as her auto approached the bottom then the rise of another hill she stayed with the machine till the momentum ran out—steering it steadily down the grade, up the hill and as it backed down the hill and up the first one repeated and repeated till the auto remained exhausted at the bottom street between the two rises. One of the coolest-headed women of her era!

* * * * * * *

I adored Auguste Chamot. He seemed to me tall, dark and hand-some. He was slender, had compelling yet kindly loving eyes, wore a small dark mustache—in short, was very French. Though I now realize he was Swiss, his must have been a French canton. The last time I was with him was in 1907 when he and Lizzie visited our home in San Francisco. Even at that time they were having marital difficulties. I knew there was another woman. I saw her once on the street with Auguste—a buxom blonde. Even my childish deductions seemed to place her as a possible result of a custom I had heard Irene say that she had discovered once when helping Lizzie make her bed. Lizzie made a long roll of a blanket and placed it firmly in the center of the Chamot connubial pallet. She was in so many ways a generation or two ahead of her time—clearly an exponent of twin beds!

Campiche comments on M. Auguste Chamot's death that he "had divorced his wife and on his deathbed married his mistress, a manicurist, Betsy Dollar." That is *not* the way I heard it! Shortly after the 1907 visit Lizzie and Auguste were divorced and he did marry the buxom blonde, Betsy, but during ill health before his death she deserted him. It was Lizzie who went to Auguste in his illness to nurse him and in whose arms he died.

Besides Lizzie the McCarthys had two sons, Gene and Will. Mrs. McCarthy (Auntie Mac—a rugged and spirited old lady who suffered the crippling ravages of arthritis before her death which occurred about 1912) always claimed that Gene was in love with Irene but had never declared himself because his younger brother, Will, had early showed Irene attention. Later they were practically engaged. All the McCarthy clan accepted their marriage as inevitable. Will was quite a gay blade and, in the midst of all this family joy at his alliance with his sister's best friend, eloped with Edith (to hear his family tell it), a "cheap and dissolute" chorus girl. Their marriage lasted but it broke the tie between Will and his family. At one time, when all was rosy between Irene and Will, passage was booked by Auntie Mac for Irene and herself to go to China to visit Lizzie and Auguste. I think the trip was canceled due to the Boxer unrest which was sensed in China long before the actual rebellion.

The McCarthys had money, plenty of money, until the earthquake-fire of April 1906 wiped them out. (They were insured by London companies that did not pay.) Father McCarthy, who had died before Irene knew the family, had collected San Francisco real estate with the ardor that other collectors acquire paintings of the old masters. He attended auctions. In San Francisco in his era items were auctioned in groups. Perhaps a sofa, a diamond ring, two sandlots would go on the block together. Most bidders were interested in the diamond and were barely aware of the "worthless" sandlots but Mr. McCarthy was aware *only* of the sandlots which he was convinced would not be worthless long. He had a hotel and office buildings to leave his family as well as the many far-flung sandlots.

Gene had his bachelor apartment in the City where he housed his valuable library of first editions. To begin with, his tall book-cases had doors of beveled plate glass, mahogany framed. Soon he discovered that the sun shining through the glass faded the book bindings. He changed to solid mahogany doors and had the framed glass ones made into mirrors; he gave one to his mother and the other five to Irene. Gene, who visited much in our home until about 1908, never came but that he brought me some lovely gift. He gave me many beautiful books, among them *Denslow's Mother Goose* and *The Guessing Book*. He could not forget that as the oldest child he grew up when the McCarthys were poor and that his only toys were trains of empty gin bottles dragged over the sand dunes in an intricate tracery of tracks.

Gene wore a full heavy beard, not uncommon in that era. Will whom I met but once, was smooth-faced and smooth looking—dashing, derby-hatted. Lizzie really was not pretty. Her nose was too pointed, her hair frizzy but trim. SHE was trim and had a tre-mendous personality though I find it impossible to describe.

Shortly after Auguste's death Lizzie remarried—a Gus Renstrom, a most ordinary and uncultured fellow, as much the opposite of Auguste as could be imagined. The marriage was not lasting. Perhaps it would have been, had their one child not died at birth. I remember Lizzie, who must have been forty at the time of her pregnancy, coming for dinner at our Piedmont home one Sunday with Gus. She wore a maternity dress of priceless Chinese uncut velvet. From this time which was about 1910 until the late twenties Lizzie was lost to us. Shortly before we began to see her again Gene had died penniless. We learned that during many of the intervening years Lizzie had been a nurse-companion to Mrs. Le Conte[3] (Mrs. Joseph Le Conte, I think), staying with her until her death. Their tie was extremely close and Professor Le Conte revered Lizzie for what she had meant to his wife.

Lizzie was down on her luck financially, was boarding, living in one room in San Francisco. Irene would have her over for weekends in Berkeley and would send her substantial Christmas checks. Lizzie was trying to sell her fabulous Russian sable and ermine coats, acquired in the Orient, to the movie industry for period pictures. They were about her only assets. At this time all Lizzie's reading was directed toward books on Tibet. Not only the wild grandeur of the country but its mystical philosophy attracted her. It was her passionate wish to visit Tibet and as she talked of it somehow one felt she was actually there in spirit riding her pony, Pepper, up a frozen mountainside to look down on the breathtaking beauty of a hidden valley. She must have died during World War II. I do not even know the date of her death.

3 Helen Gompertz Le Conte; a sister, Kate Gompertz, M.D., a fellow resident at Canterbury Woods until her death about 1971.

LASTLY LAURA'S NOVEMBER 1896 LETTERS stretched three separate and seemingly inconsequential strands of news across the miles to Irene in Chicago. First, "Kate Scott came to see me today." Second, "Alfred is here. At least he was registered at the Palace Sunday." (How did Laura know? Were registrations at the Palace newsworthy enough for daily papers to print? Was Alfred Remington's presence in San Francisco news?) Third, "Add wants you to go and see Mrs. Chambers. She is coming out here in December." Before the turn of the century the slender threads of these three items would be woven firmly into the pattern of Irene's life fabric.

Alfred Remington purchased the famous Lick Mill near Agnew in Santa Clara County for his paper manufacturing venture. Authentic source materials document the elegance of the historic buildings at Lick Mill. Beautiful woods—mahogany paneling— door knobs and escutcheons of silver, gold washed, were in Lick's flour mill and the big house which eccentric James Lick had built as proof of his financial worth because, decades past, a miller "back East" had scorned penniless young Lick as suitor for his daughter's hand.

I know of no documentation of the activities at Lick Mill under A.D.'s ownership. My childhood memories of hearsay must suffice. A.D. moved his wife, Nann, from the social whirl of Watertown, New York, to the fine house at the Mill. He installed Lew Corwin as mill manager, for A.D. had many far-flung investments to look after himself. It was not long before he was glaringly aware that Lew lacked the day-in-day-out, shoulder-to-the-wheel qualities necessary in a working-manager and that Nann lacked interest in a socially isolated life. A.D. hoped to solve both these deficiencies by hiring Jim Scott as assistant manager to supply the attributes Lew lacked and housing the Scotts in one of the various satellite dwell-ings on the mill grounds. Jim's wife, Kate, and her sister, Harriet, were jolly young women who would give Nann on-the-premises companionship. But, alas, Nann was still restless, unhappy. In a final effort to mill-break his pampered wife A.D. appealed to his Cousin Laura and Irene. Offering financial inducements he asked them to move into another of the houses at the Mill. This they did. But, about the time they were comfortably settled, Nann had had it! She left permanently for her beloved New York home.

Life at the Mill was a sort of feudal idyll. The Scott family was moved into the big house which was adequately staffed by servants, as in Nann's regime. When in California A.D. would entertain his business associates there at elegantly appointed dinners. The gar-dener, who brought out flowers to the big house daily, would make corsages for the ladies to be worn at these dinners—Irene never forgot one he made her, choosing red salvia which set off the beauty of her dark hair and eyes. Harriet and Irene were special friends. With Lick's eccentricities in mind they searched for treasures in every nook and cranny of the old mansion—and found, in a far attic corner, James Lick's old silk hat in which rats, long since routed, had once made a comfortable nest!

Days she was left to herself at the Mill Irene would take the canoe and a book of Shakespeare's plays and drift down the creek to the shade of an overhanging willow to read the Bard's masterpieces. Adelyn Porter Watrous, writing in 1964 of the Mill continues the impression of a pastoral idyll, "M (Mary Goddard) and I can remember going there on a little private rail line running through the cattails." But there was an ogre in this fairyland of Irene's. The Lick Mill property adjoined the grounds of the Agnews Insane Asylum (as Agnews State Hospital was known in the '90s when the whole terminology and concept of mental illness was quite different than now). Poor Irene would lie in bed, covers over her head, suffering tortured fear of the possibility of a crazy prowler when at night the whistle blew at the asylum to warn that some inmate had escaped. Dr. Stocking, the long-time superintendent at Agnew, a most enlightened man for his era, tried to allay Irene's fear. She was very fond of Dr. Stocking, respected him and believed what he told her in the light of day but when that whistle blew in the darkness, fears engendered by centuries of misconceptions concerning the mentally ill would grip her anew.

All this was while Irene had her railroad pass and the Southern Pacific tracks were close at hand. Up she would go to San Francisco for a weekend of yachting with the Pews, or a visit at McCarthy's or at Meehan's, or off on a cycling jaunt with the Go Easy Club, or up to Sacramento for a gay party at the Titus' hotel. So though she moved at slow temps through the pastoral idyll of Lick Mills, Irene continued to whirl in San Francisco's fin-de-siècle gaiety.

BOOK
of
ARTHUR

"HE HAVING NOW HERE IN OPEN COURT, TAKEN
AND SUBSCRIBED THE OATH REQUIRED BY THOSE
LAWS, TO SUPPORT THE CONSTITUTION OF THE
UNITED STATES AND TO RENOUNCE AND ABJURE
ALL ALLEGIANCE AND FIDELITY TO EVERY FOREIGN
PRINCE, POTENTATE, STATE OR SOVEREIGNTY
WHATEVER, AND PARTICULARLY ALL ALLEGIANCE
WHICH HE MAY IN ANYWISE OWE TO The Queen of
Great Britain and Ireland WHERE HE WAS HERETOFORE
A SUBJECT...," so declare the naturalization papers that made
George Chambers a citizen in Cook County, Illinois, on March 1,
1858.

Elizabeth Broomfield, whom he subsequently married, had sold
matches on the streets of London when a child. (Could she have
dreamed then that she was an Eliza Doolittle destined to be the
Fair Lady of a stately mansion in an elite suburb of a great American
city?) So both George and Elizabeth were born in England of pure
English stock—not of aristocratic descent but the kind of folk who
built America. How and why each came to the United States I know
not but that George Chambers and Elizabeth Broomfield with one
of her sisters, at least, *did* reach Illinois I *do* know. I assume George
and Elizabeth met in Chicago and were married a year or two after
George became a citizen, for their first child was born in Chicago
on February 2, 1861. His middle name showed how Americanized
this English born couple had become. He was christened Arthur
Lincoln Chambers *and* he was to be my father.

George was a builder—a successful contractor installing sub-
ways, bridges, an under-river tube in the fast-growing Midwestern
city. However their Chicago was growing so fast that George and
Lizzie, with another baby on the way, sought more relaxed and

ARTHUR CHAMBERS

67

GEORGE AND ELIZABETH
CHAMBERS WITH THEIR
CHILDREN | Arthur is standing
behind his mother's chair, with
his first wife, May Crosse.

bucolic environs. Lizzie's sister had married Charles Gladding. The Gladdings' son, Albert, was a little older than Artie Chambers and their son George a bit younger. The Gladdings, too, hoped for a more peaceful, more rural setting. A friend of the two men, one E. P. Ripley (later to become president of the Santa Fe Railroad), was also seeking for his family comfortable, elegant country living not too far from Chicago's business heart. Together these three men became the Founding Fathers of Chicago's select residential suburb of the era, Riverside. There the families built their stately Victorian houses—the Chambers and the Gladding houses side by side.

Except for the loss of one child, the infant Lizzie, the Chambers family steadily grew to include, after Arthur, Annie, then little George Robert—Charles—Jim—Charlotte—and, finally, Genevieve, the baby—a slightly spoiled baby perhaps, adored by so many older siblings. Her experienced parents however did not flinch at her maneuverings. One day, unable to get her way about some passing desire, small Genevieve in a rage packed her suitcase determined to run away from home. Finally packed, with bonnet and coat on, downstairs and almost to the front door, her anger cooled sufficiently so that, small suitcase in hand, the little girl stopped before her father's chair to tell him she was leaving home, running away from home. George Chambers lowered his newspaper just long enough to glance over it at her and said, "Well, goodbye. I hope you enjoy yourself." Utterly deflated, Genevieve, dragging her feet, climbed the stairs to her room—and unpacked.

Life flowed happily on in the Chambers family. George continued to prosper financially. There were servants in these Riverside homes in that gracious era—cooks, second maids, children's nurses. It was a nurse, though, to whom the only really tragic occurrence in the Chambers family was attributed. His nurse dropped baby

Charlie—a hard fall. It was noticed afterward that the child did not hear well, then little seizures began to occur, developing in later life to true epilepsy.

*　*　*　*　*　*　*

Next door in the Gladding house, too, tragedy had stalked. Mrs. Gladding, Elizabeth Broomfield Chambers' sister, had sickened and died. A widower with two small boys, Charlie Gladding, in due time, took another wife. I do not know how he met her but this time he married Sarah Adeline Remington. Their only child, a girl, was born in October of 1866. This, his only daughter, Charlie Gladding insisted should bear his mother's name, Eleanor. Apparently he was satisfied when the little one was named Flora Eleanor (to be known throughout her life either as Flora, Flo, Flossie or by her formal signature, Flora E. Gladding!).

A letter written in September by Lotte in Middlebury, Ohio, told Helen, "Add was here and we had a pleasant time during her sojourn. She has some nice clothes you better believe. She took us by surprise with a set of diamonds, pin and earrings. I don't know real diamonds, I presume there (sic) were, at least they passed for such and were very handsome.—Add wore all her fine things very quietly and very modestly. Flora is a perfect little picture and bright as a dollar." (Lotte mentioned that she, herself, had recently been given some *garnet* jewelry by an older woman friend.)

*　*　*　*　*　*　*

The Riverside of 1871 comes to life in Carrie Dieterich's diary. On July 26, 1871, she arrived for a visit at the Gladding's. "The houses are all very pretty. Some of the yards have rustic fences around them, while others have no fences at all. Uncle Charley's house is not as pretty as some, but it is very pretty. He has a little summer house in the yard. He raises a few vegetables but buys most. There is a barn on the lot, and he keeps two horses and some chickens.

"July 27th 1871. Uncle George Laurie is here. After breakfast he took me out boat riding on the river. Uncle Charley owns a boat. Artie Chambers is here visiting. So he and Albert unlocked the boats. We had a splendid row. The woods grow along each side of the river. After awhile we came to a foot bridge which was so low we had to stoop to get under it. When we had gone quite a ways beyond that we came to a place where there were some Water Lilies. We got three buds and two blossoms. Then we turned around and came home. Uncle George, after showing me the way home, went directly to the depot. He was going to Chicago—." Carrie describes the DeGolyer house nearby in Riverside. "The house is splendidly furnished. The bed in the front chamber has a canopy to it lined with blue silk." Subsequently Annie Chambers married Joseph Baldwin DeGolyer—her wedding gown, gloves, fan and shoes were on exhibit when we visited the de Young Museum in San Francisco about 1940. Annie and Joe had two sons—George born about 1892 and Joseph Baldwin Jr. (Baldwin) born in 1899.

Carrie, herself, was fifteen and coquet, eating candy and reading seemed to fill her time between calls. One night they went to the hotel to look on at a dance. Flora went to sleep and Aunt Add laid her on a sofa. After they got home the hotel band came serenading the house. "Uncle Charley said, 'I am much obliged for the music but I haven't a drop in the house'."

During her Riverside visit Carrie went to Chicago to visit friends. The journey took her one hour and five minutes. At the friend's house, "While I was sitting at the window, a man came along crying, 'Watermelon, watermelon, fifty cents apiece'."

At home in Galesburg later that year Carrie writes in her diary on October 10, 1871. "There has been a terrible fire in Chicago, and it may be burning now. It commenced Saturday night (October 7, 1871) and has been raging ever since. The most beautiful buildings in the city are destroyed, among them, Potter-Palmer's magnificent new hotel. Last night Pa came home with a lot of meat for us to cook for the sufferers of Chicago. They sent a carload of provisions there last night, and are going to send another today. There are 100,000 people burned out of house and home. Ma went to Riverside yesterday." I guess she could see the fire from there.

"October 11, 1871. Pa received a letter from Ma today. She said when the train was within 40 miles of Chicago they could discern a faint glow, and in Riverside they could see the flames plainly. Uncle Charley's houses are burned. Mr. Chambers had 14 houses there and every one are burned. Mr. Fuller's folks and Uncle Frank are staying at Aunt Add's. Mr. Chambers has four families staying with him. The prairies of Minnesota and Wisconsin are on fire, everything is so dry. We have a force of eight men to guard at night, as there is no insurance now."

CHARLES GLADDING, comfortably settled in Illinois,[4] nevertheless felt the magnet of westward migration. Only a few years after the completion of the transcontinental railroad California had become known not only for its salubrious climate for winter visitors but also for its "boom"—its burst of permanent population growth. Brick was the predominant building material of the period. Charlie Gladding knew clay and knew how it could be used for manufacture of brick and he thought possibly for other products that would be useful in the development of a fast-growing area. Hopefully roaming California he discovered and purchased the fine clay deposit at Lincoln. (The original patent for the town site of Lincoln was granted by President Buchanan in 1859 to Theodore Judah of Central Pacific Railroad fame. Building began at Lincoln the following year.) Here was a propitious site for his new venture Charlie Gladding so wholeheartedly believed would succeed.

Gladding McBean and Company was established in 1875. In Peter McBean with his aptitude for office detail, his business experience and administrative ability, Charles Gladding had just the man to balance his own technical knowledge and supervisory skill in pottery management. Gladding and McBean had the clay. Gladding and McBean had the right combination of technical and administrative skills. Gladding and McBean did NOT have the cold hard cash needed to establish their pottery. Charlie Gladding turned to his old friend and neighbor, George Chambers, who fortunately had such an adequate income from his various substantial

---

4 *The Great Persuader* by David Lavender, Doubleday, 1970, is the source of the following summary. Colonel C. L. Wilson (who could have been the donor of those three diamonds to Mrs. Haskins, Mary and Irene!), founder of the California Central Railroad, intended to push the railroad from Folsom to Marysville but reached only Lincoln. Wilson brought Judah to California re: building the railroad from Sacramento to Marysville but Theodore Judah, an engineer, surveyed first the 22 miles to Negro Bar; then the next 18 miles to what would become the town of Lincoln. This railroad was the Sacramento Valley Railroad.

investments that he readily supplied the needed funds from his liquid assets, thereby becoming the "and Company" of Gladding McBean and Company. (At his death the Gladding McBean stock ranked lowest in value of the various assets George Chambers left his heirs. At his widow's death, some twenty-five years later, that stock formed by far the major portion of the appraised value of the large estate.) In fast-growing California the glazed terra-cotta sewer pipe developed at the Gladding McBean pottery was as much in demand as were the various kinds of brick made by the company. In time, drain tiles, roof tiles and other terra-cotta products were added. By the time I visited the pottery in 1916 a skilled Italian sculptor was employed full-time to design cornices, window and door trims to be reproduced in finely glazed terra-cotta custom-made ornamentations for the façade of the Matson Building then under construction in San Francisco. In 1924, that period of giant mergers, the family firm faded into the great corporation now famous for its Franciscan china as well as brick conduit pipe and other terra-cotta products.

Charles Gladding may have left his family in Illinois for some months or even a year until the labor pains of the pottery's "borning" were over. However before 1877 the Gladding family was ensconced in their house in West Oakland where they remained until Flora was through high school.

Meantime Albert and George, the two sons of the Gladding-Broomfield union, had developed into two very different types of young men. George, the younger, had a terrific personality. No one could help loving George Gladding but he had little or no Horatio Alger worth. A nineteenth century playboy par excellence was George! In 1878 Irene wrote Carrie from Oakland, "Cousin George is boarding with us." Probably he was *persona non grata* to his father by then. I never heard of his working. At first he was far too busy with "wine, women and song." Later wine alone absorbed all his time and eventually more money than his father would supply. One scrape of George's after another had disillusioned Charles Gladding but Add would secretly give George money saved from her liberal household allowance for she never stopped loving and sympathizing with this personable but errant stepson. George died at an early age, I was told, "as a result of his dissipation," but never given a more specific cause of his demise. I like to think his end was hastened by nothing more disgraceful than cirrhosis of the liver.

Albert, steady, plodding, salt-of-the-earth dependable, lived most of his life in Lincoln. Whatever his precise executive position at the pottery he worked at it hard and conscientiously for such self-effacing devotion to service was his very essence. Albert's worth did not flash on the surface. He appeared, in fact, rather dull and stolid. One had to know Albert well to realize his depths touched veins of the purest gold. In his early twenties Albert married Carrie Chandler, whose father, Zachariah Chandler had been mayor of Detroit (1851-1852) and United States senator from Michigan (1857-1875). Senator Chandler, who had been born in New Hampshire in 1813, died in Chicago in 1879.

The Gladding McBean pottery grew and prospered. Its very growth demanded Charles Gladding's even closer attention and almost constant presence in Lincoln. He missed his family more and more as these years of partial separation continued to keep him away from Oakland. Flora's schooling over, Charlie Gladding built two Victorian houses in Lincoln separated only by a broad area of lawn and the copious shade trees he had planted. Possibly it was the year that Gladding McBean and Company incorporated, 1886, that the two Gladding families moved into these houses, so very elegant for that locale. The big two-storey for Albert and Carrie would eventually stretch to hold all ten of their children from Lois the oldest, born in August 1884, through Augustus (Gus), Charles (Charley), Anita, Grace, Chandler, Doris and Dorothy (the twins born in 1890), and Helen to Caroline, the baby.

Into the single-storey house, next to Albert's, Charles Gladding moved Add and Flora. For its era this cottage was a luxurious cottage—a truly spacious cottage. I am not sure just how long these two ladies consented to stay in residence in that charming cottage but before very long the wife and daughter so hopefully imported to the scene of his highly lucrative labors let it be known that they wanted no more of Lincoln. Charles Gladding moved them to San Francisco and soon after built the fine cupolaed house at 1611 Franklin. Add and Flora, fundamentally city women, were happy once again. (Flora became a most dedicated San Franciscan. During my childhood she consistently intimated that even the East Bay was a most benighted hinterland. Lincoln, to which she was forced to repair for the annual Gladding McBean stockholders meeting became almost more than she could endure for the duration of the meeting.)

Charles Gladding died either just before or just after I was born, died on the steps of the Coliseum in Rome—a heart attack during a European sojourn he was taking alone. Some few years before, during the coastal steamer trip on which Charles had taken Add, Flora and Irene the rough seas had caused Add to become so acutely ill that she had to be landed at Monterey, an unscheduled stop. That abortive trip ended sea travel for Add so Charlie had gone alone to Europe. Though I never knew him, Uncle Charlie Gladding stands apart in my life as the pivot of confusingly intertwined family relationships, most concisely explained by the statement that his first wife was my paternal grandmother's sister, his second, my maternal grandmother's sister.

BY 1881 ARTIE CHAMBERS' FERVOR for playing neighborhood baseball (with its souvenir of his crooked little finger that had caught a fast flying ball head-on and never recovered from the impact) had been supplanted by his lifelong devotion to the game as a spectator sport. Fact is, "Artie" had disappeared in his teens of the 1870s, and in his place was Art Chambers, a charming, very handsome young man of twenty. He had attended the select Lake Forest Academy where a lad from Indiana had been his chum. This George Ade later became an American humorist and playwright of note.

Walker Whiteside, though three years younger, had been a Riverside friend of Art's teens. Walker by 1883 had made a name for himself as a Shakespearean actor. Later he, too, tried his hand as a playwright but merited renown more as a thespian. He played the McDonough Theatre in Oakland when I was entering *my* teens and was completely enthralled by the theater. Arthur took me to see Walker in *The Melting Pot*, a play in which he had attained great success. We went backstage and I met Mr. Whiteside in his dressing room. (Oh! THRILL of thrills!) Arthur and he easily established their boyhood rapport yet to me Walker Whiteside never seemed quite to step from, nor want to step from, his role as actor. He rather demanded adulation. *I* gave it most willingly—most sincerely!

I met only one other of Arthur's boyhood friends. His closest Riverside pal, John Driver, had not only shared his enthusiasm for baseball but had been his partner in Halloween pranks and general boyhood rascality. John had married well and retired early to the Santa Barbara area. When I was ten or eleven Arthur took me on one of our earliest travel adventures, a train trip down the valley to Los Angeles where we stayed overnight in a hotel. We returned by the coast route, stopping over at the old Potter Hotel in Santa

77

Barbara. Long years had passed since he had seen John and Arthur was full of zestful anticipation at the prospect of a reunion. He hired an automobile with driver and we jolted the miles over country roads to reach Montecito and John's house which was of pueblo-type Southwestern architecture. (That stopped Arthur for a moment. He had never seen a house constructed on such lines.) John had a quietly cordial wife, John was charming. All went well till at some mention of our train time John shot out his wrist to consult his watch. That finished John for Dad! A wristwatch! Why, no real red-blooded man would wear such a contraption. Theirs was a wristwatch-wrecked friendship! Arthur had died a decade before their granddaughters, Laurie Pilling and Adele Rock were together in the Alpha Phi house at Berkeley. I am not sure he would have been too pleased. The ghost of John's wristwatch would have haunted even their granddaughters' friendship for Arthur!

* * * * * * *

Art Chambers' first job was as an underling shipping clerk for the Chicago firm of Crosse and Blackwell, noted then as now for the excellence of its food products. Arthur used to tell how embarrassing it had been for them when new federal food laws required that a manufacturer print the ingredients on the label of each product. Their higher-than-average-price, superior quality apple jelly had ignominiously to have listed on its aristocratic label, along with sugar, "apple peelings and apple seeds"—for the apple part of the apples went into that superb Crosse and Blackwell apple butter!!

Art's must have been a Horatio Alger career at Crosse and Blackwell's, complete with marriage to an owner's daughter, the charming and beautiful socialite, May Crosse. To his dying day Arthur thought I did not know of this first marriage of his. For some impalpable motive peculiar to his own reasoning, he had secured Irene's promise to keep it a secret from me. However, about the time Arthur and Irene's divorce was pending Irene accidentally (or not so accidentally?) let the story slip out. She said she had not meant to tell it before me because she had promised Arthur she never would, but that actually she saw no sense in his insistence that I know nothing of May and their marriage.

I do not see the sense either but something within Arthur dictated the wish and I am glad he always thought I did not know. Because of this curtain drawn over Arthur's twenties and early thirties I know little of that period of his life. I have no idea why he left Crosse and Blackwell but at some point this seemingly quiet, conservative young businessman, who was a plunger at heart, decided he could make a small fortune (which he sorely needed to foot the bills for May's extravagant way of life) by raising mushrooms underground in a sort of Chicago mushroom catacomb. The dismal failure of this intriguing venture was no doubt as hard on May as on Arthur. At all events May had already begun to take drugs. By the time of their divorce she had been a hopeless addict for years. (Her gracious benevolence must have remained through all the travail for when she learned Arthur was to be married she wrote Irene a warm note praising Arthur and sent Irene a pin Arthur had once given to her. The pin, now Laurie's, was a tiny blue-enamel-hilted gold sword secured by a gold scabbard.)

* * * * * * *

Arthur, his divorce final, looked for business opportunities in California, far from the scene of those last difficult Chicago years. He chose San Jose, a town of about 20,000, which he felt had promise of further development. San Jose seemed more homelike than most California cities for it had been established long enough to have tree lined streets and the general atmosphere of a small Eastern city. In 1897 or 1898 Arthur went into partnership with one Jim Kidward (later to be San Jose's chief of police) as owner of a livery stable. No ordinary stable, this, but one stocked with fine horses, up to the minute carriages of all kinds, hacks with beveled plate glass windows, a very elegant hearse and of course the tasseled heavy black nets to drape over the horses' backs and the tiny black ostrich plumes to be worn on their heads as they draw the hearse. (If my memory can be trusted there was even a smaller white hearse to be used in the funeral of a child.) In the pleasant front office of the livery stable Arthur became "Al" to his Masonic brethren and the other friends he soon made in San Jose.

By this time his sister Annie and Joe DeGolyer were installed in the cottage at Lincoln which the Charles Gladdings had so soon abandoned. Joe's entire career was devoted to Gladding McBean and Company where his meticulous technical knowledge of terra-cotta manufacture enhanced his value as a resident executive at the pottery. So this smaller dwelling beside Albert's large fast-filling abode again had tenants. Between these two highly compatible households began some thirty years of unruffled, companionable living side by side. A closeness existed among the children of similar ages. There was a visiting, back and forth, by the two couples of an evening or of a Sunday afternoon after the big midday dinners which inevitably followed attendance at church services. These were churchgoing people—good people—who lived their religion and set a fine example for all Lincoln families. With a quasi-feudal mien these two houses, set in the midst of broad flat lawns beneath the lordly shade of trees, were, figuratively, "the castle on the hilltop" in the level terrain that was Lincoln.

Albert and Joe at the pottery showed an interest in every work-man, his family, his personal crises. Carrie and Annie, working together, brought about wonders of civic improvement to the bleak little pottery town. Annie DeGolyer worked cheerfully and indefatigably for the town's good but, city-reared, she gloried in the transient sophistication that visits to the Bay Region afforded. Furthermore Lincoln's summer heat plagued her whole being. Carrie Gladding, beside rearing her ten, found time and energy in her quiet, seemingly phlegmatic way to accomplish a prodigious amount for the good of the factory families and Lincoln in gen-eral. Her crowning addition to summer-scorched Lincoln was the municipal swimming pool. The stifling hot valley summers were the nemesis of life in Lincoln yet living there for these two families was fundamentally thirty years of the GOOD LIFE.

* * * * * * *

Brother George Chambers came to California about this time to work in an executive capacity at Gladding McBean head office in San Francisco. George had married a California girl. Madeline Hood's early years were spent on her Uncle William Hood's fabulous Rancho Los Guilicos in Sonoma County. This ranch of almost 19,000 acres was originally granted to the wife of Captain John Wilson in 1839. William Hood (like Wilson a Scotchman) purchased the ranch in 1850. Hood then sold some portions of the grant but retained the beautiful area at the foot of Hood Mountain where in the 1850s he built the brick "White House," which, having withstood the shattering earthquake of 1868, still stands, a historical landmark among the modern buildings of the Youth Authority Los Guilicos School for Girls.

Aunt Madeline used to hold us spellbound with tales of life on the rancho during her childhood. The adults of the family and their frequent guests always dressed formally for dinners at the White House which followed days spent riding to the hounds. Left much to herself in the midst of all this transplanted way of life at Los Guilicos, Madeline, with her Indian nursemaid, spent most of her days down by the creek in the big Indian encampment. She herself attributed certain metaphysical leanings and her semi-occult powers to this early association with Redmen, their ceremonials and their beliefs. George and Madeline had three children, Madeline (Hazlet) born about 1894, George Robert Jr., 1895 and James Warner, 1898.

*   *   *   *   *   *   *

Though he never let it mar the warm relationship he enjoyed with his mother and his brother George, Arthur did not deny a feeling of rejection when George was given the position in the Gladding McBean head office. His mother also inevitably turned to George, her second son, for business advice. Arthur was fair enough to know that the mushrooms and related fiascoes had been his undoing businesswise in the eyes of his family. Nevertheless the rejection hurt. Whereas all his siblings inherited sizable blocks of Gladding McBean stock from their father's estate Arthur had forfeited any share in the estate for he had already been advanced equally substantial funds with which to fight his private battle of supporting May, her extravagances and her not inconsequential, though concealed, expenditures for drugs.

Having relatives scattered about in California did little to assuage Arthur's day-to-day loneliness in San Jose. He therefore sought out the one family-connected household near enough for casual visits.

Charles Gladding's widowed sister-in-law, Laura Laurie, and her daughter, Irene, were living at nearby Lick Mill. Arthur called, Arthur saw Irene. Her beauty, her charm and vivacity enthralled him. Arthur was devoted. He was a home-loving man. He proposed. And how did he show his love for Irene? Each evening, exhausted from a long work day, he drove the long miles to the Mill in one of the stable's smart equipages. Upon arrival he stretched out on the living room sofa and for the duration of his call slept soundly. Irene sat beside him sewing, but her fury burned bright for long years to come!

It was probably 1899 before the widowed Lizzie Chambers established the family home in San Jose. Almost a block of lawn behind the wrought iron fence surrounded the big red-maroon Victorian house on East Santa Clara. Even before the California move Jim had been ailing. His death from cancer of the throat followed soon after the family moved to San Jose. Jim was Irene's favorite of all Arthur's siblings. She mourned especially the suffering that preceded his death. Having finished her third year at Smith College, which she had chosen because of its outstanding music department, Charlotte joined the family in California. She graduated from Leland Stanford Junior University where Genevieve, known at Stanford as "Judy" Chambers, was already enrolled.

Arthur Chambers and Irene Laurie were married in San Jose by the Rev. Mr. J. Clarke Robins on June 5, 1899.

BOOK
of
ELIZABETH

ELIZABETH CHAMBERS |
1919

OFFICE: 68 South First St.　　　San Jose, Cal. March 26th 1900

　　　　　Letitia Building

　　　　　Telephone, John 781

　　　Mrs. A. L. Chambers　　　　194 N. 4th St.

　　　To DR. R. H. BURKE, Dr.

To Obstetric Attendance　　　　March 26　　　　$45.00

* * * * * * *

EVEN AT THE VERY DAWN of the twentieth century California was painting future trends. Dr. Burke's receipted bill above that Arthur had to pay $45 for me in 1900 while in Montana a generation later Roy paid but $35 for Laurie's delivery. Clearly by 1900 the wave of higher price levels was already washing the Pacific seaboard.

In 1964, with San Jose grown to ten times the population it claimed on my birthdate, I searched out the house where I was born. One hundred ninety-four North Fourth Street was a complete shambles as were the houses on either side of it. I should immediately have guessed from the broken window, gaping door, sagging steps and peeling paint that some form of urban renewal was afoot. Later I learned my birthplace was to be gobbled up by a clover-leaf connection for some super freeway. My horse-and-buggy memories seemed anachronistic in the San Jose of 1964!

I found this Fourth Street house divided into first- and second-storey living units. In 1900 it would have been known as a "flat"—one tenant would have occupied the lower flat, another the upper flat. (The word "apartment" was still not in common use; the term "duplex" unborn.) Perhaps #194 was always so divided. I do know that it and this house (long since succumbed to progress) in which we lived on South Second Street from the time I was a few months of age until I was half past two years were both rented abodes.

To this North Fourth Street dwelling Arthur had taken his bride and Laura had established there their first home. In this Fourth Street house Irene's charm as a young matron began to win her a place in the social life of San Jose, a small city with but one social status group. One was in this group and therefore "in society" in San Jose or one was "out of it"—out of the group, out of everything that really mattered socially in Santa Clara's county seat. It was as white and black as that). Irene's subsequent social success was a definite business asset to Arthur.

Meantime at 194 North Fourth life coursed on. Arthur, Irene and Laura joyously awaited the advent of "Jack." During my pre-natal period I was supposedly a boy. Already named "Jack." I was always referred to by that name. (Was that "Jack" for J. C. Stubbs, I wonder?)

Irene, as become a gentlewomen of this era, "had her baby at home." Only the impoverished and improvident repaired to a hospital to be delivered of their young. If a woman had a decent home and could afford the necessary help and was confined at home, a home delivery was definitely the status symbol of the diaper crowd in my day!

Irene was emotionally attached to Dr. Burke as women generally were to their obstetricians in those days of friendly and leisurely doctoring. During the first of Irene's labor symptoms she and Arthur played cribbage between her pains. Soon Dr. Burke, bringing the practical nurse, arrived to stay with Irene through (what she termed) "the very difficult time" she had. Dr. Burke, because during her pregnancy Irene had been so well in mind and body, expected a very easy delivery. However the labor dragged on for hours. Dr. Burke stood by the while, never leaving the house, seldom leaving the bedside. I was never able to elicit any precise details that marked my birth as more difficult than that of the average first baby born to a woman in her thirties but Irene was convinced it had been unusually trialsome. It was an experience she had no intention of repeating!

Upon my arrival Irene's first question to the patient Dr. Burke was not a query as to the Jack or Jill status quo but, "Is the baby perfect?" This was no idle checking against birth defects. Irene was quite sure her child "had been marked" by a prenatal incident. Poor Arthur needlessly did things that Irene held against him for "time and eternity." One of his worst faux pas had been less than a month before my advent. Stooping down to tinker with some minor repair in the kitchen Arthur stood up quickly forgetting the open cupboard door above his head. The door's corner cut his scalp. Like all scalps his bled lustily when cut. With a man's inevitable helplessness with home surgical dressings he called, "Irene." Coming from the next room and startled by the bloody scene Irene threw her hands up in surprise and shook as she stood before the window's bright light. I know these details for this was an incident Irene oft repeated. She felt it had been a terrible shock for her to sustain "in her condition." She was sure it would "mark" the baby she carried, then sure it had. My hands were darker on the backs than the palms and it had been so with Irene's hands as she had thrown them up in shock at Arthur's bloodiness, palms toward the window's light. Though not every mother delivered of a perfectly normal baby had Irene's ingenuity of imagination the concept of marking a baby, well supported by old wives' tales, was generally accepted up to and including the early 1900s.

I was a colicky baby. But when Irene told the story it sounded so much worse than that, so quite dramatically terrible. I am sure to Irene it was all of that. I not only cried but screamed almost constantly during my first months. For Irene it meant much getting up at night. Irene took her baby troubles to Dr. Burke who said, "You are spoiling the baby. Let her cry it out. Don't pick her up!" *Very* soon after that Irene had the widower Burke for dinner. I was crying, was screaming loudly in fact. Irene sat calmly being a charming hostess, showing no sign of concern. Before long Dr. Burke blurted at her, "For God's sake do something for that child! Can't you tell by the cry she needs some attention?" So did Theory and Practice meet head-on in 1900!

Irene accepted Burke's reversal. Night followed weary night of repeatedly getting up in answer to my screams. Arthur proved a frustratingly sound sleeper. Irene took cold doing this strenuous night duty and developed a cough. Arthur mentioned one morning that her coughing had kept him awake a good part of the night. Irene never forgot, nor *forgave*, that remark.

One night, thoroughly exhausted, Irene decided to try taking me to bed with her, cradling me snugly in her arm. We both promptly fell asleep. Such a welcome, such a deep sleep for Irene. Then for me, all too soon, the colic and piercing screams. Irene suddenly wakened, quickly jumped out of bed, forgetting she had taken me from the crib till she heard my head thump against the floor and rocker of a nearby chair, then a more than normally anguished scream. As Irene often said it had been a terrible thing for her to go through, to realize she had unwittingly flung her own darling baby across the room. She was unsure just how vital my contact with that chair's rocker had been so that for once she was thankful to hear my lusty piercing yell. Though I am sure she never guessed her stories had such an effect on me, it was not till I had babies of my own that I escaped from feeling pretty damn guilty about all the suffering I had caused Irene.

So much for hearsay!

The locale of my first conscious memory is the edge of a pine wood pushing into a broad meadow of soft tawny grass cut across by a rustic fence. The path from the tall pines leading to a stile over this fence. Arthur and Irene are trundling me in my baby carriage—a cumbersome wicker gondola perched high on a fragile chassis. The pastoral idyll of their stroll is interrupted—physically and emotionally—by the stile. This, my first memory, is of Irene and Arthur at odds—Arthur saying no need to take me out of the buggy that he can safely negotiate the stile with carriage tenanted. Irene insisting she will hold me while he tugs the carriage over the up-and-down steps of the stile. Oddly enough I remember only the setting and the slight altercation not the denouement.

I'll put my money on Irene though! Unlike most early childhood memories kept alive by adult repetition of an incident, this is an independent memory. When my own awkward manipulation of baby conveyances brought it to mind I recounted the recollection to Irene. At first she could not remember anything about it. On further cogitation she did recall such a situation.

Grandma Elizabeth Chambers had "discovered" Pacific Grove, a refined Christian summer retreat quite unlike Santa Cruz with its "sporty" element or the obscure literary colony at Carmel-by-the-Sea. The summer of 1901 she rented a house on Lighthouse Avenue in the general location of the present-day post office. We were her house guests for a few days. My baby carriage had been checked on the train. Irene recalled the walk to the woods.

COUSIN CARRIE COMES
***

IRENE FELL IN LOVE WITH PACIFIC GROVE! It was summer cool. San Jose was hot. The following summer when I was two Arthur rented a Pacific Grove house for us in the same area but just above Lighthouse. I remember the Fourth of July there. The strings of tiny sizzling-popping Chinese firecrackers set off all together in one delightful swoosh on the soft sand-earth of that backyard.

It was the turn of the century, the Fourth was still a Great Day replete with bangs and thrills and home fireworks. At this season this area added a colorful festival of its own, the Feast of Lanterns. Complying summer residents, as well as the natives, strung front porches with gay paper Japanese lanterns. The chief event was the best parade, mainly the fishing fleet. All the boats, decorated with lighted paper lanterns, sailed in single file from Monterey to Pacific Grove in the early dark of the long, crisp summer evening.

By the summer of 1903 we had a home of our own at "the Grove." With her life savings of one thousand dollars Laura had bought 512 Willow Street from the locally famous watercolorist, Adams. Irene had chosen this artist's studio-home in the pine woods. Most summer residents preferred locations at the bay shore. Irene found the powerful ever-moving ocean made her restless; the pines bespoke peace. She knew that living in the woods the magnet of the ocean would draw her; she would walk to the shore. If she lived at the ocean's edge she doubted the pines' peaceful power could call her from the sea. Therefore 512 Willow would assure her forest *and* sea.

For me summers in Pacific Grove were like the word picture of a happy childhood drawn by the wife of Finland's president, Sylvi Kekkonen—"a secret garden, full of ineffable beauty, morning dew, bird song, the fragrance of flowers, murmur of trees, light and shadow." Because these were seashore summers, the prancing

6512 WILLOW STREET,
PACIFIC GROVE COTTAGE |
Arthur and Elizabeth
Chambers beneath the
pergola of the cottage. *1904*

waves, the crisp ocean breeze, the sea-smell of kelp, the miracle of the tide's bounty strewn on the firm damp sand to be trod barefoot with squishing, probing toes, even the lonely sea-sound of the whistling buoy as I drifted to sleep in my crib are early memories as filled with enchantment as with nostalgia.

Carrie Manny, I believe, during the period she held the office of National Secretary of the Women's Christian Temperance Union, attended that organization's 1905 convention in California and visited her Remington relatives as well. Descriptions from Carrie's letters written on this trip to her children (John, Edward, Helen, Vernon and Catherine, the baby about ten at the time) offer objective appraisals made by a mother of five visiting a cousin with an only child and seeing an ocean shore for the first time in her life.

"Pacific Grove Nov. 1, 1905—We all came down here yesterday afternoon, and in the evening went to the beach to see the tide come in. The beach here is rocky in some places and sandy in others,

& among the rocks the water dashes clouds of spray as the tide comes in.

"Aunt Laura's little cottage is very cozy & convenient. It is finished in Japanese style. The walls & ceilings are all covered with burlap, fastened with strips of wood. The woodwork is stained red in the guest room, one bedroom blue & one green. The living room black (Carrie's error, it was very dark green) with wide border and ceiling of red (burlap), & the sides painted with vines and chrysanthemums." (Irene not only painted the lovely sprays of red mums with graceful green foliage on the natural-colored burlap walls but stretched the burlap and painted the battens which held it in place as well.)

"This morning we went to Monterey and took a trip in a glass bottomed boat. The glass through the middle, with a railing around it we look over that & see everything beneath us." (Carrie might have added that a dark blue canvas curtain fastened around the edge of the deck sheltering the glass section was pulled down behind the seated passengers darkening the viewing area. The sunshine lighted the sea bottom making brightly visible the submarine wonderland.)

"The rocks are covered with mosses, seaweed, tall green grasses waving constantly, sponges, quantities of sea urchins & star fish in red, purple, pink, grayish green and brown. Then there were abilone (sic), octopus, a big crab, rock cod—with as many colors as a calico quilt—little striped fish called convicts, key hole limpets and sea anemones. Some very tall seaweeds, almost like trees.

"Elizabeth is a slender, dark-eyed little girl, with straight dark hair. She lisps very much, & is not very strong, & is sweet and obedient. She has not been much with other children & talks in a grown-up way which is often quite amusing. She was delighted with a little purse I gave her, though she had quantities of nice toys."

Carrie writes from San Francisco where she visited Flora after Irene. "Nov. 17, 1905-One afternoon at Pacific Grove we went down to the beach and looked for shells but did not find many. I got a few pretty specimens of seaweed & small shells & two abalone shells. One was not very perfect, but beautiful colors.

"We took a trip to Del Monte, which is a popular hotel with beautiful grounds. All sorts of plants and flowers and trees can be seen there. Immense pines & live oaks are native to the soil.

"There is a maze. Paths bordered by thick hedges of evergreen higher than a man & which get higher as they reach the center. In the center are benches. We walked around in that awhile & came to an outside opening. Then Elizabeth and I sat down under a tree, & the others tried it again until they reached the center.

"We saw some white and black swans there, & some little ones that must have been quite young, others half grown. These were all gray."

*   *   *   *   *   *   *

By the fall of 1902 we were in the house that Arthur and Irene built at 570 South Sixth Street in San Jose. The only "new" house on that block (between Williams and Reed) lined with wonderful old Victorians, it was considered quite ultra in 1902. A pseudo southern colonial, the house must in actuality have been as architecturally atrocious then as now. In 1964 even after interim remodeling accomplished with brick and composition shingles, it was rundown and dilapidated. The room-for-rent sign on the front porch was no added attraction yet this was the house in which Irene had given her fabulous parties. This was the house to which all San Jose had clambered to be invited.

In 1905 Carrie wrote of her stay at the South Sixth Street house, "Arthur and Irene met me at the depot. Aunt Laura looks much like mother" (Laura's sister, Helen Remington Dieterich) "and still more like grandmother. It seems good to be with them. Elizabeth is a dear little girl, very quiet & well behaved, not at all like her mother used to be. This morning we went on the electric car" (known to us San Jose natives as the Interurban, the car went as far as Los Gatos, I think) "through the prune, plum & cherry groves. This city is in the midst of miles and miles of fruit groves, which are planted over the Hillsides & in some cases over the hilltops, & make a very pretty picture. Irene says they are something beautiful in the spring when the trees are in bloom. One of the largest and best fruit canneries in the country is near there."

In a letter written after she had left San Jose Carrie says, "We rode every afternoon at Irene's. She has a horse and surrey, & they ride a great deal to get Aunt Laura and Elizabeth out."

Before Irene had her own horse and surrey, jaunts to town were made in a hack, an enclosed vehicle, from Arthur's livery stable. My first words, after "papa" and "mama," were therefore "dark-down-town."

Today the road names on all freeway exits in the San Jose area ring familiar from those long-ago surrey rides—Trimble Road, East Julian, McKee Road, Brockaw Road, Gish Road, on and on. The orange glory of spring's carpet of California poppies stretching end-lessly vies in my memory with delight at the white-washed trunks of orchard trees. "Those trees all have sore throats," I insisted, recalling the white flannel that had swaddled my neck when once my throat had been afflicted.

SPRING'S FULL IMPACT REACHED MY CONSCIOUSNESS first as I sat amidst green grass and wildflowers during a picnic at Almaden— noted then as now for its quicksilver mine. The Chambers clan had come in force from San Jose, bouncing and jolting over the bumpy horse-and-buggy roads of the day. Ginger ale, a current popular drink (and quite possibly fairly new beverage), had been brought along for a cool drink. When Genevieve opened a bottle, the terrific pressure built up by the rough jouncing trip blew the cap off with great force cutting her chin severely, a star-shaped scar and always carried.

Charlotte Chambers and Maynard Wright were married at the Chambers home in East Santa Clara. Vaguely I recall following imperative instructions as I descended the stairs strewing rose petals before the bride. Baldwin DeGolyer, less conforming, more bashful, retired determinedly to a remote corner behind a large sofa. No ring-bearing for him! I felt quite superior about having played my role gallantly. I was two at the time, Baldwin a full year older.

Relations must still have been intact at this time between Irene and Arthur's family. Such a situation did not long endure! Irene and Charlotte, both sensitive, both artistic, both deeply aware of Nature's beauty, two people made to be highly compatible, instead of becoming the warm friends they were in later years, had a terrific falling out. I am not sure of the basis but have the impression it had to do with Irene's friends who were not of the churchgoing type approved by the Chambers family but were more suggestive of Bohemians—that ambiguous term of the fin de siècle in California.

At all events, newspaper clippings of Irene's parties do not include Chambers family names in the guest lists. However, as the clippings are undated some of these parties may have been given after Grandma Chambers moved her family to the Linda Vista district on the Oakland hills just below Piedmont.

One clipping from a San Jose newspaper tells us,

A novel event last week was a "housewarming" given Thursday afternoon by Mrs. A. L. Chambers. This was not, as it might seem, the formal opening to guests of her new home, 570 South Sixth Street, but a reception to a number of ladies who had watched the growth of the marvelous doll house, constructed by Mr. and Mrs. Chambers for their little daughter Elizabeth, and who had expressed their desire to see it when completed.

The house occupied a table in the parlor and was closely inspected by the guests, who found it perfect in every detail. The absence of sides allowed a perfect view of the interior, which is a marvel of ingenuity and skill. The first floor is divided into reception hall, dining and living rooms, kitchen and pantry. Three bedrooms, a bathroom and nursery occupy the second floor, a broad stairway leading up. The rooms are about ten by twelve inches. They are tinted in different shades and each is carpeted and fitted with hangings to correspond in color. Tiny pictures hang from mouldings and the furnishing throughout corresponds to that of the thoroughly modern fashionable house. Such furniture was made by Mr. and Mrs. Chambers and is exquisite in design and workmanship. One set especially, after the old mission style, is unique and artistic in the extreme.

Tables have the daintiest of d'oylies upon them, tiny curtains hang at the windows and the beds and couches are perfectly fitted out with hemstitched sheets and pillow cases, blankets and counterpanes. The kitchen has its stove, table, tiled sink and pots and pans of every description. The bathroom has tiled floor and sides and enameled tub. Incandescent bulbs project from the walls of every room.

No detail has been overlooked in the making or furnishing and the result is a doll house of unusual perfection and beauty.

Captioned "A Shirt Waist Luncheon" one news article relates that,

A novel and well-carried out "shirt waist luncheon" was given Saturday by Mrs. A. L. Chambers, at her artistic home on South Sixth Street, in honor of her guests, Mrs. Nellie (sic) Porter of Ashtabula, Ohio, and Mrs. J. W. Tew (sic) of Belvedere. The state flowers, buckeye and eschscholtzia were chosen for decoration, the house being in the buckeye, and eschscholtzia being the table flower. The name cards carried out the idea, each being hand decorated with white shirt waists, having dainty embroidery of eschscholtzia, the name being on the front box-plait. They were the clever work of the hostess.

Irene always referred to the California poppy by its botanical name. She had a special way to trick the beautiful brilliant blooms that normally tightly close their petals and 'go to sleep' by late afternoon. When Irene used them for dinner table arrangements she shut them up in a dark cupboard all day where they would sleep, petals closed tightly. Brought forth, the electric lights would waken them to full open bloom for the evening.

Irene's originality in entertaining reached a zenith in her Hobo Party. The local paper did it full justice.

One of the jolliest parties, most original in the plan and most completely carried out, was the 'hobo' party given last Monday night by Mr. and Mrs. A. L. Chambers in their artistic home on Sixth Street.

The invitations to this unique affair were written on butcher paper, the rough edges of which had been burned to give them a scarred and battered appearance. They read: "After dark find shack with sign 'To Let' in windows, first door north of Reed on Sixth Street, next to vacant lot. Each pal will be given four slugs for slot machine and twelve checks for sandwiches. Come for a good time and wear your old rags. Ring up John 2086 and let the Chambers know you're coming."

On the eventful night the hoboes bidden all found the house with the "To Let" signs, which Mr. Clayton kindly furnished, and they all wore their oldest clothes. The make-ups were very clever and it was more than usually baffling to find out who your neighbor really was. "The Tough Girl," "The Blind Lady," "Happy Hooligan," "Flying Liz," and "Cross-Eyed Sue," the tramp whose shoes were not mates, the old soldier, the one whose clothes were so patched that it was hard to tell the patches from the original suit, and he who was dressed in someone else's cast-off finery, were all there.

True to the promise made, each pal was provided with four slugs for slot machine and twelve checks for sandwiches. These checks were of butcher's paper cleverly tied together with a bow, each of the men's having a tiny metal hoe tied through the bow.

The slot machine was in charge of Mrs. W. E. Robson and Mrs. C. Jesse Titus of Mountain View. It was placed in an alcove off the reception hall, and a bar was run in connection with it. The men played the machine for cigars and the women for gum.

In the living room fruit punch was served, though it was necessary to win a check at the wheel of fortune, presided over by Mrs. A. M. Barker and Mrs. Chace, before one received any punch. If one was unlucky in winning, perhaps he might be able to persuade some more fortunate 'pal' to treat him; and if one had good luck he could treat his friends. Mrs. Van Dalsem served punch.

In the dining room sandwiches of cheese, fish, meat and pate, piled high in market baskets, were served, buffet style from the sideboard. But here, too, it was necessary to present one's check.

In the living room flinch and five hundred were played and upstairs there was a smoking and club room for the men. Everywhere there were signs for trespassers to beware, advertising matter and notices of interest for hoboes.

Wild mustard was the appropriate flower, it being gracefully disposed in vases.

The prizes of the evening were given for skill in a guessing game and for the best sustained characters. The guessing game was to tell the name of familiar 'ads' from the picture only. In a cut, Mrs. A.M. Barker won the women's first prize, a handsome silver inlaid teapot, and Mrs. Alexander, the men's, a cup of the same ware. The consolation prizes fell to Dr. Barker and Mrs. Van Dalsem. Mrs. Hobson and Mrs. Lumbard cut for the best sustained woman's character, the prize, a brass drinking bowl, going to Mrs. Hobson. Mr. Woodrow was adjudged the best of the men and carried off a brass lantern to help light the hobo home.

MY FIRST MEMORY OF LIFE IN THE SIXTH STREET HOUSE is of being on Laura's lap, examining the backs of her hands. The prominent veins and dehydrated loose skin of age that I could gently pull into peaks that would slowly level back into place, were never-ceasing wonders compared to my baby-plump hands. This day Laura told me the phenomenon of her hands was because she was old, that she had been seventy-two years old when I was born, that she was seventy-two years older than I. I was appalled! But all the while, I was in that best of all places—on her lap, surrounded by her ever-present love. Always there was Laura to love me, to be interested in all my doings. Besides that there was the extra bonus of watching Irene, the glamorous, my adored mother, at her various creative pursuits. She was as delighted to have me watch each brush stroke or pencil mark as I was happy to watch. Another thing I never tired of was watching her dress to accent to the fullest her vivacious beauty as she prepared to leave for some social event. Though many things *did* make Irene nervous, including getting dressed for a party if the slightest time pressure was involved, my watching never bothered her. Deep down within me I knew I had the happiest childhood of any little girl. How I did love Laura and Irene!

My best remembered doll is "Tiny," (now in Phyllis Williams' doll collection), a big bisque doll that Irene "dressed" for my third birthday. Tiny's trousseau brought Irene much acclaim. As a doll companion for me she proved a bit difficult being near my size, breakable and hard to dress as her clothes were tight fitting in the fashion of the day. She came after the triumph of the doll house for Irene who said one saw baby dolls and little girl dolls but never a lady doll—quite true for this era. Irene was going to dress a lady doll. To start she made Tiny a corset, properly padded to give the

RANDOM MEMORIES
***

ample-bosomed, small-waisted, full-hipped lines then in vogue. Next followed underwear—corset covers, drawers, petticoats, all with insertion for ribbons, embroidery, tucks. The wardrobe consisted of a tailored suit of gray woolen material trimmed with black braid; a small flowered toque; a dark blue taffeta shirtwaist suit with parallel lines of bright red stitching; black lace over light blue satin evening gown with short train; an opera cloak of brocaded silk with copious lace rufflings; a Japanese kimono, complete with padded roll at bottom. Tiny wore the latter over a nightgown of one of my old baby dresses which I felt an outrage to her elite wardrobe. Irene made her bedroom slippers, very warm and cozy they were, too. Irene even made Tiny long black silk stockings but, of course, her long black silk gloves were bought as were her high button shoes and her low shoes. Some admiring relative or friend presented Tiny with long lavender kid gloves which were a mite too small and had to be carried in her hand as no amount of tugging could get them on, even though the tugging was done by a grown-up. All Tiny's dressing was beyond the clumsy learning fingers of early childhood so she was really a grown-up problem, a grown-up showpiece. I was very proud of her but I felt much more warmly toward a toy cat. Though unfortunately hard and flat-bottomed this cat wore real cat's skin of semi-Persian calico-like type and looked so real with its cold green glass eyes that one day as it sat on the porch ledge at 512 Willow a caller, who had knocked at the door, while awaiting a response, reached down and stroked the cat, thinking it alive until her fingers touched its hard motionlessness.

Another favorite plaything was my duck. I was especially fond of him. I would stroke him by the hour. Some sportsman friend of Arthur's, who had gone on to bigger game, presented him—a mallard drake of taxidermic skill with webbed feet firmly nailed to a ten-inch square board! I was very fond of Duck.

The great lot between #570 and Reed was vacant. I would linger there in the spring growth, almost hidden by tall grasses and weeds, playing at making scissors from filaree pods or, a bit later in the season, clocks—by counting the number of twists in the self-winding brown filaree seed-end I would have the time, not accurate, but a prescribed diversion of childhood. Here, too, on a mallow-like plant I found seed pods, like tiny green squashes, which children called "cheeses." I happily would munch on these.

In 1964 looking quite as I remembered it was the old Enwright house on the northwest corner of Seventh and Reed. Margaret Enwright, with her long golden curls, was my friend, my glamorous friend! Straight dark hair braided, big-eared I went to my first birthday party at her house. I wore a bright yellow dress of a satin-like material and I am sure there was no other dress anything like it. Irene was so handy at making modish apparel out of some cast-off Gladding garment. I always had great faith in her sewing ability and was most pleased to wear her creations. (The thought only now crosses my mind that my clothes were probably—at best—"quite different.") Surely my everyday clothes were different for a little girl. Irene dressed me in boy's clothes—rough little tweedy knickers and jackets.

Neighbors across the street on Sixth acquired a new contraption—a battery. I was invited to come try it. As it was supposed to be health-giving and generally beneficial Irene was in accord. To my best recollection it was a black box-thing some two feet long, a foot wide and a foot high. The front panel was beset by gadgets and controls. There were two hand holds, one at each side. Six or eight people holding hands would form a semicircle with the person at each end grasping a battery handle with his free hand. The sensation was much like an electric vibrator as the current passed through the group tingling hands and arms. Quite a parlor trick!

Whether my first marketing was a result of Irene's forgetting to order extra cream from the milkman that day or merely her attempt to build self-confidence in a rather shy almost-five-year-old I do not know. Be that as it may, I was sent from #570 with a pitcher to the corner store to buy ten cents worth of cream. Bulk buying meant not quite our concentration on pure uncontaminated food. Irene put the dime for the cream in the pitcher so I would not lose it. The obliging saleslady I can see yet in her neat gingham dress and big apron. Her hair was in the big pompadour style of the time but a bit scraggly and straggly. I told her I wanted ten cents worth of cream. She poured the cream in the pitcher and held out her hand for the dime. I said, "Oh, it was in the pitcher!" Resourceful saleslady that she was, she took a large wire hairpin out of her hair, successfully fished the dime out of the cream and I trotted home with my purchase. I must have had some prescience thought of things to come. Somehow that hairpin-in-cream sequence stayed with me through the years with a slight question as to the sanitary suitability of the hairpin. As Irene had put the dime in the pitcher I never did sense any sanitary problem from that source.

Random memories of this period crowd. Some are hard even for *me* to believe. Irene had a pearl-handled revolver that she kept close at hand—honestly! A holdover from protecting her honor in the old days I was given to believe. The revolver's presence at #570 was due to Irene's timidity at night when Arthur was away. His Masonic work kept him away many evenings, a misdemeanor Irene could not forgive yet to Arthur his work in Masonry was close to his heart, was his creed, was almost his religion.

(At the time of his death in December 1929 he was a member of Friendship Lodge No. 210 F.A.M. of California; of Oakland Commandery No. 11 Knights Templar of California; of Royal Arch Masons of California; Oakland Council No. 12 which is a regular council under Grand Council F&SM of California; of AAHMES Temple of the Shrine and of the Red Cross of St. Constantine No. 23, Oakland. His was a Masonic funeral. His ashes were placed in the California Memorial Columbarium, 4999 Piedmont Avenue, Oakland, Section I, tier 5, #20.)

In 1904 San Francisco hosted the Triennial Conclave of Knights Templar. Our entire South Sixth Street household trekked from San Jose to stay with the Gladdings at 1611 Franklin for the event. Arthur, in full regalia and looking very handsome, marched in the great parade of Knights Templar gathered from all parts of the United States. Arthur was proud of his plumed hat and crossbelt with gold-hilted sword; not silver, for by this time he had risen to Commander of the San Jose Knights Templar.

Add, Flora, Laura, Irene and I had grandstand seats on Market Street in a vacant space between two two-storey buildings. Parade day was one of San Francisco's hot days. The long wait for the parade between sun-reflecting walls is stamped in my memory but no glimmer of the event itself. I remember the evening, though. While Arthur was "conclaving," Add hired an open phaeton-like carriage (the Gladdings did not own a "rig" but rented carriages with drivers from Kelley's Fashion Livery Stable, which was located nearby). We womenfolk drove forth to see the great illumination in the city which honored the Knights. Electric lighting was in its infancy. A few clear glass incandescent bulbs strung on a few buildings elicited "oh's and ah's." Even in Oakland almost a decade later in the area of Grandma Chambers' house between Monte

Vista and Bayo Vista on Walsworth Avenue (now Harrison), gas streetlights were still in use. A black-mustached lamplighter, long lighting stick in hand, went his rounds at dusk.

My memories of "being amused" at #1611 are few but warmly precious. Flora would let me stroke her "cooey" sealskin coat to my heart's content. She would play the perforated steel discs on the tinkling music box in the upper hall. Irene would take me out "for fresh air" and hold my hand so I could walk the rounded curbings that held the terraced lawns above the sidewalk level. I would pick a few of the pink-tipped, white-petaled English daisies that inevitably grew low and close to the grass in scatter pattern on these lawns.

This 1904 visit at Gladding's was the last time I saw my Great-Aunt Add and the first time I saw my Cousin Flora's friend, Mrs. Madeline Victoria Brooklebank MacAdam. Mrs. MacAdam had come to San Francisco directly from an engagement on the New York stage where she had been playing a boy's part. Her hair was cropped fairly short—unheard of for a woman. In this era the number of brush strokes to a woman's tresses marked her femininity and was supposed to enhance her shining "crown of glory." The more and the longer the hair the better. Nearly every woman upped Nature's bounty by adding "a switch" to supplement an already ample coiffure. So from the hair standpoint "Mac," as Flora called her new friend, stood apart.

This particular morning she was calling at #1611. Add, Laura, Irene, Flora—all of us—were in an upper sitting room. I, lolling on Flora's lap, finally lay on my back across her lap, head down. In that uncomfortable position I remained, fascinated, till Flora realized what was hypnotizing me and cuddled me to an upright position. With head lolled back I could see Mrs. MacAdam, upside down, as she sat behind me *smoking a cigarette*! Such a thing was almost beyond belief! She was the first woman I had ever seen smoke.

Probably she was also the first woman Add had ever seen smoke. Poor, dear Add would have liked to believe that Mrs. McAdam did not exist but what she had to believe was what she saw develop before her eyes, Flora's attachment to this mannish stage-struck New York divorcée. Mac was establishing herself in the real estate business in San Francisco. A business woman was as unheard of among one's acquaintances as a smoking woman or as a woman with short hair. Mac had an eleven-year-old daughter, Katherine Madeline (called Madeline), in the East staying with her grandmother until Mac could provide an adequate California home. Mac, who adored her child and wanted the best for her always, had her eye on the proper and adequate home—Flora's home. Add refused to let "that woman" live in her house. Mac compromised by spending the major portion of her time there and being most charming to Flora all the while. Accommodatingly Add died within the year and Mac moved to #1611. Within a couple of years she brought Madeline from New York to round out Flora's household.

Irene kept me close to her most of the time. Often she mentioned she felt it the duty of a mother who really loved her child to care for that child herself. Sixth Street to the north touched the grounds of the Normal School. That embryo of San Jose State University in the early 1900s was primarily a teacher training institution, and a progressive one. Normal had an experimental kindergarten. A new-fangled idea was this, children going to school before they were six and mainly on a group play-to-learn basis. Irene unhesitatingly said that only a mother who wanted to shirk "being tied down" by her child would send her offspring to a kindergarten. Irene felt strongly that the place for me was at home, close to her. No murmur of the value of socializing with peers, no slight whisper of child psychology reached the ears of the mother of Irene's era. Well before I was six Irene purchased the current reader for first grade use and began my education single-handed. I struggled with writing. "No, Babe, the pencil in your other hand; you mustn't write with your left hand!" Had I been in school, my teacher too would have insisted on right-handedness. (Maybe not the worst idea, it has seemed to build a certain ambidextrousness.)

Irene continued my instruction (except for one week in 1907 that I attended the Pacific Grove Grammar School and for a month or two in 1908 when I was in Miss Merriman's School in Oakland) until I entered the Piedmont Grammar School (now Frank Havens School) at the age of nine and a half years. At ten I went into the low fifth and ranked highest in that class with a 99% grade average. Irene had repeatedly said, "Babe will learn more with my teaching her at home than in any school." This home tutoring privilege (or was it a privilege?) was enjoyed by no other child I knew or ever heard mentioned. It resulted in my heartily disliking school *on the principle of the thing*!

IN 1964 THE KINDLY BRONZE PRESIDENT MCKINLEY of my
childhood was still in San Jose's St. James Park. The news of
McKinley's assassination lurks an early shadow-memory. My San
Jose recollections of poor McKinley's successor are intriguingly gay.
Irene was a fine horsewoman. Many a horse that she handled well
no other woman would dare to drive. The family horse, Nobby,
was well named. He was a stunning, fine muscled black gelding
with style in his every step. Naturally our surrey was the best and
smartest to be had. Arthur always liked to provide his family with
the best (actually whether or not he could afford it). In this case
we were an advertisement on wheels for his business so the family
equipage was naturally the very snappiest.

In 1904 President Theodore Roosevelt visited San Jose. Irene, at
the prime of her beauty, dressed in the latest mode, with her friend,
Mame Hunt, beside her and with Laura and me in the back seat,
drove forth to halt the surrey along the line of the Roosevelt parade.
Teddy had been bowing from side to side in a perfunctory, rather
bored manner but when he saw Nobby and Irene he rose in his
carriage, doffed his hat, bowed and smiled that toothsome famous
smile. (I remember this quite well.) Irene knew the line of march.
She whipped Nobby into some fast shortcuts so that we intercepted
the presidential carriage further along its route. President Teddy
repeated his performance of cordial bowing and even more smiling
recognition. Irene was delighted and said she had been sure all the
time that Nobby was a handsome enough horse to attract Teddy's
attention, big smile, gallant bowing but I never felt sure in my
own mind that it was Nobby who drew the presidential eye. Irene
was exquisite!

I have 1904 in mind also as the date of my first ride in an automobile; in fact, in the first automobile to run on the streets of San

Jose. Mame Hunt's husband, Ed, owned this Oldsmobile run-about—no windshield, no running boards, not much of anything, but a car that hobby shops commonly have to offer—that was it! One late afternoon Ed and Mame drove out to #570. I got into the Olds by means of the granite stepping block near the hitching post at the curb in front of the house. I clambered onto Mame's lap and Ed drove us around the block. Even before we turned the first corner there, walking down Sixth toward #570, was one of Irene's bachelors, Vic Scheller, a local lawyer. The coincidence of timing was God-given as far as I was concerned. Feeling no less important than Queen Victoria must have at her coronation, I waved regally and lustily called, "Hello, Vic." It was no mean accomplishment to make myself heard over the throaty chugging of the Oldsmobile but I put my all into my queenly greeting.

Aside from Irene's wonderful creative parties, when I think of social life at the South Sixth Street house I think of Irene's bachelors. Vic Scheller was local but of a Sunday, George Burdick or Gene McCarthy was want to drop down for a visit. The Southern Pacific service between San Francisco and San Jose was excellent. Another San Francisco bachelor, Goff Wakeman, also came occasionally. I am vague as to just where, just when, just how he and Irene met. I do know she was very fond of him and he of her. He was younger than Irene by a few years. She used to tell me that he had always insisted that if she were not married by the time she was thirty he was going to marry her. As Irene told it—anyway as it registered in my adoring ears—she sounded like a jilted suitor. Checking the facts now I realize Irene was well beyond thirty when she married Arthur in 1899 and Goff had done nothing to assuage her spinsterhood.

I remember when Goff's son was born, in 1907, a year or so after his marriage; he phoned Irene immediately, ecstatic with the news. I believe his feeling for her was touched with younger "brotherliness." I am not so sure Irene's had an iota of "sisterliness." Irene invited Goff and Wilbur McColl, a San Jose bachelor, to Pacific Grove for a weekend in 1904. She said she wanted her two favorite boys to meet. I sensed, young as I was, that Irene was weighing their charms, one against the other, that she wanted not so much to have them meet as to be there together before her eyes for comparison. By the time I reached adulthood I had the feeling that Goff had side-stepped something, somehow, sometime. I felt Irene might easily have assented had he pressed his point as she turned thirty.

Though I assess Goff with a certain degree of vagueness I was fond of him—big, handsome, sweet Goff! Irene last saw him in the mid-'20s when she and Arthur called on the Wakemans in Seattle where Goff was then a semi-retired local bank president. Though they met but two or three times, Irene made no secret of her dislike of Goff's wife. Strong feelings were rampant in the Irene-Goff relation!

Irene had four other San Jose bachelors besides Vic Scheller. Of course, Arthur perforce had them too! Professor Schemmell, a German violinist and professor of music at the College of the Pacific (which was then in San Jose, out in the general direction of Santa Clara) was actually a widower, not a bachelor. He taught me to say *auf Wiedersehen* as we parted and was delighted by his accomplishment. Two Alsatian French Jews, the brothers Loeb—Isaac, tall, thin and dignified, and Gabriel, short, fat and jolly—owned and operated the City of San Jose which was THE dry goods store of town. (Raphael Weill, founder of the White House in San Francisco, was their cousin.) Gabe was my especially beloved favorite. The brothers Loeb would come bearing gifts of jewelry for me. (An enameled pin with pendant irregular pearl is now Laurie's; the amethyst bracelet, now Ann's). Of course the fifth bachelor was Wilbur McColl. I was extremely fond of him. He was also a music professor from College of the Pacific; piano and piano composition being his fortes. But more of Wilbur soon!

Irene served marvelous gourmet dinners when she and Arthur entertained "The Bunch." (That phrase "The Bunch" predated Mary McCarthy's "The Group"—but the same general idea!). The Bunch included Herman and Pauline Pfister, husband and wife, Professor Schemmell, the Loeb brothers and Wilbur. Pauline could even out-gourmet Irene in her cooking. She and Herman, who held a nepotist's job in the office of his brother Rick, Santa Clara County Recorder, were of German descent. Big people, both, with great warmth of personality. Pauline, though, was more exuberant than sweet, phlegmatic Herman. This was Irene's—and Arthur's— Bunch. Their dinners were replete with conviviality, delectable foods, excellent wines. Pauline had a fine singing voice. I wonder if many such evenings transpired elsewhere in the United States even at the turn of the century. They belonged more to continental Europe.

*   *   *   *   *   *   *

San Jose's nearby ostrich farm admitted visitors for a slight fee. How small I did feel in the viewing area outside the stout wire fence, looking in at the great feet and legs of those huge birds stepping majestically about in a teeming mass of legs and ever more legs. In the exhibit room was an ostrich egg. I was staggered by its size! Had not these ostriches figuratively laid golden eggs the farm would not have been. The birds were raised to produce the plumes coveted by women to adorn their hats and bonnets—as well as by Knights Templar for their helmets. Though plume-plucking must have been humiliating and transitorily painful to the ostrich its life was not endangered thereby—not so fortunate the egrets, birds of paradise and many other beautiful feathered creatures. No conservation of bird life, to speak of, in 1900! No Audubon Society to protect. Not many years hence the movement to protect wildlife from the needless waste got underway. In little more than a decade the sale of aigrettes, the plumes of the egret, at least was banned. Public sentiment swung in support of the law so that soon hats trimmed by feathers of rare birds were looked at askance. Finally even the ostrich plume disappeared from all but the crest of the Knight Templar.

Meanwhile Irene busily made stylish hats to go with her modish frocks. This pursuit was aided and abetted by millinery stores that carried hat frames of white and of black buckram in all shapes and sizes plus materials with which to cover them and to trim them. Straw, usually one or two inches in width, was sold by the yard in every imaginable color and texture. Starting at the center of the crown this straw was sewn on the buckram frame in ever widening circles of the ribbon-like length of straw selected. This was but the base. Hats were well adorned in the early 1900s—feathers, flowers and furbelows. In winter instead of straw a hat frame was covered with velvet fitted neatly to the frame's contour. No flowers on a winter hat but feathers were especially appropriate—also expensive. Irene discovered a mine of feathered treasures at a surprising source. The owner and operator of Monterey's glass-bottomed boat, mentioned by Carrie Manny, was Manuel Duarte, a hearty character, he, with a great spiel about sea bottom wonders. Irene and Manuel became buddy-buddy enough so that he showed her the product of his taxidermic hobby, the preserved skins of shore birds. Irene became his prize customer. Some of the lovely white-breasted grebe skins she even fashioned into a short cape, black velvet trimmed. Always after the Manuel contact was established her hats had lavish wings at stylish angles. At first Manuel *shot* the birds whose skins he coveted. That practice outlawed, another source had already developed. Oil tankers cleaned their holds near enough the coast so that the plumage of many shore birds became matted with great splotches of tar. Such birds were unable to fly. Manuel was saved the expense of shotgun shells; he had merely to pick up the poor disabled creatures and continue his hobby.

Opposite the old customhouse on Monterey's Alvarado Street, only a door or two from Manuel's fisherman's supply store, was Oliver's Curio Store. Oliver's had everything from simulated mer-men to beautiful abalone pearls. The latter immediately caught Irene's eye. For several years all her spare pocket money was used to buy matching specimens. Irene loved rings. She had two abalone pearl rings made, one of the dark pearls, the other of the light. She also had one of the pearls set in a stickpin for Arthur's tie. These pearls were so rare that their value was not too great. As Mr. Oliver (father of Myron Oliver) explained, "Tiffany decided not to stock them ....Mrs. Vanderbilt would want some like Mrs. Gould's but Tiffany would be unable to supply her. It would not be good busi-ness." Far more lustrous than oyster pearls, Irene purchased these abalone pearls comparatively reasonably.

AT THE BEGINNING OF EACH SUMMER our trunks were shipped by express and Irene drove Nobby with Laura and me in the surrey from San Jose to Pacific Grove. The trek took two days! We always stayed overnight at the old Plaza Hotel in San Juan Bautista. I not only remember the thick adobe walls of those hotel rooms at San Juan but also its rarity of rarities—a two-storey privy. Very convenient it was, too, for us second-floor hotel guests. The balcony at the rear of the hotel led by a trestle-like structure to the door of this remarkable necessary house. (My vivid recollection of this device seemed so bizarre that to make sure my memory was not playing tricks I questioned the ranger in charge when in the mid-'40s I revisited San Juan. He said, "Indeed you are right! It was right over there.") Our stay at San Juan let Nobby start fresh the following day on the San Juan grade that rose steeply before dropping to the Salinas valley floor. Often Irene repeated the story of Grandma Chambers and three members of her household who, less thoughtful of an animal's welfare, once made the trip in one long day, driving Molly, the family horse. They had left San Jose almost at dawn but it was dusk when they reached the Grove. As the family clambered out the surrey old Molly dropped dead in harness.

Irene, Laura and I would stay through the whole summer at "Go Easy Lodge," as Irene had christened 512 Willow in honor of her old cycling club. Arthur would come by train for weekends. During the summer we would take the Seventeen Mile Drive probably twice. The entrance fee for horse and surrey with occupants was fifty cents. We could not be *too* extravagant. On those great days we would take a picnic lunch and enter the Drive by the Forest Avenue toll gate (which was in about the location of the present Pacific Grove High School). By driving so that a wheel of the surrey would go over a raised wicket a spring automatically would open

THE GROVE
***

117

the gate. Simultaneously the gatekeeper would appear from his lodge to collect toll.

Once as we drove along the forest road nearing Point Joe ahead of us some two hundred yards at the meadow edge of the woods a mountain lion crossed our road. I clearly glimpsed the long-tailed, lithe, slinking body as Irene, who saw it first, exclaimed her thrilled astonishment—a most unusual sight, even in the early 1900s!

We would always stop at "Point Joe" to enjoy the phenomenon labeled "Restless Sea." Eventually Irene learned the scientific explanation of meeting ocean currents. At the left of the Drive on this point in a rambling shack of gray driftwood among the smaller rocks lived Joe, the old Chinese who gave the point its name. Around his slapped-together abode his chickens, an unusual feather-legged variety, scratched endlessly in the rich loam to supplement meager rations. Beyond the point, on the grass just above the sandy beach, lay a carpet of drying seaweed and kelp gathered by Joe and Chinaman Charlie, whose driftwood-gray dwelling nestled at the far side of the next rock mass beyond the point. From the sale of this dried product of the sea these industrious Orientals hoarded funds toward a hopefully affluent return to China.

Along the meadow between the ocean and forest edge in the area from Point Joe to Bird Rock were hurdles used to jump-train horses of the U.S. cavalry regiment stationed at the Presidio of Monterey. (This unit's uniformed, white-gloved, mounted band, which was a commonplace in local parades, was a marvel of the precision and synchronization of many skills.) On this meadow and other places along the Drive, we would see small herds of cattaloes. These great black, humped creatures were a cross between American bison and Galloway cattle. (The attempt to introduce these hardy beasts as a popular beef cattle strain failed because the animals proved too ornery and unruly to wrangle successfully. Until the mid-'20s their descendants haunted some areas of the Drive.)

At Bird Rock we would stop to watch the shags. (Irene later learned that "cormorant" was the more correct name but shag was the vernacular.) We would look ahead toward Cypress Point to see the fascinating Ostrich Tree. This great striding ostrich was formed by two cypresses, leaning one toward the other. Their trunks formed the legs; their foliage grew in the shape of a giant ostrich when viewed from afar. Next we would walk Fan Shell Beach to gather the fragile pink-toned bivalve shells along the tide rip. Probably we would be rewarded besides with at least one beautiful lustrous tiny abalone shell, no larger than a thumbnail.

The fiords of Cypress Point drew Irene like magnets. Gazing down the sheer cliffs to the jagged rocks and seething sea below, unfailingly she would assert, quite seriously, "This is where I am going to commit suicide!" On the far side of Cypress Point was The Loop. Only occasionally did Irene drive that tricky narrow road that looped the edge of a tiny peninsula with sheer sides dropping to the wild ocean waves. Less a peninsula than a round island connected to the mainland by the narrowest ribbon of land, it has long since succumbed to the eroding elements. How delightfully scary just to look at the Loop even and decide *not* to drive it *that* day!

At Midway Point we might walk out to the Lone Cypress though the chances were equal that we would be so hungry that we would immediately select some idyllic spot nearby and spread out our lunch. Along the way we would have stopped at a watering trough or two to let Nobby drink. At lunch time he would have his snack of oats from a nose bag brought along for his picnic. After luncheon we would drive through the cypress trees till we came to the shore at the Witch Tree. The foliage of this cypress formed the silhouette of a hatless witch, with hair in a bun, riding on her broom. A bit beyond her we would admire the Ghost Tree, a whitened cypress skeleton standing to the left of the road.

We would by this time be nearing Pebble Beach but we preferred white sand beaches. We would not stop but would have looked forward to reaching this part of the Drive, because the daughter of the Chinese fisherman, whose home was in a cove on the shore below, offered abalone shells for sale at a crude driftwood stand. A pretty young girl, she dressed in her native costume: bright-colored silk brocade oriental blouse, black trousers, embroidered Chinese slippers. After she was left behind we would vie with one another to determine who could say "She sells sea shells by the seashore" the fastest without tongue-tripping. Then there would be the long pull up to the Carmel Hill gate, the only other gate to the Pacific Improvement Company's vast land area that was traversed by but one road—the 17-Mile Drive. Seventeen miles it was from Hotel Del Monte, which was also owned and operated by the Pacific Improvement Company (the P. I. Company, a subsidiary of the Southern Pacific Railroad), through Monterey and Pacific Grove via Forest Avenue gate, around the shore, out the Carmel Hill gate, down the Carmel Hill, back to the Del Monte Hotel. Just seventeen miles it was and Hotel Del Monte's guests came from over the world to take that famous 17 Mile Drive!

THE walk from 512 Willow was to the dunes at Moss Beach (Asilomar). Those high so-white sand dunes, one of the wonders of the world, should have been saved for future generations as "White Sand Dunes State Park." Their destruction for the manufacture of glass constitutes the strongest of arguments for state ownership of California's shore line.

Another trip Nobby would take us on each summer was to Seaside where a sign proclaimed "The World's Largest Oak Tree." In the low sand dunes this oak covered an area stated in acres as it sprawled, branches growing low, close to the warm sand hills. But by 1905, summers when we would have our own horse and carriage to roam the lovely Monterey Peninsula were at an end.

TERRA-NOT-SO-FIRMA
***

ARTHUR BOUGHT A GOLD MINE IN PLUMAS COUNTY. Not letting Irene know, even when he left, the extent of his financial involvement, he went to Quincy to stay in order to "look after his mining interests." Not long till Arthur and all of us knew there were no interests worth looking after in Plumas County. The former owner had cleverly "salted" the mine to lure Arthur to invest. Before Arthur's return Irene found out that he had even sold his share of the livery business in the vain hope that further operation might strike another vein in the mine and result in retrieving at least some of his capital.

Arthur was the husband of his era who did not confide his business affairs to his spouse and who kept the bank account in his own name but generously paid all his wife's bills and supplied her with ample pocket money. Irene caught up with just how low the family finances really were by inveigling the bank president into telling her Arthur's current balance—sixty-four dollars, if I remember correctly! Irene was more than upset. She felt Arthur had been dishonest in not telling her what he was doing financially. (Any wife today would agree but this did not happen today, but about as the calendar turned from 1905 to 1906.) Also Irene was, naturally, very unhappy about the family's near bankrupt state. Irene must have known that Arthur's mother would come to his financial rescue to some extent but feeling as she did toward Mrs. Chambers (whom she had always refused to call "Mother Chambers"), aid from that source would have been humiliating.

In later years I truly felt that someone at this time should have been thoughtful enough to tell me about the poorhouse. I did not know such a haven existed so, having absorbed the gist of our debacle, I spent hours mentally checking over friends and relatives to figure how many meals each might be counted on to feed our starving family. As a grown woman I delightedly rechecked my rating and found that, though not quite six at the time, I had the friends and relatives in about the order of sacrificing concern that I did as an adult!

After Arthur had returned to San Jose from his mine and with the family finances shaken to a shambles, on April 18, 1906, at 5:30 a.m. came a very real earthquake. Six years old, my crib abandoned, I was sleeping now in the big bed with its high solid oak head and footboards. Against the wall, opposite its footboard and separated from it by only a narrow passage way, stood the great oak secretary, a ponderous piece of furniture some six feet in height. Placed atop that secretary for safekeeping, on its own small black lacquer tray, reposed my treasured Japanese tea set—lustrous green glaze on dainty white china. At five thirty on this April eighteenth the shaking of my great bed awakened me. In the dim light I could see the huge secretary teeter, then lurch forward. Arthur by then was ricocheted into the room—thrown against door jamb, banged against the wall. Even as he scooped me into his arms I saw my precious tea set fly off its perch and shatter to the floor. The stout oak footboard of my bed had caught the impact of the secretary which tilted there.

Laura from her room, met Arthur, with me in his arms, in the upper hall. Within seconds, like all our scantily clad neighbors, we were out in the middle of the street where our houses could not fall on us. But, by and large the houses did not fall. Being frame structures they "gave" with the swaying quake and held more or less together. (Not so fortunate the great fashion-hotel, the Hotel Vendome, in its opulent grounds north of the Southern Pacific Railroad station on First Street. Much of that hotel crumpled to a rubble of fallen timbers and chimneys.) Arthur, at full daylight, surveyed his neighbors' toppled chimneys and announced triumphantly that ours seemed to be the only house unharmed—not a single brick displaced in our chimney even. When some hours later he repaired to the basement his triumph quickly faded. The chimney, the whole house, had shifted several inches on the foundations!

Awakened so suddenly from deep child slumber, not till the sanctuary of the street was gained did I realize why Irene was not with us. San Francisco, that music loving city, was having its opera season. Irene, with Elizabeth Meehan and Wilbur McColl, had gone to the opera on the evening of April seventeenth to hear Enrico Caruso. As that disjointed day of April eighteenth wore on, Laura and Arthur explained that the earthquake had disrupted train schedules, that Irene might not get home till the next morning. But Irene *did* get home! About four-thirty that afternoon she walked in the front door, walked into Laura's arms and buried her head on Laura's ever-comforting shoulder. I heard her tear-choked words, "Oh! I don't even know where HE is!" Such a confusing day as it had been from the very beginning and now I didn't know what Irene was talking about! I asked, from the sidelines, "Where WHO is?" Irene cued me in—perhaps farther than she realized—by answering, "Wilbur! I don't know where he is. I haven't seen him since the awful earthquake!" Up to that moment Wilbur, to me, had been just one of Irene's many bachelors—the one of whom I happened to be very fond. Now I knew he stood apart, a very important person in Irene's life.

Following the opera Irene had crossed the Bay with Elizabeth and spent the night at the Meehan's. Awakened by the violence of the earthquake Irene had panicked; had run down the stairs, bric-a-brac falling from plate rail and stands had bruised and cut her feet. She had dashed out the front door. Clad only in her nightdress, she had sprinted halfway down the block before Jesse Meehan had caught her and asked her where she thought she was going. Irene had her destination clearly in mind. She was going to get home to her beloved little daughter and her mother just as fast as she could! Brought back into the house by Jesse she hurriedly dressed and walked quickly to the nearby East Oakland Southern Pacific Station. The agent told her no trains were running to San Jose—that the tracks had to be inspected before the San Jose train schedule would be resumed, that the quake had been very severe on the East Bay shore. Irene took the local commuter train and ferry to San Francisco intending to get a San Jose Southern Pacific train from the Third and Townsend station. As her ferry approached San Francisco the water front buildings were ablaze. The captain turned his ferry without attempting to land and returned to the Oakland mole. Irene took the first south-bound train from there. Crews preceded her train, testing and, in places, repairing the tracks. It was a long, trialsome but historic journey, those fifty miles with Irene frantic to get to her beloved child and adored mother.

Meanwhile Arthur had been preparing for the safety of his family. Frequent tremors and even short sharp shakes punctuated the day. No one cared to sleep upstairs in a house, no one dared start a fire in a cook stove until the chimney had been thoroughly inspected for safety. Arthur shopped for canned goods and other imperishable goods against a possible food supply shortage. With the next-door neighbor, Edwin Coolidge, Arthur set up temporary sleeping quarters and outdoor cooking facilities in our backyard for the two families. The Coolidges had a tent that was pitched near our hopvine-covered summerhouse at the far rear of our lot. If our house fell we would be out of danger at that distance—even from falling chimney bricks.

The Coolidge household consisted of Edwin, a bachelor, editor of the *San Jose Mercury*; his spinster sister, May, a teacher (after whom one of San Jose's schools was subsequently named), and their mother. As this enforced encampment got dinner, then began to settle for the night outside, there was one forgotten item after another to be retrieved from the houses. Edwin, the ever willing, literally jumped into the breach and loped off to get this or to bring that. As the evening wore on his lope became more and more unsteady. The typical failing of the newspaper man was his; each time he left us he "hit the bottle" to fortify himself for the disrupted way of life.

After two or possibly three nights, as the earth became more quiescent, our backyard campers retreated to the comfort of second-storey beds. At the end of each of these days the sinking sun had burned blood-red and the night sky had glowed ominously, tinted by San Francisco's blazing tragedy.

Finally San Francisco lay in ashes. Monumental work must be done to clear the rubble so that the City could rise again, phoenix-like. Arthur moved quickly to take a lucrative part in the clean-up job. Contracting for the removal of debris from various properties he soon had many teamsters with their horses and wagons in his employ. As our San Jose house figuratively went down the Plumas mine shaft Arthur moved his family to San Francisco. Twelve-twenty-seven Waller Street, out in the Sutro Forest area, was a lower flat. Built into the hillside at the back, in that foggy climate, Irene found it a somewhat damp abode which made her cough worse. She was not happy living there. Looking back I would guess other factors than climate entered into her feeling of wanting to escape this San Francisco home Arthur had established.

Waller Street was the locale of my entire musical education. One day each week Wilbur had to be in San Francisco. Those nights he stayed in our front basement bedroom at #1227. He gave me private lessons and tried hard to teach me piano. I was a miserable failure. A piece I had memorized and could tap out by heart on the keyboard sounded to me quite like some piece I had never even heard before. I honestly could not tell the one from the other. Wilbur told Irene that if I continued to study music, my piano performances would be purely mechanical, completely uninspired. I was mercifully allowed to escape from the practicing and the confusion of trying to understand my lessons.

At #1227, two or three times Arthur put down his newspaper after dinner and on the backs of his business cards drew little pictures of squirrels for me. I was entranced! I thought them beautiful drawings! It is the only time I remember his doing anything like that—just specially for me. Irene let it be known that she was sure that Arthur was all at once being so nice because he was jealous of Wilbur. I treasured those little card-pictures just the same!

"THE CITY"
* * *

WHILE WE LIVED IN SAN FRANCISCO Irene and Flora usually talked on the phone each day. The earthquake had figuratively shaken Flora out of 1611 Franklin for all time. As the fire swept through downtown San Francisco, then began to lick its way up the hills, #1611 was threatened. Flora and Mac, with the few valuables they could transport, were evacuated, like hundreds on hundreds of other San Francisco refugees to the sheltering care of the U.S. Army at the Presidio, where hastily pitched tents and soup lines provided survival essentials. Mac was a master go-getting-organizer so before many days the two were established in a hotel in Berkeley. As soon as possible Flora leased a spacious lower flat out on Jackson Street in San Francisco. Mac brought her daughter, Madeline, from New York to live with them. Here it was that they lived during our tenancy of 1227 Waller.

Actually the fire had been stopped before it crossed Van Ness, one block below Franklin and #1611 remained standing, at least superficially unchanged, until the early 1930s. Flora, from 1910 until her death, lived in a large and, for its time, luxurious apartment house next to the Christian Science Church on Franklin, a scant block from #1611.

One of the subjects of Irene and Flora's phone conversations was "shanghaiing." Their friend of many years, Effie Thompson's husband, Charlie, had disappeared. No trace of him could be found. Had he been shanghaied? To be sure this custom of acquiring seamen (to replace those who jumped ship) by drugging, or blackjacking some unfortunate male, leading him aboard ship and weighing anchor, was about at an end. Not so definitely ended though but that everyone suspected it, rather than amnesia, to be the reason for Charlie's disappearance. Everyone was wrong! Given a couple of weeks Charlie's "amnesia" cleared and he returned home to Effie, a rather stolid and uninteresting type of woman. Never to his dying day did Charlie Thompson have another amnesia attack—the one, apparently, lasted him out!

Our Waller Street flat, near the Golden Gate Park's Panhandle, was in the Haight Street district. Irene, taking the Haight Street trolley car and transferring a time or two, would go each week to visit Flora on Jackson Street. Irene knew Mrs. MacAdam had Flora firmly in her clutches but Irene was not for giving up. Mac's influence led Flora to a rather dissolute existence—smoking, an absorption in restaurant-cocktail life, eventually to far too much drinking. In 1908 Irene took me with her to the Gladding McBean head office for a confidential appointment she had made with Mr. McBean. Irene hoped "Pete" McBean might still have some influence with Flora to counteract the almost complete control Mrs. MacAdam exercised over her and her considerable financial resources. Later Mr. McBean did plead Irene's case versus Mac's to Flora thereby making Flora absolutely livid with rage. Nevertheless the fact that she did will her estate (or rather that part of it which Mac had not wrangled away from her) in equal shares to Irene and Mrs. MacAdam indicated that Flora may have heeded his advice. More likely Flora had always intended to recognize the blood-tie to Irene which everyone seemed to assume had been irrevocably financially strengthened by Add's insistence, half a century before, that her widowed sister and small daughter come to live in her home. Irene never wavered in her frequent contacts with Flora—letters if away from San Francisco, calls if in the Bay Region—though for the last decade of Flora's life Irene firmly believed Mac had every penny of Flora's safely in her grasp. Despite that belief Irene, ever aware of Flora's financial worth, left no stone unturned.

Irene's weekly streetcar trips to visit Flora were interrupted by a motorman's and conductors' strike. No trolleys were running in San Francisco. Irene and I walked across town to Flora's, going through old Calvary Cemetery. The earthquake had left Calvary like a scattered Roman ruin—headstones broken, curbings awry, vaults askew. Rather picturesque it was; Irene had done a couple of sketches there one day. Rather eerie it was this day as we hurried through it returning home at dusk!

In 1907 the U.S. was suffering so major a financial crisis that I heard it referred to as The Panic. San Francisco was further suffering through the Mayor Schmitt-Abe Ruef regime. Nineteen seven was a year of unrest. One day on Haight Street we saw a work gang of stocky, swarthy Latins throw down their picks and shovels and run off shouting. I was mystified. Irene explained, "They are striking."

San Francisco was ever colorful. Irene spoke wistfully of some of its lost attractions. The old Cliff House, a low rock-hugging building, warmly hospitable, had been unlike the ungainly turreted castle-like structure that was the Cliff House I knew. Woodward's Gardens, which had occupied the area bounded by Thirteenth, Fourteenth, Valencia and Mission Streets, had been a delightful family recreation spot. One of the daughters, Mame Woodward, who had been a bridesmaid at Mary Haskins Porter's wedding, had married George Raum. George subsequently became Sir George, knighted in England for his exploratory work in removing the desert sand to expose the long-concealed paws of the great Sphinx at Giza. He accomplished this feat, which brought him such great acclaim, by using Mame's inherited Woodward wealth to hire natives who carried the sand away in great squares of clothing—a primitive, long, laborious process. The Raum's extensive world travels were similarly financed. A charming and cultured couple,

Sir George and his "Lady" spent their last years in comparative poverty in the King's Daughters Home in Oakland, Mame surviving till the early '40s. With the changing fortunes of the years, it was our Christmas gifts of Yellow Cab scrip which enabled dear Mame Raum to occasionally escape the home's confinement for a call or a bit of shopping. She used to tell us of her childhood and how the beautiful gardens surrounding the Woodward home were admired by the public. On Sundays families would stroll round and round the blocks trying to see what they could of the lovely garden. Mr. Woodward decided to further develop the area and open it to San Franciscans for a charge. One attraction which he added was a boat trip through a "Tunnel of Love" with various pastoral and garden scenes. After church on Sundays Mame and her sisters, dressed in their frilliest, would sneak into one of the Tunnel's scenes to become living statues as the boat slid through the grotto. Sooner or later an adult family member or nurse would round up the truants and put an end to the fun. But another Sunday would come!

San Francisco was most exciting when entered from the Ferry Building at the foot of Market. Eastern tourists as well as East Bay residents came into the City on the ferries. I remember the day I returned to San Francisco from my first overnight visit alone away from home—at Meehan's. Katie Meehan crossed the Bay with me. We took the local Southern Pacific train from the East Oakland station to the mole, detrained and walked up the ramp so as to sit on the upper deck of the ferry. (The rougher element stayed on the lower deck.) Had I been with Irene we would have sat outside, even though it might have been breezy, the better to watch the maneuverings of the scavenger gulls that hopefully followed each ferry, more interested in refuse from the galley, which served short orders en route, even than in the pieces of bread tossed them by the tourists. My Aunt Katherine being more conservative we sat "inside" as most ladies did. Inside, that horrible loud whistling-toot as the ferry left its slip was not quite as ear-splitting but I never could help jumping anyway.

The Bay crossed, boat landed in its slip, secured by hawsers, aprons lowered into place, one of the uniformed crew loosed the rope that held back the teeming passengers. Holding Aunt Katherine's hand I started to run off the boat. She said, "We have plenty of time, let's not run, we don't have to, you know." Indeed I did NOT know! Because everyone always did run off the boat, up the apron, down the corridor—until that moment I had thought you *had* to run!

On the ground floor of the Ferry Building was the lovely flower stall with orchids and a profusion of colorful blooms and the fruit stand with its exotic produce—pineapples and pine nuts always and not infrequently, alligator pears (avocados), which were scandalously expensive. The San Francisco of my childhood was a horse-drawn city. Once in front of the Ferry Building we faced a "frenetic jumble of traffic," the various horse-drawn hotel buses. Occasionally a waterfront freight train would chug by. Always drays were about in a plethora of confusion.

I remember well the horsecars that came to the Ferry Building where the driver would unhitch his huge team from one end of the car then hitch the horses in place at the opposite end, ready for the return route. One day Irene told me that horsecars would soon be out of use. I could hardly believe that horsecars, which I took to be a fixed part of life, would not always greet me at the ferry. The Clay Street cable car is said to have been the first in the world. Nevertheless, by my day cable cars were taken for granted. Neither uniquely new nor antiquely old, they were just cable cars, not as grand as the trolleys but highly acceptable for the steep hill routes.

Blue-helmeted policemen with wide-belted tunics and large dangling billy-clubs would drive by in horse-drawn patrol wagons taking some unfortunate drunk to the station. In those days San Francisco's mounted police wore the same English-bobby high blue helmets. How odd that uniform would look on Chief Cahill's officers today!

After the rebuilt stores were once again doing business in their old downtown San Francisco locations, one day when Irene was shopping with me in tow she showed me what must have been a replica of Colonel Andrews' original Diamond Palace—"a glowing mirrored cavern of jewels." Always I associated with childhood shopping in the City the balloon vendors. Straight out of story books, they were mustachioed Italians holding great bunches of varicolored balloons on long strings. I loved those balloons and held tightly to the string of the particular bright colored one I had chosen to be sure that I would get it safely home. As it began to shrivel a tiny bit on the morrow, it would be time enough to free it. Off it would sail to a speck of nothingness in the sky. I loved that venturesome freedom of my balloon, too! Market Street inevitably had sidewalk vendors of small mechanical toys. San Francisco charmed even the very young with its gay carnival air!

Having soloed as a house guest at Meehan's I was ready for flights afar. Irene left me in San Jose to stay a night or two at Barker's. The Barkers, aside from The Bunch, had always been Irene's closest San Jose friends. Irene could not possibly have chosen friends who differed more radically than The Bunch and the Barkers, who were quite conventional and strait-laced. Albert Barker, DDS, at one time was president of the California Dental

Association. He was a crack shot and the hunting dogs pictured on the label of his fancy-packed Imperial prunes were doubly appropriate. Minnie Barker's parents, the Wings, were undoubtedly the chief money source that purchased and nurtured the prune orchards but I believe Dr. Barker in 1914 or 1915 may have been the first to develop such especially fine large Imperial prunes and possibly the first to fancy-pack any kind of dried fruit in small quantities, for this was still the period of bulk buying. The Barkers lived on the Alameda in what was such a large imposing stately white-pillared mansion that when they sold it, unchanged, it became a funeral home and looked to have been built for the purpose. But when I visited them in 1907 they were quite out in the country, had fruit trees and chickens. To the delight of their son, Chester, some six years my senior, when asked to come along and help gather the eggs I promptly put the porcelain nest egg in my basket! Chester Wing Barker was connected with Stanford's drama department until his retirement. One of his daughters, Margery Barker (Blockley) and Beva knew one another during college years. In the summer of 1966 Marg was our tour-guide-hostess in the sugar plantation area north of Hilo, Hawaii.

In 1907, while we still lived at 1227 Waller, Laura was nicknamed Maltie. She was very ill for quite some time with one of the debilitating attacks of diarrhea that were the only curse of Laura's old-age good health. Her condition seemed to show little improvement from the daily visits and recommendations of the neighborhood physician so a consultation was called. That day the regular M.D. communed for a long period with his bewhiskered colleague after the latter had seen the patient. Finally Irene was given the verdict. "Give your mother tongue broth." Then the learned two departed. During this long illness of Laura's, as I would look in on her, her gray head so still on the pillow reminded me of a Maltese cat sleeping quietly on a cushion. I would stroke Laura's head a bit and call her "My Maltie, dear." From that time on it was a term of endearment used by both Irene and me.

PACIFIC GROVE RESIDENTS
***

BY THE FALL OF 1907 IRENE, LAURA AND I were in permanent residence at 512 Willow. Irene had felt that dampness in the San Francisco flat was aggravating her cough. No doubt she felt other aggravations as well. Be that as it may, I was happy to be at the Grove. We had a chance to know Pacific Grove, devoid of summer residents, pared down to quiet small coast-town life. Just one block through the woods on Granite Avenue lived the Smith family with their five daughters. Esther was a year older and Gladys only a few months younger than I. What wonderful times we had playing together! Occasionally I would go with them to Sunday School in the huge high-steepled old Methodist Church on Lighthouse Avenue.

During this period of residence at #512 we first became acquainted with Miss Louise A. Wilson, who lived a block down Willow. Soon we learned that she and Mary Haskins (Porter) had known one another as girls at the Napa Seminary for Young Ladies. Louise Wilson was sensitively attuned to the beauty of the outdoors; flowers, birds, the sea waves were her friends. Each year Auntie Louise became more and more a part of our lives during the Pacific Grove months. In later years, the fact that she and Laurie are November twenty-third "twinnies" strengthened the bond.

Next us, toward town on Willow, in a tiny white green-trimmed toy of a cottage, lived a widowed librarian from Boston, Mrs. Merrit. Our rapport was instantaneous and complete. She must have been lonely for she was grateful for the hours I spent in her gentle presence. A Theosophist, she firmly believed that I was a "very old soul." To my surprise, when half a century later I read Bhagavad-Gita, various terms, various words explained in Aldous Huxley's introduction were already a part of me from those far off visits with "Grandma Merrit."

Meantime Arthur came to Pacific Grove to be with us whenever he could get away from his work—likewise Wilbur! By careful planning on Irene's part their visits never coincided. I was ecstatic when Wilbur was with us. I adored him by this time. He was kind, affectionate and loving with me.

By this time, too, Grandma Chambers had built twin cottages next 512 Willow toward the woods. During the summer and at odd vacation periods family members would occupy these cottages. Irene found this arrangement a bit awkward. The slight twitch of a curtain, a passing face at the window made her sure that Wilbur's comings and goings were (quite naturally!) being spied upon. Long before this I had been carefully coached that if questioned I was to know "nothing." I was on Wilbur's—and Irene's—side! In actuality I was never "pumped"—Irene's word for what she expected would happen.

Each afternoon about four-thirty I would leave #512 with a covered tin quart pail and trot across lots through the pines to Congress and Spruce where lived an elderly widow and her spinster daughter whose cow, Sally, was the source of our milk supply. If I got there early, because I was very quiet and because Sally had become used to my presence I could watch the milking. One day, with warm milk in pail, trotting home across lots, I tripped on a pine root and went sprawling. The cover rolled off the pail and every drop of milk spilled! Unaware of the proverb and humiliated by my awkwardness, I ran home crying over my spilled milk.

Old Miss Wood, her black shawl about her frail shoulders, tended the little grocery store on Lighthouse Avenue, a block from Forest Avenue. Walking along the board sidewalk we went into her store for purchases shortly before Christmas. She gave me a little paper bag with fine stripes of green and purple, filled with hard Christmas candies. She gave to all children who came to her store that season. Such largess was beyond my ken. I never forgot that gift!

We had our own Christmas tree at #512 in 1907 and decorated it with ornaments which we bought and which I still believe to have been the most beautiful of all Christmas tree decorations. The tree, too, had many small lighted candles. This was the only Christmas tree I ever had in my own home until I had a home of my own.

If you were a Chambers you and your family spent Christmas at Grandma Elizabeth Chambers'—period! I followed Irene's lead and resented those big Chambers family Christmases. Even now I have no nostalgia for them but looking back on them objectively I realize they were rather marvelous occasions. Like the horse and buggy, such clan gatherings seem to have given way to a swifter more independent pace.

At those Chambers Christmases the gift receiving, a confusion of acquisition, which Irene felt devoid of the true spirit of the day, waited till the plethora of the two o'clock dinner on Christmas day had dulled our sensitivity. Always beneath the tree, beside the general welter of gifts with criss-crossing destinations, were tiny Christmas gift boxes, one for each grandchild, each containing a shining ten-dollar gold piece.

Those Christmas dinners of which everyone heartily ate each one of the almost countless courses, were not only culinary achievements but, for the diners, were psychological feats. At the climax, with Grandma at the head of the long table and with Arthur opposite her at the far end, a huge golden-brown turkey would be placed before each of those expert servers. Eventually, though the dining room was very large the Christmas dinner group had to be seated at two tables. The children's table was through the wide folding-doorway in the big reception hall. Being teenage by then I never had to submit to the indignity of this second table.

Every year for this Christmas celebration the DeGolyers, four, came from Lincoln; the five of the George Chambers family came the few blocks from their Santa Rosa Avenue home; Maynard and Charlotte Wright with Muireen and Elizabeth walked over from their home next door but Frank and Genevieve Case with their Elwell and Elizabeth trekked by train all the way from Seattle (no plane travel in the era of those big family Christmases). Grandma Chambers' widowed niece, Gertrude Gee Knox, and her son, Morris, who lived on Kingston Avenue not far from 155 Monte Cresta, always joined the family group at Christmas, too.

A HOUSE
IS BORN
✳✳✳

BY 1908 ARTHUR, IRENE, LAURA AND I were living in a rented house on Glen Avenue in Oakland. Several histrionic events marked my life in this house. Buffalo Bill's Wild West Show, measles, the Great White Fleet, gambling at poker, coffee drinking. Irene must have decided I had reached the age for a degree of sophistication. Each morning at breakfast I was given a thimbleful or two of coffee disguised by liberal amounts of sugar and cream. A week or two of that and my coffee drinking ended forever, with only the taste for coffee flavored desserts remaining. Then Arthur and Irene taught me the fundamentals of poker till I knew fairly well what I was doing at the poker table. Next Irene, saying poker was really a gambling game, suggested that if I would like to we could play for money. Excited and feeling very grown-up I raced to my dresser drawer and brought my entire financial resources to the gaming table. Thirteen cents, if I remember correctly. A few deals later I had lost every penny of my wealth. I remember very correctly being told I was a poor sport, that if one gambled one must be ready to take losses. If a teetotaler devoid of any interest in gaming is the desired result I heartily endorse Irene's method. I have always been grateful to her for much rearing which began when at age two and a half I asked, in effect, "May I have some?" then swigged from a great gulp of the beer Irene proffered. Bitter, awful taste—no more of THAT stuff, EVER! Later, the same with martinis, wines, highballs! Irene always offered me a cocktail as they were served but I always refused. What better method than Irene's? When a parent has been trying as long as you can remember to choke the stuff down you, how, as a teenager, can you have one iota of interest in "experimenting" with liquor?

Colonel William Cody's Great Spectacular was something else again! Arthur and I went alone to the tremendous tent out

Broadway a few blocks beyond Fortieth. That Wild West Show is history now. I have read many accounts describing it but to my mind all descriptions fall short of the reality—Buffalo Bill in spotless white fringe buckskin frontier suit doffing his hat to the audience—the Indians—the pounding of horse's hoofs—the dust—the speed of animals—the stagecoach careening!

Measles surely was a horse of another color! Irene, modern in her approach to childhood ills, was contemptuous of Grandma Chambers' comment that it was just as well for me to have measles young and get them over with—that she would even have approved of exposing me to them. Her old-fashioned ideas incensed Irene. Ah, how Time's pendulum doth swing!

My measles seemed to have come at the worst possible time. Mary Porter and Mary Porter Goddard, out in California to see the fleet sail into San Francisco Bay, came calling on Glen Avenue. Irene was busy making the beautiful heavy hammered-copper light fixtures and door escutcheons she designed and executed for her Piedmont house. Immediately E. Goddard decided she *had* to learn hammered-copper craft from Irene before returning to Ohio. She would come alone for the full day on Tuesday next. Come she did, on Tuesday, to a house peppered with open saucers of camphanol to disinfect against the malady of the fevered child who lay in an upper bedroom. Irene taught all, hammered-copperwise, to Mary at a feverish pace. Meantime Laura offered a cool hand and comfort. The sick room was darkened by heavy blankets over the windows excluding every crack of light, for light might weaken for life the eyes of a measles victim. Thin gruel (repulsive) and, in a day or two, scraped beef (tasty) were proffered the measled one. Eventually health was restored but not in time for that GREAT EVENT—the coming of the Great White Fleet.

Irene attended with Chambers family members and watched from a hillside in San Francisco as the ships filed into the Bay. On her return she intimated I had not missed much, but in those years everyone got so white-hot about EVENTS. Each Stanford-California Big Game meant careful wearing of the colors for a couple of weeks before the event. Talk focused almost exclusively on the Big Game for at least that long. Presidential elections were likewise great events of white-hot intensity for small fry. Then there were the polar expeditions. Their attraction was comparable to, but much more mysteriously and thrillingly remote than, space missions. Radio and TV have made the heroic and seemingly impossible adventure a commonplace. Not so the meanderings of Cook and Peary and their ilk!

Our Glen Avenue house was half a block from the Fortieth and Piedmont Key Route electric train terminal. Across Piedmont Avenue from the Key Station were a bare half-dozen stores—the Piedmont Grocery, the Piedmont Meat Market, a bakery, a notion store. The neighborhood did not appeal to Irene as one in which I should grow up. First she sent me up the hill to the more elite Linda Vista District, to Miss Merriman's, a private school, for a month or so. Then she laid plans to build a house of her own in a good neighborhood. Over the years, from occasional birthday and Christmas checks from Flora, and pocket money from Arthur, Irene had squirreled away enough, she hoped, to build a modest home. She chose a fine view-lot on the Alta Moraga Road and Pale Avenue. She paid $1000 for that lot, number 10 Monte Avenue. Next she took her tentative house plan to Charlie MacGregor, a building contractor, and awaited his estimate for the house she wanted on her lot. A two-storey house it was, shingled with low slanting gabled roof, downstairs; large living room with fireplace,

10 MONTE AVENUE,
PIEDMONT, CA

dining room, butler's pantry, kitchen, food pantry, back hall with "stationary" laundry tubs, maid's room, toilet—upstairs: four bedrooms, sleeping porch, store room, toilet and bathroom—the furnace in the partial basement was piped to each room. The contract price for this house, $3500, was a bit more than Irene had hoarded. Walter Lamert gladly took a small first mortgage which Irene cleared well before its due date.

Irene's Piedmont house was well built; in fact was even bolted to its concrete foundation. Irene wanted none of that earthquake funny business that had taken place in San Jose. Besides as #10 was on the hill side of Monte a few strong bolts engendered a feeling of security even sans earthquake. Some fifteen or more steps up from the sidewalk one reached the front door! As the house neared completion, each morning Irene packed a lunch and took the Piedmont streetcar to watch 10 Monte's progress and to make sure that no mistakes were made. The carpenter foreman, because he really did look quite like a parrot, we referred to as "John, the Parrot." An old-time cabinetmaker, John was readily empathetic to the perfectionist in Irene and worked in accord with her wishes. The finish in the living room and dining room was in pine, torch-burned to bring out and darken the grain, then waxed. Irene went to the lumberyard and herself selected each piece of this wood with an eye to the beauty of the grain.

* * * * * * *

(Irene was not the only woman to practice this sort of meticulous selection. Mrs. Varney Gaskell, Oakland's gorgeous Lillian Russell-esque beauty, when, a decade before, her home was being built, arrived early one morning at a West Oakland lumberyard to similarly select the paneling for the beauty of its grain. The lumber merchant, making out a bill, suggested that while he finished with his customer making out a bill, in the office, Mrs. Gaskell stroll ahead to where the paneling was stored at the far side of the yard. Her stroll did not go unobserved. A degenerate tramp, who had slept the night in the shelter of a stack of lumber, awaited her approach. As Mrs. Gaskell, beautiful of face and form, impeccably groomed, ineffably poised, rounded the corner of that particular lumber pile the man stood up, exposing himself to her. Mrs. Gaskell stopped short. Losing no whit of her poise, she raised her lorgnette, gazed earnestly through it a second or two at his exhibit, then turning on her heel, said, "Humph! I've seen better!")

I HAVE NO IDEA just what Arthur and Irene's arrangement was during this period. I do not recall that Wilbur ever came to Glen Avenue nor to 10 Monte while Arthur was still there. At least once a week Irene was off to San Francisco for the day. Arthur may have believed that she was meeting Flora for lunch; I knew she met Wilbur. In the spring of 1909 when we moved to 10 Monte, Arthur, handy as always with tool chores, tended to the myriad small items that needed tending to in a new house and built a fence around the sides and back of the lot as well. He even came home one day bearing a bunch of red roses from the florist's with which to woo his wife. Irene was coldly polite to him about the roses but let me know he had never before thought to bring roses even on her birthdays. Almost as soon as the last nail was pounded into the fence Irene started divorce proceedings. Arthur reluctantly moved out of 10 Monte and into his mother's home, but not before he made one last horrible blunder. I was grown and married before Irene confided this final offense of Arthur's to me. Seems he intimated that sooner or later Irene would get over the Wilbur syndrome. Quite blankly he told Irene that if it would help to get it out of her system to go ahead and sleep with Wilbur but for God's sake to hold the family together. Irene figured she had been grossly insulted! To me Arthur's love for Irene remained a constant element through all the years—something I never once doubted.

One morning when I was midway between nine and ten—and the divorce was midway between interlocutory and final decrees—I was busily helping Irene make the beds. Suddenly she asked, "Now, if I *were* to remarry, who would you want me to marry?" Her remark jolted me! It was coy and childish, certainly not worthy of the mother I so devotedly adored. —I was even a bit "put out." I knew Irene wanted me to say, Wilbur. Instead I answered, "Just

145

who you intend to marry." When *will* parents learn that children KNOW? I may even have known before Irene consciously knew, that she was going to marry Wilbur. I felt her question to me, over the morning bed-making, to be an insult to my intelligence. It rankled!

The divorce from Arthur granted, Irene and Wilbur were quietly married in San Rafael, went to Muir Woods for a few days, then returned to 10 Monte to live a compatible year or two. I loved Wilbur dearly and was as happy as the bride. Always Wilbur spent certain days of the week in San Jose, teaching. After the marriage he was organist, first at Oakland's Baptist Church then at St. Paul's Episcopal Church. All was serene at 10 Monte until it became quite apparent that alcohol was becoming more and more of a problem for Wilbur. He would miss choir practice. He would fail to come home. Irene would cry and cry. Because his behavior was making my adored mother unhappy I began to actually hate Wilbur, whom I had loved for so many years. By early 1917 Irene had stood all she could. She again started divorce proceedings. At the time I was not happy at the prospect of Arthur and Irene's inevitable remarriage. As their marriage had not worked once, I saw no reason for it to a second time. (Time would prove me to be very wrong!)

Another family wedding, at about the time of Irene and Wilbur's, was Genevieve Chambers to Frank Elwell Case of Seattle. The actual ceremony is a blank in my mind but the reception which followed at Grandma Chambers' Walsworth Avenue house impressed me because various Chambers family friends, of whom I had often heard but never before seen, were present—Mr. and Mrs. E. P. Ripley, Mr. and Mrs. Peter McBean, and son, Athol.

Madeline Chambers' 1913 marriage to Earl Palmer Barker (son of the Barker brothers of the Los Angeles furniture firm) was the next family wedding. Quite a wedding it was, too—twelve bridesmaids, yes! The ceremony in the Plymouth Congregational Church on Piedmont Avenue, was followed by such a whing-ding reception at the George R. Chambers' that it was necessary temporarily to remove a side wall of the dining room and add a large extra room to accommodate the guests. A scraggly little girl of thirteen, I was far too old for a flower girl, far too young for a bridesmaid, yet Irene was furious that I was not among the bride's attendants. She was determined therefore that at the wedding I would look so mature and attractive in a modest girlish way that my absence from the wedding party would point a finger of shame. She created a dress of cream-colored point d'esprit net over light pink with hit-and-miss bunches of tiny artificial rosebuds showing through the net. A sophisticated knot of pink ribbon held tiny rosebuds in my hair *which was done up*! (Otherwise I wore my hair in two thick braids down my back till I was well past sixteen.) Irene put her all into my wedding outfit and despite Nature's deficiencies I looked rather well.

Irene had her reasons to be a bit furious about that wedding. Madeline Hood Chambers' expensive demands tended to keep the George R. Chambers family finances in the red. With his only daughter about to make what appeared to be a most desirable marriage George was "broke." What could be done about the big wedding daughter Madeline so keenly desired? Simple! Arthur said, "I will foot all the bills. I love Madeline. I want her to have the kind of wedding she wishes." To me this was logical—all of it. Madeline was everything I thought a girl should be—a pretty blond, very feminine, utterly charming. Irene saw no logic whatsoever—period. To her mind all that wedding money—and in truth it must have taken a pretty penny for that blast—should have been mine, not Madeline's. As I said, Irene had her point but Arthur's generosity knew no bounds, ever. His heart was big enough to dearly love both his pretty niece and his gangling daughter.

WITHIN A YEAR we had next-door neighbors at 10 Monte. Max Cohn built a large shingled house at 12 Monte Avenue. (Max, then a Zellerbach Paper Company executive, after his company's merger with Crown Willamette, became president of Crown Zellerbach.) The Cohn's only child, Ruth, was my age. Next our lot line in the Cohn's backyard sprouted Ruth's playhouse—a sturdy, completely shingled building. Irene had a theory (founded on more, it seemed, than mere coincidence) that Ruth's playhouse was so grand because the Cohn's delighted in outdoing us; inevitably they topped every possession we acquired. Close to Cohn's lot line in our back yard at 10 Monte my well-furnished playhouse, though a sizable wood structure, had *canvas* sides. Three steps led to the door which had a real lock with key. My wonderful doll house, my dolls and other toys were kept in that playhouse ready for playtime. I had plenty of neighborhood playmates and school friends but the hours spent with them made lighter memory patterns than those spent with Irene, Laura and their friends. Irene was a vivacious raconteur who with only a soupçon of exaggeration could make some simple incident into a fascinating story that held the lively attention of her audience. How I loved to sit quietly by and listen to the grown-up chatter interspersed with those sparkling stories of Irene's! When Mary Porter was a 10 Monte house guest my joy knew no bounds. The stories Mary and Irene resurrected from their youth undeniably were far more interesting than the chitchat of my peers who had but a decade of experience to draw upon!

Despite the fact that Laura was in her eighties, her attitude of youth rather than age, her sprightly sense of humor and her acute interest in affairs of the day made her such a stimulating companion that when Irene's friends came calling inevitably they would gravitate to Laura's room to visit with her.

LAURA LAURIE AND ELIZABETH
CHAMBERS | At 10 Monte
Avenue, Piedmont, CA. *1912*

Every few months, despite her dislike of the East Bay, Flora would trek to 10 Monte to see her Aunt Laura. She would bring Laura the latest "best seller" to read and bring a box of bonbons and chocolate creams with candied violets and little silvered sugar-balls sprinkled over the top layer. During those years we lived in Piedmont, Flora had a ritual for my birthday and the pre-Christmas weekend. She would invite Irene and me across the Bay to lunch at San Francisco's finest restaurant of the hour. Those gourmet-restaurant luncheons were served in elegant style by San Francisco's French waiters—a species of waiter now extinct—who knew better how to serve unobtrusively and well than any waiters I have since come upon—or am likely to! Always, the luncheon conversation was sparkling. Irene hoarded incidents so as to have amusing stories with which to regale Flora. On the late December occasions after lunch we would visit the White House and the City of Paris to browse their marvelous displays of Christmas toys.

* * * * * *

The 10 Monte years were years with Irene sewing as Laura, sitting in her steel-caned rocker, read aloud in the front bedroom with its long view over lower Piedmont, Oakland and the Bay to the Golden Gate. (How Laura loved to watch the sunsets from that rocker! From it, too, she saw Halley's comet for the *second* time in her life.) Laura kept abreast of the times, not only by assiduously reading the daily paper, but also by reading the latest books of outstanding authors. From infancy, I heard good writing read aloud.

Irene kept us all well-dressed. Laura's clothes requirements were relatively few but Irene made her apparel of dignity and quiet charm. When I was small Flora delighted in buying me an outfit or two each year but by the 10 Monte years Irene was making all my clothes. (My college wardrobe was so outstanding that decades later girls who had known me at Stanford inevitably mentioned one outfit or another that they had admired and still remembered. All these were Irene's handiwork.) Irene, herself, always had several striking costumes. The wizardry of her skill let her look at some stunning, fabulously expensive creation exhibited in the window of an exclusive San Francisco or Oakland store then go home and copy it for herself. Irene's sewing was self-taught. She *had* learned one trick, though, from Aunt Add's early days–San Francisco French dressmaker—to fill those little round pads, which were the ancestors of today's falsies, not with cotton but with birdseed, -"Ah! Zee FEEL; eet eeze much more like zee real flesh! Mais non!"

That second-storey storeroom played no small part in the miracle of Irene's economical output of elegant frocks of the latest mode. A small section served as linen closet leaving rows of shelves that were filled by large suit boxes, each carefully labeled with its contents—white lace, black velvet, linings, ribbons, flowers, trimmings, feathers—on and on. Every hand-me-down was ripped to pieces, the pieces washed and ironed, then stored in one of those boxes ready to be drawn upon to create some dazzling new costume.

Despite the storeroom, with all the sewing that went on, necessarily there were frequent shopping trips to Oakland. Irene never liked to be alone or to do anything alone. Knowing that I loved to be with her on these jaunts we would wait till school was out, then take the Piedmont streetcar and go to Fourteeth and Broadway to shop in Oakland at Kahn's, Capwell's, and Taft & Pennoyers' for the needed supplemental findings. Irene had no charge accounts at these stores but always paid in cash, in coins. Paper money was something used in the East. The West knew only coins—five-, ten- and twenty-dollar gold pieces. (Irene kept three twenty-dollar gold pieces in her safety deposit box at the bank "just in case"—of what, I never knew!) In California in those days silver dollars were as much the rule as they are today at Harrah's Club. We never spoke of quarters and half-dollars or of twenty-five or fifty cents but always of two bits and four bits.

*   *   *   *   *   *   *

In my preteens there were the inevitable fads that swept the growing generation. Sample collecting was one craze. Innumerable companies put out miniatures of their products which could be acquired by sending in a coupon, sometimes accompanied by a dime. I had a candy box full of intriguing samples. Next door Ruth Cohn, a more dedicated collector, had one large bureau drawer given over to her treasures in miniatures. Another rage was monocles. Like every girl that I knew, I wore one on a narrow black ribbon round my neck. Useless clear glass though the monocle was, it was precious to me, during the peak of the craze, that is.

September Morn was the *Venus de Milo* of 1912. What a storm of censure that modest little maid engendered! Now owned by New York's Metropolitan Museum, the French artist, Paul Chabas' mild, sweet picture titled, *September Morn* was regarded as the zenith of sexy daring in modern art during my early teens. However I was exposed to better art than *September Morn*! Irene attended all available art exhibits and always took me with her. By mid-teen age, I could generally tell by one glance at a picture who the artist was! I was that familiar with our California painters. Because of his musical talent, Wilbur had been made an artist member of San Francisco's Bohemian Club which had an art show each year. Occasionally Wilbur would take Irene and me to this annual Bohemian Club exhibit. Once he took us to his friend Amédée Joulin's studio. Joulin, an eminent portrait painter, graciously showed us all his canvases and was most charming to "the little lady."

Piedmont Park had a permanent gallery—a good one, too. The park was in the approximate area now occupied by Piedmont High School. There was a ten-cent park entrance fee. Beside the entrance "George," a pleasant, swarthy, short Greek candy-maker, had his stand where he sold the delicious sweetmeats he concocted. Just inside the entrance was the park café. Otherwise the lovely lawns, flowers, shrubs, trees, benches, swings and gallery (for which I think there was an extra ten-cent charge) sufficed to attract numbers of people. On Sundays and holidays whole families would come by trolley to spend the day in the greenery of Piedmont Park.

Streetcars were THE mode of transportation. The fare was five cents, with transfers available to connecting lines. Not infrequently Irene, Laura and I would go forth for a luncheon and visit at Meehan's or at Scott's (whose home by then was in Alameda). Hours would be consumed by travel on the streetcars because of their stops made at each corner, plus the periods we waited at transfer points. At the end of these precious visits with old friends which Laura so gaily enjoyed, after the long trolley trip back to Piedmont, she would have those two steep blocks of Parkway to climb to Monte Avenue. That climb was slow going. One of us would take her arm to help but many stops to rest and get her breath were necessary.

THE THEATER
***

IRENE HAD TO BE ON THE GO, doing something to keep enter-tained. Always I was taken along. She never wanted to be alone. She abhorred a vacuum. Irene delighted in good food. Constantly she sought and found unknown small restaurants that served epi-curean menus. Little Italian and French places in San Francisco for a very small charge offered much to gratify the discriminating palate. Sanguinetti's* was rather well known but Irene discovered Locatti's,* which like Sanguinetti's was in an "off location," had sawdust on the floor, in short had atmosphere and served good red wine (Dago red) for free with a big Italian multi-course dinner that cost about thirty-five cents. I would be there always, eating heartily with Irene and Wilbur! (* spelling of the names of these restaurants is suspect!)

Until well into my high school days Irene, Wilbur and I would attend one or two matinee vaudeville shows each week. (Though at the time I did not realize it, this avid indulgence in matinees was not only a palliative for Irene's restlessness but her ruse to fill Wilbur's afternoons to keep him from drinking.) For vaudeville, beside the Orpheus which had a new show each week, Oakland had a Pantages Theater which was not only less expensive but also changed shows twice each week.

The Orpheum, in addition to the usual vaudeville turns of acro-bats, comedians, impersonators, jugglers, song and dance teams, contortionists, banjoists and what-have-yous, brought before its audiences some of the notables of the stage. There I saw, among other celebrities, Sarah Bernhardt, Lillian Russell, Harry Lauder, Annette Kellerman, Will Rogers, Ruth St. Dennis and Ted Shawn, Vernon and Irene Castle. Sometimes a short-short play would be the final attraction.

One featuring Mme Alla Nazimova, made an indelible impression on me. This little drama was a veritable *Uncle Tom's Cabin* of New York's divorce laws. The July 23, 1965, issue of *Time* magazine told that "by virtue of laws going back 178 years New York is the only state that recognizes only one ground for divorce; adultery proved by third-party testimony. Couples determined to divorce often resort to staged infidelity."

At the Orpheum fifty years earlier the scene was a room in a cheap hotel. Nazimova, a streetwalker, entered with a well-dressed distinguished looking gentleman. Their rendezvous was a rendezvous only to the extent that the man flung off his coat and tie, unbuttoned his shirt as, by prearrangement, the door was forced by a "private eye." Nazimova's curtain-closing soliloquy not only pointed the fact that she was truly a fine actress but also that even a poor wretched streetwalker could feel, at least fleetingly, a righteous satisfaction in her profession when so used to correct such lagging laws as those of New York state.

In recalling this Nazimova drama, and it alone of all the Orpheum "playettes" I saw, my memory treasured a play with the zeal of reform which caused such controversy that Nazimova's contract to play it was canceled and she received $11,000 to bow out. In 1923 Denver's famous juvenile court judge, Ben B. Lindsey, called Nazimova's act "the finest production ever presented in the interest of public morals." But the zeal of reform must be a patient zeal. In 1967 a new section on prostitution in New York law will go into effect. Passed late in 1965 this law provides that the *customer* of a prostitute, as well as the prostitute, is guilty of violation of the Criminal Code. In the spring of 1966, with that law pending, the New York legislature finally reformed its antique divorce law (toughest in the U.S.) drafted in 1787 by Alexander

Hamilton—adultery the sole ground for divorce. Nazimova was justified—after half a century!

Irene made one of her "discoveries" when she learned of the Dillon and King performances in a little theater on Tenth Street in Oakland. Judged by its location it should have been a third-rate burlesque house; instead Dillon and King, clever comedians themselves, each week staged a different and quite good musical comedy with some fine voices among the performers. We usually went on Friday nights to this "off-bounds" theater. (All socially acceptable playhouses were in the general area of Fourteenth and Broadway, Oakland's business hub.) Friday nights Dillon and King's musical was followed by a "talent show" that was always an excellent olio. Admission to this not-too-elegant palace of drama was ten cents, the same as to the Pantages.

Ye Liberty Playhouse on Broadway just above Fourteenth Street presented Oakland's stock company. This excellent repertory company put on fine plays. The Ye Liberty players, some of whom later became quite well known in Hollywood, had a family flavor; George Webster, Mina Gleason, James Gleason (son of Mina), Lucille Webster (daughter of George, wife of Jimmie Gleason), Henry Schubert, Frank Darien, Marjorie Rambeau, J. Anthony Smythe (who in later decades played Henry Barbour, the father of radio's *One Man's Family*). Each week this intrepid troupe presented a different play. Eventually the theater added a revolving stage, a very modern innovation to obviate set changing. Ye Liberty had tone and drew a discriminating audience.

Oakland's McDonough Theater, on Fourteenth Street just east of Broadway, booked the best road companies in current New York successes. The "greats of the stage" played there and I saw most of them during my teens. The tariff for McDonough shows was high.

Sometimes Arthur would take me to evening performances but when he had to be out of town he would get matinee tickets for Irene and me. On such matinee days I would board the streetcar at the Ransom School stop when classes were over at 1 p.m.; Irene would get on the car at Parkway and off we would go to the theater. At the McDonough I saw Sir Johnston Forbes-Robertson (in *Hamlet*), Margaret Illington (in *The Lie*), John Drew, Margaret Anglin, May Irwin, Nat Goodwin, Maxine Elliott, Nat Wills, David Warfield, Ferris Hartman (in *The Prince of Pilsener*), Edward Everett Horton (in *Too Many Cooks*), Maude Adams (in *Chanticleer*) and such delightful productions as *The Merry Widow*, *Peg O' My Heart*, *Chocolate Soldier*. (Maeterlinck's *Blue Bird* is the only performance I recall having to take the trek to San Francisco's Geary Theater to see.) Besides the fine legitimate shows the McDonough occasionally offered outstanding movies which we always attended— D. W. Griffith's *Birth of a Nation*, the Johnson African wildlife films, Burton Holmes' travelogues.

Movies eventually began to push vaudeville aside. By 1917 we even had a movie theater at Fortieth and Piedmont and one at Pacific Grove. Some of the stage greats began to take leads in movies—Geraldine Farrar, Walker Whiteside, the Barrymores, the Castles; but we had our early coterie of just-movie stars—Mary Pickford, Douglas Fairbanks, Mae Murray, Francis X. Bushman, Bill Hart, Charlie Chaplin, Theda Bara (the vamp), and a host of others. The handwriting was on the wall for live theater. The moving picture was in ascendancy. In 1904 I had seen my first motion picture—a fire engine drawn by horses that dashed toward me on the screen. Two decades later, in the early 1920s the movie had become the foremost theater medium.

HOUSEHOLD COMMERCE— CIRCA 1910

***

DURING THE PIEDMONT YEARS, various sounds heralded the approach of wandering artisans and tradesmen. A ringing bell told us a scissors-grinder would soon be available to sharpen our knives and scissors. Down the sidewalk he would saunter, heavy grindstone strapped to his back, his right hand tracing an arc as he rang his sizable bell. A sing-song "rags, sacks and bottles" preceded a decrepit horse and rickety wagon as the junk man drove down the street, hoping to buy our cast-off possessions. I cannot describe the chimney sweep's cry but we knew by it that he was coming long before this sooty artisan, garbed in black, wearing a high square hat and carrying the tools of his trade, came into view.

The postman's whistle was a familiar 10 Monte sound both morning and afternoon for we had two deliveries of mail daily. Half a century has made but little change in the mail carrier's uniform and leather pouch but it seems to have silenced the whistle he used to blow as he delivered the mail. Our letter box was on a landing up some five steps from the sidewalk—as far as the law allowed. Despite those steep Piedmont hills, year after year the same mailman—complete with bushy dark mustache—continued on our route.

Best of all was "the sound of music" as an Italian organ-grinder, monkey atop his instrument, came strolling along. He would crank out a tune on his hand organ. His green-jacketed monkey would go through a repertory of tricks. All the neighborhood children would gather round in delight. The musical selection would end. The monkey would take off his little red hat and pass it to collect the pennies the children clutched to pay for this at-their-very-door entertainment.

One passer-by we always looked at with interest was Joaquin Miller, who used to walk down our block on his way to Moraga

Road which led to his home estate (now preserved as a park). He wore a sash and Western hat and was quite the character poet!

*   *   *   *   *   *   *

My Piedmont childhood world was a different world of household commerce, everything was weighed out by the pound from a bulk supply. I can remember no foods in packages. Some canned foods could be bought but such foods tended to be inferior. Those were still the days of do-it-yourself cooking. Definitely it was not an era of going to the store for one's food supplies. Each morning Irene would compile a long list to order by phone from the Piedmont Grocery (Sachs') where she ran a monthly bill. Once, when paying her bill she said to Mr. Sachs, "You must find a small account like mine a nuisance to carry on your books, but I do appreciate the service." Mrs. Sachs said, "Believe me we appreciate your account; you pay promptly! You wouldn't believe if I told you the names how hard it is to collect on grocery bills from many of the very wealthy families in the Crocker tract." The Piedmont Grocery, like the Piedmont Meat Market, had two daily deliveries made by horse and wagon but despite all these deliveries neighborhood borrowing of food stuffs went on at a rate unheard of today.

Our milkman, Mr. Brusseau, a typical short thick pleasant French peasant sort, wore dark coarse peasant woolen clothes. A kind of "cat-door" in our back-porch-laundry accommodated delivery men when no one was at home. Each morning a clean round shallow enamelware pan was set on the floor just inside the little door. Into this pan M. Brusseau would pour a quart of delicious, rich unhomogenized, unpasteurized and unsanitary milk which we would put in our louvre (a screened, slatted cooler on the north side of the pantry) for the cream to rise for skimming. We did have an ice-box on the back porch but Piedmont is comparatively cool and we were an economical family. When we had ice, company was usually in the offing. Occasionally for a party dessert Irene would freeze a delicious tutti-frutti concoction, for which she had a very special recipe, in a tin half-melon mold. The mold, surrounded by cracked ice and rock salt in a galvanized pail would be put in the basement, the coolest place in the house, to freeze the mousse. No electric refrigerator, no freezer, very little refrigeration of any kind in the 10 Monte days!

Most colorful of our delivery service was Ah Him's. (More colorful even than our taking-away service of great, open, green garbage wagons pulled by teams of huge work horses and manned by swarthy, shouting, long-mustached Italians.) Vegetables and fruits we bought from Ah Him's well-stocked wagon with its dangling scale for weighing out the pounds of produce. Irene seldom went out to the wagon, but would have a list to read to Ah Him when he knocked at the back door. If string beans topped the list Irene would begin the buying transaction by questioning Ah Him in pidgin English, "You catch 'em velly fine stling beans today?" If assured by Ah Him, "Stling beans heap good, you buy him," she would tell him, "All light then, 15 cents stling beans." (Irene never could seem to think in pounds. Most of her recipes read, quite unhelpfully for today's economy, "10 cents round steak" or "5 cents worth of celery.")

If perchance we were lunching in the dining room and did not hear Ah Him's knock at the back door he would walk right in, through the back porch to the kitchen, raise the "slide" (used to pass dishes to and from the kitchen and dining room); poke his head through the opening and if I was visible shout, "Hello, Girl!" He was a big, gaunt weathered Chinese who loved children as all the Chinese who served California households seemed to. Ah Him continued to call me "Girl" till I left Piedmont in 1918. I had a sort of affection for him but once he rather embarrassed me. I was sitting sedately in English class at Miss Ransom's select school. (Ah Him was also vegetable Chinaman for Ransom's.) Looking through the open classroom window as he drove by toward the kitchen entrance he spotted me. In great glee, big, gaunt Ah Him shouted, "Girl!" and pointing at me with his whip, "Hello, Girl!" I was almost as amused by the preceding as I was embarrassed—which, at thirteen, helped.

HELP (!)
***

IRENE MOST CERTAINLY WAS NOT DOMESTIC in the Victorian implication of the word. She disliked practically everything to do with housework but she had one special hate—cooking. To be sure in later years she could prepare an occasional epicurean feast for guests and serve it with style. As Laura put it, "All Irene can cook are darn fool society dishes!" Laura seldom used such strong language—but I am getting ahead of my story.

In the early California years Laura, dedicated as she was to Irene's having a good time and herself a very domestic widow with nothing to do but the housework in small living quarters, quite naturally did all the cooking and household tasks herself. Irene was creative, was an artist at heart. Irene's was not a work-a-day housekeeping orientation. For all that—came THE DAY—to Irene, a grim and terrible day. At the time, Laura was touching seventy and Irene had passed thirty. On THE DAY Laura put their dinner on the dining table in the Lick Hills abode and calmly said, "This is the last meal I am going to cook. It is just too much for me at this age. You will have to take over, Irene." Irene adored Laura but many times she recounted this story. Quite apparently she thought the dictum rather unfair, certainly hard to bear.

Soon after this episode Irene became engaged and married to a man dedicated to giving his family the best of everything. Irene started by hiring a servant to do the cooking and all the manifold other chores that household help of that day did, in exchange for $15 or $20 a month plus room and board.

The rooms these servants occupied give one pause. I do not remember the servant-room at San Jose except that it was similar to the one in the Piedmont house. Ten by ten at best with one small window, it was furnished starkly with a narrow bed, chair, small chest of drawers and wash stand with bowl and pitcher. There was running water in the "sanitary laundry trays" (wash tubs) on the back porch from which the room opened. A toilet opened off this same back porch. Strangely enough in Piedmont, even though at the time 10 Monte was considered quite lonely and isolated, Irene was able to hire girls at $20 a month (though by 1910 the wages were pushing up toward $30, even $35) *because the room was so nice*!! Often the servant's room was a damp basement cubicle. Chinamen never objected to these but hired girls were becoming fussy!

Irene always hired "help" in San Jose or Piedmont but each "girl" was taken to Pacific Grove for the summer with us at 512 Willow. At Pacific Grove the equally small servant's room was off the pantry in which was a sink with running water. Because #512 had originally been built as an artist's one room studio-home in the unsewered woods, then added to as need arose, the only bathroom (tub, basin, toilet) was off a back hall beyond the kitchen. We all used the one toilet including the hired help.

Chinaboys were marvelous household servants. Descendants of the Chinese who had originally drifted to California to work at railroad-building or mining produced a population of Chinese workers who, by my day, served the whites mainly as cooks and household help. Wonderful cooks they were! Very independent but able household workers, inordinately faithful to the families for whom they worked. They were always paid a considerably higher monthly wage than the "hired girls." Most of these Chinese worked in this country just long enough to save sufficient money so they could return to China to live and support their families in comfort. On serving notice that he was leaving, inevitably the departing China boy brought around "his cousin" as a replacement. Just as inevitably, this cousin lacked the skills and good traits of his avowed kinsman who had sailed off to his homeland.

For long years the Gladdings had Sam, who not only did the cooking and all other housework but could be glimpsed on a stormy day taking the cat out and standing patiently with a sheltering umbrella. Twice Add, angered by Sam's autocratic independence in the kitchen, discharged him—outright fired him! But twice, too, she took him back into the fold when he sneaked into the house, by climbing in a window, and came to kneel before her begging, "Oh Missie—Missie, please you take Sam back." I remember less of Sam as a person than as the creator of the marvelously complex meringue ducks he made for the floating island dessert when we visited at 1611 Franklin.

These Chinese house servants always gave generous gifts to "their families" as a part and parcel of their own celebration of "China New Year." Besides lichee nuts, candied melon rind, coconut and ginger they would also present some lasting gift. These gifts, which were usually samples of China's fine old ceramic arts, are now irreplaceable. The de Young Museum in San Francisco, in the early '40s, exhibited a pair of Cantonese vases, replicas of, though smaller in size than, the fine pair given Flora Gladding by the China boy she had in about 1906. We still have those vases, which Irene at one time had made into lamps.

Wei (pronounced way) was Grandma Chambers' longtime Chinese cook in Oakland. Like all of his kind, he dressed in white starched coat and black cotton pantaloons, wore black Chinese slippers, had a blue-shaved forepart of his head and a long queue, which in Wei's case, instead of hanging down his back, was held with a Chinese hairpin in a coil at the back of his head. He was chubby with a smile almost as broad as his round face. Yorkshire pudding, ladyfingers and popovers were his fortes.

In the Walsworth Avenue house during his reign (for all the Chinaboys *did* reign) George DeGolyer was living at Grandma's while attending the University of California. George's room was directly at the top of the stairs. Wei's Sunday breakfasts, besides finnan haddie and half a dozen other goodies, always featured popovers—his pride and joy. George, out late of a Saturday night, wanted to sleep in. Grandma gave Wei orders—explicit orders— not to disturb Mr. George. Wei thought otherwise. His head would pop out the door from the back stairs to a common landing to assess whether the coast was clear (i.e., that "Missie Chambers" was not in sight), then in remarkably swift motion for one of his rotundity he would dash up the stairs, burst into George's room, grab the bed covers, strip them off and chortle, "Time to get up Georgie, time to get up!" Then back to his kitchen instanter. No hope of sleep after *that* treatment. George always appeared for Sunday breakfast, for this was a repeat act each week!

I have but two recollections of Sing, the first of our servants whom I remember. Understandably the first, for we had Sing before we moved into the Sixth Street house when I was two and a half. My first memory of Sing concerns one early morning when he called excitedly, "Hully up quick, bling baby, come see!" Jack Frost had etched intricate trees and ferns on the kitchen windowpane. Irene lifted me up. I still remember the frosty white wonder of the tracery.

Not long after that cold morning Sing had to leave us. There was a Tong War. (Always during my youth newspapers were erupting with headlines about Tong Wars.) A frightened Sing came to Irene to tell her that a highbinder of his tong had killed a Chinaman of another very powerful tong. Sing was the only member of his own tong in San Jose. He was a marked man—a far too easy target for a retaliatory killing. He must get out of town immediately and go into hiding. Irene said, "Get in the surrey; I'll drive you to the train." Sing would have none of that; an impetuous highbinder might aim at him but accidentally wound Irene. She insisted on a compromise which proved enough protection to save Sing. I remember Laura held me on her lap in the surrey as Irene slowed Nobby's gait to pace Sing's as he trotted along the sidewalk toward the station. I hated to have Sing go! All these Chinese loved the small children in "their" families and their love was usually reciprocated. Besides I had Sing slightly confused in my mind with Jack Frost!

My only other brush with Tong Wars came when I was seventeen. We were still getting gas from the single hand pump at the local garage in a town—no service stations, no restrooms. In making the trip from Piedmont to Pacific Grove we customarily stopped at the Southern Pacific station in Gilroy—a good halfway point—in order to avail ourselves of the station "facilities." Across the street, where Mexican town now is, in that day was the Chinatown. As we stopped one morning a shot rang out. We saw a Chinaman who had been casually leaning against a door jamb of the building opposite the station slump over. Almost before he hit the ground seemingly disembodied hands from within the building dragged him out of sight. In fact no one was in sight in all of Gilroy's usually crowded Chinatown. Next morning headlines about a Tong War—the last I remember ever seeing, too.

In addition to their acclaim as house servants and cooks, San Francisco's Chinese were famous as the city's washermen and noted for the lotteries they consistently ran—even after the law frowned. Laura, the quiet, the conservative, given the opportunity—and somehow not infrequently she found the opportunity—would buy a Chinese lottery ticket. Not long after 1907 the Law had its way. We heard no more of Chinese lotteries.

Chinese laundries were not confined to Chinatown but were found as well on convenient neighborhood shopping streets. Looking in the front window of one of these steamy little establishments one invariably saw a patient Chinaman at his ironing board carefully sprinkling the clothes as he ironed by the age-old oriental method of blowing a fine spray from a mouthful of water through his teeth. The Chinese vendor who toted his wares in baskets suspended from the ends of a long wood pole over his shoulders, though a commonplace in San Francisco, seldom penetrated to Piedmont.

After Sing's precipitous departure, Irene's cooks were "hired girls." Martha, hair parted in the middle, fluffed out a bit at either side then drawn into a bun at back—Martha, calico-neat, was the most typical hired girl we had—strong, able, willing, probably thirty—in her prime.

Mrs. Etlin, a beautiful dark-haired German woman, loved by us all, had come with her husband to America to seek better economic opportunities. Their two daughters, ten and twelve, had been left with her mother in Germany until the Etlins could become established in this new country. Sweet, warm, beautiful Mrs. Etlin had a well-trained, full-toned, enchanting singing voice. We all chose to call her "Mrs. Etlin" because it seemed fitting to do so.

The girl just returned from the Klondike gold rush was the one fiasco on our list of hired girls. Indicative of the nature of psychological blocks I do not remember her name—we all wanted to forget *her*! She came to us shortly before the yuletide and was hardly "broken in" when off we went to the gathering of the clan at Grandma Chambers' in Oakland. We returned to find "Klondike" had funneled all her Christmas cooking urge into candy making. Plate after plate of highly colored candies hid the sideboard top, hid the dining table. Irene took one look, then one bite. The Yukon must have learned to substitute lard for butter. Lard was not a pleasing taste in candy! Candy et al., Irene thought Klondike must be crazy and promptly sent her on her way. Miss Klondike however left a not-to-be-disregarded reminder of her sojourn with us—bedbugs.

It was Ida next. She rose to the occasion with the help of eradicating kerosene. Irene was mortified not only about the bed bugs but that Ida should be the victim to follow Miss Klondike. Ida was our special girl. She and Irene were more like friends. We had her for only a few months. She was working her way through college and when the fall semester started Ida, the comely blonde, left us.

Despite Klondike, of all the characters on our list of help, May Deloe took the prize. She was in her thirties and we called her, not May, but Mrs. Deloe—by *her* choice. She was the nearest to an Okie of any girl we had. Early she endeared herself to us by saying of a girlhood friend, "Me and her went to college together."

This hired-girl situation could be lonely for a newcomer in even so small a city as San Jose. We had not had Mrs. Deloe long when she announced that her brother was coming to San Jose. Long, lanky Mr. Lown, this brother, certainly assuaged her loneliness. He spent long hours every evening in her room, took her out Sunday after dinner, then brought her home early for more "visiting" in her room.

Once when Uncle George Chambers was staying overnight with us in San Jose I remember calling on him for a morning cuddle in bed. (I must have been pushing five.) He told me that Mrs. Deloe had been taken ill in the very early morning hours, that Arthur and Irene had taken her to the hospital. I remember the great dark reddish splotch on the dining room carpet where, coming to call for help in her illness, she had fallen in a faint and had, Irene said "had a hemorrhage." I gathered not of the lungs but at not quite five I knew no alternative source.

May Deloe rallied at the hospital but returned to us no more. Instead she married Mr. Lown explaining, "He is only my half brother you know." They moved to a fine two-storey house in Pacific Grove down Willow Street from #512. For long years after, Mr. Lown was Pacific Grove's garbage man, a highly respected citizen, as was his wife, May. She was an excellent cook, too!

Our Piedmont hired girls were not girls but middle-aged women due to our less propitious financial circumstances in those years. By 1910 a good girl in her prime of robust strength could demand thirty or even thirty-five dollars. Irene paid twenty dollars in Piedmont and took what that would buy and even at that could only afford to hire a maid for a few months at a time—just long enough to give a respite from that hated kitchen routine.

Actually Irene didn't mind cleaning and scrubbing nearly as much as cooking. I drew the dusting which I surmise Irene disliked as heartily as I did. Between hired girls and between her spurts of thorough cleaning of the house Irene hired, by the day or half day, Jap cleaning boys. These Japanese men were just beginning to dominate the house cleaning field. A few years later these "Japs," as they were consistently referred to, seemed all to have become gardeners but in Piedmont from 1910 to 1918 our by-the-hour gardeners were Italians.

One of our Piedmont maids, Mrs. Flynn, was Irish but not the typical Irish hired girl. Ponderous, slow-moving with orange-gray hair pompadoured not too neatly, she wore a black waist, limp white rushing at her neck, a black skirt. She gave one the feeling that she would have been in a more fitting role cushioned in an easy chair wafting a perfumed handkerchief before her face on a warm afternoon.

Christine Hulba was a flat-footed German woman *mit* accent. With brown hair drawn tightly to a bun atop her head and a well-scrubbed look, she too was middle-aged. When we took Christine to the Grove she was enchanted with the nearby woods, which reminded her of the Black Forest of her homeland. Off to the woods she went with a gunny sack to gather pine cones to kindle fires in the cooking stove and airtight heating stove. One beautiful vine she did not know in this New World forest. She brought one scarlet leaf of it home to Irene to be identified—holding the leaf between her lips as she grappled the sack of cones with both hands. There was no mistake as to identification, Christine was in bed for two agonizing weeks; her face ballooned from poison oak.

Of them all, we really had but one typical hired girl—Martha, Mrs. Etlin, the refined lady, was working at what she could do best in order to attain a goal for her beloved family. The Klondike gal was fairly typical of the young women who followed the gold strikes. Ida was a college woman. Mrs. Deloe was not only poor white trash but dangerously deceitful. Mrs. Flynn, besides being very Irish, had that slight air of condescension. Christine was German, trying in her clumsy way to adjust to a new country. But Martha was the epitome of the American hired girl. "I am the hired girl, Martha. I am what I am—a hired girl." One felt perfectly comfortable about Martha!

Next door to us in Piedmont the Max Cohns had a thirty-five-dollar-a-month type of hired girl. Katherine, an efficient cook and housemaid, was a sweet pretty young Irish woman. Under our very eyes blossomed the prototype of all hired-girl romances. The Cohns, like ourselves, traded at the Piedmont Meat Market. Short, thick, jolly, red-haired Frank delivered for the Market. Before long Frank began to lose considerable time making the Cohn's delivery. His horse would nervously shift feet at the curb and wait—and wait. When Frank did come to his cart he came running, making up for lost time. Only his time was not lost, for Frank and Katherine were married by the year's end. Such a romance was as typical of the era as the butcher's cart itself. Not many years passed before Frank King, Horatio Alger–like, was part owner of the Piedmont Meat Market and Katherine was happily tending their brood of small redheads.

BODY AND
SOUL
✳✳✳

SOME AFTERNOONS AFTER SCHOOL Irene would say, "Let's take a walk." Such lovely country we had to ramble! When the first curve of Moraga Road, beyond Monte Avenue was rounded, civilization was left behind—not a house in sight. Only one vacant lot separated 10 Monte from Moraga Road and Moraga Canyon which dipped on its far side. This was all wild country! Not infrequently at night the yipping howls of coyotes furnished a background chorus as we drifted to sleep. I must have been all of thirteen when one night I was awakened by insistent coyote howls that seemed so much nearer than usual that I quietly got out of bed and crept to my window which faced Moraga Road. The glow of the corner arc light helped the moon to illumine the vacant lot where a lone coyote, muzzle raised, yodeled his desolate night call.

On those afternoon walks Irene and I might go up Moraga the half mile or so to the Red Rock Quarry with its fascinating funicular cars that brought rock from upper levels to the crusher below. (All Piedmont streets were paved with this fine-crushed red gravel.) At the crusher we would drop down the trail to Moraga Canyon through whose leafy tunnel flowed an all-year stream. Tramps, asking for food, were not infrequent during the 10 Monte years. Once or twice Irene and I encountered such "gentlemen of the road" resting in this soft duff along the stream's bank. Though those we came upon were indeed true gentlemen with a courteous word of greeting as we passed, this was remote country and Irene decided it would be wise to eschew the canyon walks for hikes in the hills back of 10 Monte.

This walk to the reservoir became our favorite. Often we took a roundabout path to it so we could drink from a spring Irene had discovered which flowed diamond clear from the hillside to drop a foot or more to a moss-rimmed pool below. How refreshing was

172

that pure cold water we intercepted before it reached the basin below its source! (In our farthest hill rambles we never so much as reached the near boundaries of the present Montclair district.) In season we would return from the spring-green hills with great bunches of Brodiaea, which we learned were also known as "wild onions," the bulbs of which Indians had prized as food. Indians had indeed been in this gentle area, for one day I found a fine obsidian arrow point in the backyard at 10 Monte. Of all the joyous times I had doing exciting things with Irene, to me none compared to the thrilling walks in those lovely remote hills.

* * * * * * *

The summer I was eleven Arthur thought I should learn to swim. It was a good thought. He intended to pay for lessons from an experienced instructor for me that summer at Pacific Grove. Irene agreed it would be fine for me to learn to swim but amended Arthur's plans, suggesting that if he would pay the entrance fee for the two of us at the Pacific Grove "tank" (a very large indoor swimming pool at the Pacific Grove Beach) she would teach me to swim. Arthur agreed. I wonder if he did so because he felt disagreeing with Irene to be hopeless or if he actually had that much faith in her teaching ability. At any rate, the swimming under Irene's instruction did not come along as swimmingly as the schooling had. I was not too apt a pupil in the tank, a few yards of floundering breast strokes, head held high above the water, being the result. The fact that Irene, herself, could not swim *may* have had some bearing!

When I was fourteen Irene decided I should learn to ride. As usual at her suggestion Arthur was more than ready to foot the bill for lessons and horse hire for us both. Miss Graham, at her riding academy, then located in Oakland on Telegraph at about

Twenty-Fourth, did her best to make a horsewoman of me but I did not have Irene's skill with equines. However that summer at Pacific Grove, with Arthur paying the charges, we rented horses from the Gardner Stable on Grant in the block above Lighthouse Avenue. I never felt at all at home on horseback and with that summer my equestrian life came to an end.

*   *   *   *   *   *

Early in 1912 Ned and Mary Goddard left Ohio to drive via the southwestern route to California, where they had decided to make their home. Coming through Arizona they lingered, taking the desert side roads to visit remote Hopi villages. Arrived in California they stayed with us at 10 Monte for two or three weeks till they selected Marin County as a home location and bought their place in the Sleepy Hollow area. (When the Goddards arrived they presented Irene with a woven Hopi plaque which stood near our fireplace at 10 Monte for years. On leaving they gave Irene an electric iron—until that time heavy flat irons heated on a gas stove burner had sufficed at 10 Monte.) Not long after the Goddards were established in their own place the Watrouses—Wint, Adelyn and Bun—joined them in Marin County. A bit later Mary Porter followed. After that, each spring and summer vacation I would spend some idyllic days at the Goddard's family compound in Marin County.

I loved jaunts away from home. After the divorce, Arthur took me on various trips. One of the first was to Tahoe where we took the trip around the lake on the little steamer that plied the lake waters daily. Next we went to Yosemite, where we rode burro-back to Glacier Point.

The following summer (1912) Maynard Wright, wishing to try his luck at trout fishing, chose Rubicon Springs for summer vacation. Annie, George and Baldwin DeGolyer as well as Maynard, Charlotte, Muirson and Elizabeth Wright planned to join this vacation venture. Arthur suggested that I go along. So I did, and fell in love with the Sierra streams and lakes, forests and granite slopes. Getting to Rubicon was not too simple—the Southern Pacific train to Truckee, then the local railroad to Lake Tahoe, the steamer around the lake to Koana Villa (near the better known McKinney's Resort on the west shore) and finally a four-horse stage via steep, narrow, curving mountain roads—in our case in a torrential electric storm which landed us at Rubicon Springs, drenched to the skin. The resort was delightful, a log lodge in the evergreens beside the Rubicon River. We had floored tents among the trees. The food was wonderful—cooked by a negro woman complete with red bandana tied around her head and marvelous starched checked-gingham apron deeply bordered in white cross-stitch designs. Rubicon had a laundry service also. Old Sally, an Indian squaw, tattooed dark lines on chin, wove baskets of native grasses when not at her wash tub. Tahoe and environs have changed with the passing years.

The summer of 1913 Arthur took me on the long Pullman trip to Denver for the Knights Templar Triennial Conclave; in fact, took me even further, to show me Colorado Springs, the Garden of the Gods, Manitou (where he had summered during Chicago years) and the old mining town of Leadville. Though Arthur had planned the trip to Denver via the Western Pacific so I would see the lovely Feather River Canyon by daylight, the return trip was by Southern Pacific. At Benicia, he impressed on me the phenomenon of the whole train, broken in sections, being transported across the Strait of Carquinez on the *Solano*, the largest ferry boat in the world. (Beginning in 1879 the Southern Pacific used the *Solano* in this service for more than fifty years.)

The next trip with Arthur was to the Grand Canyon via Santa Fe Pullman. We ate at the Fred Harvey restaurants at stations. (The Santa Fe chose to make real stops at these fine eating places, run by their concessionaire, Harvey, rather than maintain dining cars as did the Southern Pacific and most other railroads.) Our train stopped at Needles long enough so that I was able to buy from an old squaw on the station platform a long necklace of tiny beads strung to look like a lei of small, yellow-centered, blue forget-me-nots. Ten cents purchased this strand of her beautiful handiwork. In Arizona we saw vast grazing herds of long-horn cattle—amazing, unreal-looking creatures. In our Pullman we became acquainted with a family from Germany. Delightful people, they were elegantly dressed but wore no jewelry except the iron-cross ring each proudly showed. They explained that the ring signified that they had given the family jewels to help the Kaiser's cause.

The Knights Templar Conclave in 1916 was in Los Angeles. Arthur and I stayed with Madeline and Earle Barker in Pasadena for the event. Then Arthur took Madeline with us for several days in San Diego, which had an exposition of its own that year.

Arthur was a delightful traveling companion—handling suavely the mechanics of travel, frequenting the best hotels and restaurants, full of information about the countryside. I loved to travel! Before I left on one of those fine jaunts Irene always told me how happy she was that I could have these fine trips with Arthur. She mentioned once that had she not been divorced from Arthur, it would have been she, not I, who would be going on these wonderful expeditions with him. I am sure Irene never intended me to feel unhappy about her having to stay home—with Wilbur!

*   *   *   *   *   *   *

Shortly after our move to Oakland, Arthur had established himself in the municipal contracting business, which proved lucrative. He worked hard and spent much time, long before air-conditioning, in the insufferably hot valley towns—Porterville, Fowler, Hanford, Lindsay, Reedley—installing water and sewer systems in the fast-developing San Joaquin Valley. Meanwhile he made his home at Grandma Chambers'.

By the time Elizabeth Chambers had moved from Walsworth Avenue to the big square stucco house (razed in 1964) that she built at 155 Monte Cresta Avenue, Oakland her household was quite a household indeed! In the full basement were bedrooms for the cook (if a Chinaman) and for the chauffeur. Grandma had a little black box of an electric automobile which she herself usually drove down to Fortieth and Piedmont to do her marketing but her big seven-passenger Haynes touring car was driven by Stewart, familiarly referred to by the younger generation as "Stew." Short, stocky, red-haired, he proved as good-natured and kind a nursemaid for her young grandchildren as he did an expert chauffeur for her automobile.

The first floor at #155 was given over to reception hall, living room, library, glassed sun porch, dining room, butler's pantry, kitchen and so forth. The second floor had four large bedrooms and a second-storey glassed porch. On this second floor Grandma Chambers and her "retainers" lived. Cora Hotchkiss (a widowed niece who had lost husband and two children within a few weeks to diphtheria) and Louise Sieferle. Miss Sieferle, a not-too-young graduate nurse, had been conned by Madeline Hood Chambers into leaving her profession to become housekeeper and what-have-you for the George Chambers ménage. Children grown, Madeline had no further need for "Aunt Louise" who by then was far-from-young.

Grandma adopted her and adapted her into the #155 household. There was friction, but minimal friction between her and Cora.

In the third-storey were three bedrooms—one for the cook if a woman, which for many years she was—Mattie, a black-as-the-ace-of-spades negress. The second room was occupied by George DeGolyer as he finished at the University of California, then worked for Arthur. The third room was Arthur's. Four bathrooms, plus one toilet off the back kitchen porch sufficed for this household, basement to attic.

* * * * * *

Sunday School at Mowbray Hall, Piedmont's one and only meeting place, located next the Piedmont Grammar School grounds, had been the sum total of my religious education until I pushed into middle teens and quite regularly attended the Plymouth Congregational Church each Sunday with Grandma Chambers and her retinue. At Plymouth, Grandma always sat in the front pew where there was a connection into which she could plug her Acousticon, the large, awkward, box-like hearing device she wore. The sermons by the Reverend Mr. Kloss made sense to me and I quite enjoyed the churchgoing. Besides my Sundays belonged to Arthur, in my "divorced way of life," and he wanted me to go, as the possibility of saving my soul gave his mother satisfaction. In my youth Sunday was rigidly observed by church people. One was not supposed to lift a finger for anything—if a button fell off, it stayed off till Monday. Grandma Chambers frowned on any work or play on Sunday. After church she sat in her living room with hands folded until dinner was announced at two o'clock. Serving that dinner, Mattie, bearing a great prime-rib roast, would stagger into the dining room, face moistly shining from the exertion of labor necessary to prepare those inevitably huge Sunday dinners that helped to fill the idle after-church house. (Irene, from afar, shouted, "hypocrite!")

ALADDIN'S LAMP
***

TWO SOCIAL EVENTS at 155 Monte Cresta stand out. The first in 1915 came out of Arthur's pocket in toto. To return such courtesies extended to me in the past my guests were invited to a dance given at Grandma Chambers'—live music, everything swish as swish could be, with dance favors of a crepe-paper orchid corsage for each girl and for each boy a boutonniere of a crepe-paper Cecile Brunner rose. (Though Irene had made these remarkably realistic flower favors she had known she would not be present at the dance to see them worn. While married to Wilbur she was *persona non grata* in Chambers homes—not by Arthur's decrees, I think, but by his mother's.)

The second party, in 1916, was an evening card party for the Belgian Relief Fund. Guests paid a fee for this bash which was in a careful color scheme of blue and white, the colors of Belgium— ice cream molds, cake frosting, favors, prize wrappings, all blue and white. Herbert Hoover had made us Americans aware of the Belgian's plight and this whing-ding marked the depth of sacrifice we were more than willing to undergo to help our fellow man.

On my sixteenth birthday, war or no war, Belgians or no Belgians, Arthur decided I should have an "auto." He gave me a Jeffrey roadster, which I had for all of two weeks. By then Irene had pointed out to him that I really needed a larger car—one in which, for instance I could take my group of girlfriends to Pacific Grove for the weekend. Irene's suggestions to Arthur worked like Aladdin's rubbing of his magic lamp. Almost immediately I had a seven-pas- senger Jeffrey touring car and Irene chaperoned my little clique on a Pacific Grove weekend. Somehow I always felt that car was more Irene's than mine. Arthur could not very well give Wilbur's wife a car so I got the Jeffrey. Arthur made the point that the car would give Laura a chance to get out more. I am sure this gave him sincere satisfaction for, like everyone, he loved and admired Laura.

* * * * * * *

Though Piedmont had its own grammar school, Piedmont youth had to attend Oakland High School. Perforce they must take the Piedmont streetcar and transfer in mid-Oakland to another trolley in order to reach the old high school building some distance west of Broadway. Irene decided my health would not stand the strain of the long day of streetcar travel plus a full day of class work. Further Oakland High School's student body was a pretty rough cross section of East Bay youngsters. Irene felt I should be in a more elite school. In 1912 "Little Madeline" (as we erroneously continued to

IRENE DRIVING | *1917*

refer to the George Chamber's daughter) had graduated from high school at Ransom's, a girls' private boarding school that took a few day pupils. Irene's suggestion to Arthur that I go to Ransom's met with his instant, pleased approval. As to the money involved Irene had a theory which she repeatedly expounded to me. "Get all you can out of your father; if you don't get him to spend on you he will spend his money on someone else for Arthur is generous. You work him for all you can get!" To be sure *after* 1913 Irene had the specter of Madeline's wedding to haunt her!

Arthur happily "pungled up" the cost of my day scholar tuition to Miss Ransom and Miss Bridges' School, a select place of learning for girls of socially acceptable families. Oddly enough, I was the only daughter of divorced parents there—divorce was not too socially acceptable in my youth. Perhaps because Madeline was a recent graduate there was no hitch about my joining the ranks at Ransom's.

Ransom's school day started at 8:30 a.m., ended at 1 p.m. I walked the approximate mile from 10 Monte to the school at "the End of Hazel Lane" (Ransom's expensive-sounding address), off Highland Avenue, beyond Piedmont Park, and near the ugly Victorian pile that was the old Requa home. Alice Requa, a granddaughter, was already a friend. I palled with her group—Eunice Roeth, Elizabeth Bliss (St. Sure). I loved the girls but not the school.

Arthur had insisted that I prepare for college. For once Irene had to bow to Arthur's dictum. Miss Marion Ransom had her eye on me as a candidate for Bryn Mawr, her own alma mater. She thought once there, I would "do her school proud." Being no genius I worked for all my A's (and in the simple high school courses then offered my marks *were* all A's). Marion Ransom was happy. I was miserable. Never having liked school, I had no desire to go to college and I *heartily* disliked *her* hard-driving school—mainly because home, with Irene to keep the action going, was much more interesting. I was growing very fast, was very thin, was very sleepy an incredible percent of the time. The action Irene took at the end of my second year of high school at Ransom's led to the recommendation from a San Francisco "specialist" (i.e., a good internist) that I stay out of school for one year, eat well, rest and relax. That was fine with me; that year was the year of San Francisco's Panama-Pacific International Exposition. Irene and I spent many diverting and educational days on the lovely grounds of that exposition, which I will always remember specially for the Brangwyn murals and the Palace of Fine Arts (the controversial shell of which still stands) with its thrilling contents of painting and sculpture, old and new.

To spend one of those days at the Fair we would start early in the morning, walk the three blocks to Parkway and Highland Avenue. We might have to wait ten minutes for a streetcar to take us to Fortieth and Piedmont where we would board the Key Route electric train. These trains ran every twenty minutes and took just twenty minutes to get from the terminal to the mole. Between San Pablo Avenue, the last stop, and the mole the conductor would walk through the train to collect the ten-cent fare from each passenger. At the mole we would board the Key Route ferry for the twenty-minute Bay crossing. At the Ferry Building, after waiting some minutes, we would catch a streetcar that went to the Exposition via the wholesale produce district. One team of ponderous dray horses after another would be standing at right angles to their wagon in order to give sufficient room for the streetcar to pass on the narrow cobbled streets crowded on both sides with horses and wagons

GIRLS OF PIEDMONT
GRAMMAR SCHOOL |
Elizabeth Chamber in
front row, far right. *1913*

loading in front of the produce warehouses. Transportation, public and private, was neither fast nor simple in 1915.

The fall of 1916, I entered my junior year at another private girls' school, Merriman's, on the southeast corner of Santa Rosa and Oakland Avenues. On May 29, 1918, I graduated from Merriman's. I had enjoyed those two school years thoroughly—the academic work, my group of friends: Grace Ziegenfuss (Volberg), Marian Ish, Helen Rosenberg (Aunt Rose). Merriman's had one true teacher, an inspiration to all who took work from her. Fortunately she taught English so everyone did have the privilege of classes with this one-in-a-million teacher, Edith Hunt, an aunt of Eleanor (Sis) Hunt Henshaw's.

IN 1964 WHEN SCOTT SEATON CAME from the Hollywood home of his latter years to revisit the Bay Area, famed columnist Herb Caen heaped encomiums upon him as the patriarch of all actors— in his mid-90s Scott was still playing bit parts in the movies.

*   *   *   *   *   *   *

One day of the week that Wilbur moved from 10 Monte Irene, in a palliative for her lagging spirits, went lunching in San Francisco with Elizabeth Meehan. Irene was glad to have divorce proceedings started, nevertheless she was at a low emotional ebb. As she and Elizabeth walked up Grant Avenue, Irene glimpsed a handsome gray-haired man coming down the block. Some far off memory instantly tugged at her. She looked at the man again. He had actually passed, going in the opposite direction, before Irene's memory jigsaw fitted into place and she said to Elizabeth, "Why, that was Scott Seaton!" Knowing Scott, as I subsequently did, I am sure he not only had an eye but also an ear out for any vivacious, good-looking woman he might pass on the street. This day he turned and overtook Irene and Elizabeth saying, "Pardon, but I thought I heard my name mentioned. I am Scott Seaton." From that day Scott was more or less a fixture at 10 Monte and for summer visits at 512 Willow as well. He was better than a psychiatrist for Irene's emotional state. Indeed he was good medicine for us all with his light touch to life, his silly harmless fun, his utter nonsense:

"Driving over here I saw a cute little dog!"
"What kind of a dog, Scott?"
"Oh, the kind with four legs, one on each corner."

We would roar with laughter, for somehow Scott made one *feel* like laughing.

Irene had not seen Scott since they were teenagers in Oakland. His mother was a sister of Collis P. Huntington—one of the Big Four of early California railroad fame. The Seatons had then lived in a specially magnificent Victorian house in the elite Jackson Street area. A ballroom with a large adjoining conservatory full of growing flowers were among the many rooms of that house. Scott had one sibling, Etta, who married Raliegh Hooe. (Before long these people were Grandma Seaton, Aunt Etta and Uncle Raliegh to me.) Scott made a very early marriage which ended in divorce. (He was a grandfather by the time of that Grant Avenue encounter.) Scott had had but one real ambition in life—to be an actor. His family had disapproved but when his first marriage ended, he finally followed his own desires and espoused a stage career. He was a fine character actor. For years he traveled with a repertory company. He fell in love with and married the ingénue Ruby—the love of his life. The Seaton family frowned on Ruby. She tried so desperately to win their approval that it killed her! Scott's mother, Etta and Raliegh were devout Christian Scientists. Ruby embraced their faith. She died of peritonitis, caused by a neglected burst appendix, only a few months before Irene and Scott met.

Dixie, Scott and Ruby's daughter, was ten years old. Scott was in the real estate business. His mother, a semi-invalid, and Dixie lived with him in a big two-family residence on College Avenue near Ashby in Berkeley. Poor Dixie, for mother substitutes, had an ailing grandmother and a straitlaced, overly formal aunt. Scott would drive over to 10 Monte evening after evening bringing Dixie. The four of us would go to a movie, or for a ride, or Irene and Scott would visit in the living room while Dixie, open-mouthed with interest in the doings of a girl six years her senior, would come to my room to be shown my latest treasures; clothes, snap shots, dance programs. Sometimes Scott would come alone and take Irene out to dinner or for a ride.

One early evening, the doorbell rang. I opened the front door. There stood a minister—black suit, white high-front collar, flat crowned black hat, Bible in hand. I looked at him questioningly, awaiting his explanation for the call—then finally it dawned—Scott!

Once, riding a Pullman overland, Scott had bet a fellow passenger he could disguise himself so he could pass through the car unrecognized. The man laid a sizable bet that he could not—and watched alertly for an hour or more after Scott left their car. Watched alertly enough but paid little or no attention to a wrinkled old woman making her way laboriously down the aisle as she passed from car to car. Scott collected the money! He was a make-up artist par excellence and heaps of fun to boot. Besides, he filled what *might* have been a vacuum for Irene.

One Sunday early in 1918 Irene, Arthur, Scott and I drove to join San Jose friends of past years—Jack and Lill Kocher, Herman and Pauline Pfister and Calvin and Lena McBride with their son, Lux—on a jaunt to the Paul Masson winery at Saratoga where we were Paul's guests for a barbecue at his lovely villa. A rift (though no divorce) between Paul and his wife accounted for the fact that neither she nor their daughter, Adele, were present. (Later I did meet Adele in the Masson's home not far from the charming rustic building that was the first Pebble Beach Lodge. This home of Paul Masson's, the first to be built in the immediate area, was on the side of the Drive away from the ocean and Paul had the promise of the Pacific Improvement Company—predecessor of Del Monte Properties Company—that no home sites would be sold on the

Ocean side of the Drive so that nothing would ever obscure the view from his house. With the construction of the Crocker-Fagan, Clark, Murray and other homes on the ocean side of the Drive that promise to Paul was broken before many years. The Massons, feeling their home had been ruined, never forgave the Del Monte Properties Company.)

The Pfisters, Kochers and McBrides were close friends of Paul's and had been at his villa many times. For the rest of us it was a new and thrilling experience. I remember Lux McBride that day particularly as supplying the power for a precarious wheelbarrow ride I took. (Lena McBride had been a Miss Lux—of Miller and Lux fame. Calvin, her husband, had won the battle against alcoholism long years before the birth of Alcoholics Anonymous. Lux, their only child, was interested in drama. After Calvin's death Lux and his mother lived in Hollywood where Lux's bit parts in the movies made a meager living for the two of them. Calvin's poor investments of Lena's wealth plus the Depression had wiped out her ample share of the huge Lux fortune.)

That Sunday at Paul's was fabulous—the weather a delight, the barbecue the delectable ancestor of all future barbecues, and the wines!! Ah, the wines! Paul pulled aside an oriental rug on the living room floor. The trap door disclosed, when opened, a staircase descending to the opulently stocked wine cellar. We trooped down, walked through vault after vault of Paul's fine wines. (For years his wines had had a market in France where, under French labels, they were reshipped to the United States to receive the high favor and high prices that California wines at that time were not acknowledged to merit.)

Paul was a jolly, fairly rotund, courtly Frenchman. That day he was wearing a tan corduroy suit and low-crowned hat and somehow looked as though he might take off any minute to climb an alp. I always think of him, surrounded by his other guests, as he sat happily in a lawn swing with one arm around Lena McBride and the other encircling Lill Kocher, chatting away in his warmly hospitable manner. At about this juncture somehow Lux inveigled me into the wheelbarrow and took off. It was an innocent Sunday filled with the good food and good drink with which Pauline and Irene seemed inevitably to be surrounded. Whether there was any truth to the many stories that parties at Paul Masson's villa were wild, drunken orgies I would gravely doubt. Surely there was no evidence that day to support such rumors. Besides, Paul was born and raised in a country that knew how to handle liquor, that respected its quality, not its quantity, for consumption.

Today it is difficult to realize with what distress the church-going public of my childhood regarded a wine bottle. The church-goer thought the very Devil might lurk in a wine bottle! However a four-ounce bottle of whisky in his satchel when traveling was something else again—a precaution considered necessary for "medicinal purposes." Irene *never* thought of taking a trip without such a bottle along yet *never* to my knowledge did she use it!! On the other hand at home, Irene, whose attitude toward alcoholic beverages was the antithesis of the church-goers', frequently resorted to a stiff snort of whisky to "brace her up." She was "nervous" as she frequently reminded us. Instead of this symptom humiliating her she seemed to be rather proud of being nervous. When her sewing "went wrong" she needed to be "braced up." Everything Irene did was touched by drama, each meal she cooked being no exception. She always needed "bracing" to face the trauma of getting dinner. Whisky had become a staple at 10 Monte. One day early in 1918, noticing how low the current bottle was getting, I added whisky to the shopping list. Later when Irene picked up the list I saw her cross out whisky. I said, "Oh, didn't you notice? The bottle is nearly empty. You need to get some more." Irene answered, "Yes, I know about the bottle but I realize I am getting too dependent on whisky to brace me up. I have decided to cut it out altogether." And that is what she did—just like that! After that day Irene never touched liquor except when she drank socially, which she continued to do the rest of her life. Social drinking in Irene's era consisted of *one* cocktail before dinner, wine with dinner, perhaps an after-dinner liqueur. How shocked Irene would have been at the extent of social drinking today, the accent on quantity, the comparative disregard of quality.

Never at any time in her life did Irene *show* the effect of liquor, though she admittedly felt it helped to control her nervousness. To me her sudden and complete eschewing of whisky when she realized she had become dependent upon it shows more than any other incident the strength of her character and her ability, when she felt it necessary for her long-term future welfare, to change her own mores. Knowing her as the Grannie so quietly and selflessly adapted to our household only one who had known, also, the Irene of early years, a volatile, "nervous" woman concerned that everything and everyone around her conform to her particular mood, could begin to appreciate her adjustments in later life. Irene was a woman of as much strength of character as charm of personality!

THE SUMMER OF 1918 FOUND IRENE, LAURA AND ME back
under the five sheltering live oaks at 512 Willow. I was enrolled at
Hopkins Marine Biological Station of Stanford University. Before
that summer "the Lab" had been a stark gray-painted two-storey
frame structure across the road from Lovers Point. In 1918 we
christened the awkward stucco cube of a building on Cabrillo
Point at the Pacific Grove end of what only a few years before had
been Chinatown Beach, lined just above the high tide mark with
one Chinese fisherman's ramshackle hut after another, all of them
together looking like a mass of weathered gray driftwood cast high
on the shore.

At the marine laboratory I took five units of zoology and five
units of physiology. We covered a lot of territory in those six
weeks! I fell completely in love with biological science and as a
result have a straight-A record for Stanford courses!! I decided then
and there to register at "the Farm" that fall as a zoology major with
the thought of possibly becoming a bacteriologist.

In physiology, Ernest Martin gave the lectures, Frank Weymouth
shepherded the lab work. Alice Jenkins Weymouth bore their second child that summer, but Mrs. Martin and the Martin's pre-teen
Lois were always along on the all-day field-collecting trips in the
Midway Point area of the Drive. "Daddy" Starks was teaching the
zoology course. Because Edwin Chapin Starks' only child, Dorothy,
was taking work at the Station for college credit between her junior
and senior high school years, I became close to the Starks family as
represented at Pacific Grove that year. Dorothy, too, was keeping
house for her father because her mother, Chloe Starks, was teaching
a summer art course on the Stanford campus. Dr. Starks gave me my
treasured copy of the delightful book, *Tire Tracks on English Roads*
(an account of a cycling trip with one of his former students) that

he and Dorothy had printed on their Attic Press. In 1918 Dorothy already had her course set for an M.D. which she subsequently obtained to specialize in roentgenology. She became Mrs. Willis Rich, second wife of the eminent oceanographer. (No one knows more of the movements of the Pacific salmon, I have been told, than Willis.) Dorothy and I still keep in touch with yearly letters.

Up till this wartime year of 1918, Stanford summer school at Pacific Grove was noted for its "boy-girl fun" or perhaps I should say, "fun for girls." The usual top-heavy percentage of Stanford men was augmented by the pre-med (always predominantly male) undergraduate courses available at Marine Lab, for at that time Hopkins Marina was heavily slanted to undergraduate courses with comparatively little graduate research underway. After four years at girls' high schools I was not averse to the top-heavy boy ratio. I approached the first day at class with joyful anticipation. Besides Dorothy my classmates turned out to be a lame gray-haired spinster whose name I have lost in the passing years and Mrs. Hilyer, who kept a motherly eye on her six-year-old son who played on the beach below the lab window as she absorbed the marine biological terms that she hoped would help her to better translate works of the German scientists for Dr. Branner at Stanford. Then there was Miss Preston, with a tinge of gray at the temples. She was teaching her way to an M.D. (In due time she became a successful pediatrician in San Jose.) I am sure Miss Preston disliked me with zest. I butterflied about. Not infrequently one boy or another would meet me after class to see me home. I would probably be off dancing with said boy all evening but despite all my frivolity I would better her in grades the next day.

However the day came when she had her revenge—of a sort. That morning she was all smiles, "Miss Chambers (we were formal in 1918), I went out on a little collecting trip of my own yesterday. See the fine specimen I found. Here, don't you want to hold it?" She held out to me a live snake, a good eighteen inches of live snake. It must have been a marine species or she would have had no possible excuse to have it in the classroom but any scientific classification has long been lost in my memory while what strongly remains is my feeling that I was confronted with a brand-new kind of test in zoology. If I did not take that horrid snake she would feel justified in classifying me as too squeamish and rattle-brained to deserve the space I occupied in class—no matter what my grades. I took the snake—quite firmly in my two hands in a body-hold. What I was not prepared for was the strength of the muscular convolutions of the body in my grasp. There was an awful moment when I thought I was going to flunk this test but I held on! I continued to hold on for an interval that even Miss Preston would have to recognize as not being chicken—but no longer—before returning her "specimen" with a light and airy, "Oh, what a lovely snake!" And I continued to get A's!

Who were these boys? It seems I was "queening" (we did not say "dating" in 1918) all summer. How did it happen? My high school days had been rather devoid of such. Toodles Dinsmore was the popular girl. At Ransom's she wore a border of fraternity pins around her sweater. I was the quiet wallflower. In my own eyes I was the plainest and least popular of girls. I still feel that is how it was, yet if so, why, when I did go to a dance in post-sixth-grade days, was my program always filled? We had program dances then, for of course no one went steady. Sort of tallies of dances were these programs. The boy signed his name for as many dances as he wanted and felt proper to take (or, no doubt in some cases, did not want but felt obligated to take) and put the girl's name opposite the corresponding dance number on his own program. A girl's partner of the evening took dance number one and two, the supper dance and the last dance. Always!

After long years of going to dancing classes at Mowbray Hall I began, at about the seventh-grade level, to attend the quite fabulous parties which were given in the Piedmont homes of my friends. The Thomases, the Abbots, the Requas, the Roeths all had homes with large dance floor areas. Always there was live music. Always the parents were present. I felt it a special honor to dance with the hostess' father, especially kindly, "bouncy" Mr. Roeth. Carlton Osgood was sure to be at each of the many dances given at Roeth's. I think the two families were friends. Carlton always took several dances. I liked him; he was stolid and kind.

The Osgoods had a large drugstore in Oakland. In high school I had the pleasure of knowing Carlton's elder sister, Consuela. However the Osgood family was to some extent frowned upon. Mr. Osgood had started his substantial drug business on gains from the thriving bail bond business of his earlier years.

But always, though I had a good time, I felt wallflower-ish and unpopular, yet I had been elected president of my grammar school graduating class (as well as my senior high school class). Also perhaps no other girl was getting as much attention from a boy as I in grammar school (we did not say "grade school" in those days). Herbert Dickey was a nephew of the Hawaiian Doles of pineapple fame. Herbert, had he lived, might have had a fantastically brilliant career. His hobby was sciences. He had a chemistry lab in his basement and had his own wireless. (The word radio, not to mention short wave, was unknown.)

The afternoon before we left Piedmont for that 1918 summer in Pacific Grove, Herbert, who had by then finished his freshman year at UC Berkeley and had enlisted, suddenly appeared for about the first time since our graduation from eighth grade. He came to call, wearing a white shirt and a good suit over his working clothes. He could not idly wait for his summons after enlistment but had secured a job working at a Pacific Gas and Electric Company plant. He had to go to work immediately after our visit. He loved hiking, planned a walking tour just before he would leave for the service, expected to come to call on me at Pacific Grove. But Herbert was not one of the boys to wait for me to come from class at the Marine Station. Shortly after I had started summer school there was a boiler explosion at the PG&E plant. Herbert died within a few hours from the burns received. It was my first brush with death and was hard to grapple with. I had my first experience with the very real, and not at all pleasant, dreams of someone who has had some meaning in one's life and has been taken by death. I had never really cared for Herbert but he had always been attentive and kind to me despite his reputation as the class bad boy. Little wonder that reputation, for he was far too brilliant to be really interested by any class I was ever in.

Baldwin DeGolyer, a year my senior, had been attending Stanford for a year or two. Not infrequently, with Irene as a chaperone, I had been at dances at El Camino, his house on the campus, which later became a Theta Chi fraternity chapter. Leland Ellis of El Camino (a medical student in 1918 and subsequently an Alhambra M.D.) spent a week with us that 1918 summer. I always claimed Leland was Irene's beau for they were most compatible. Leland had asked me to a Stanford dance or two and of course we contrived to go dancing each evening he was at #512. Irene did not chaperone these summer dances. One evening Leland took me dancing at the Del Monte where I ordered a horse's neck—I had learned that trick;

though the drink looked and sounded vicious, it was only a spiral of lemon peel in a tall glass of gingerale.

Del Monte, as in Laurie's dancing days, was popular not only with youth but with the older generation as well. Leland had to yield a dance to Francis McComas the noted artist, whose second wife, Gene Makey McComas, was the older sister of my high school classmate, Margaret Baker Clark. Mag's had not been the typical teenage marriage of our early twentieth century. When she was a high school sophomore, Mr. Baker, her father, editor of the *Oakland Tribune*, had died within a month of her mother's death. Sister Gene, temperamental and much older than Mag, was hard for exuberant Mag to live with. Their older brother, Cecil, a navy officer, was married and serving in the Philippines. In the early summer of 1916 Mag, the orphan, set out chaperoned by the navy chaplain and his wife to become a member of her brother's household. Shipboard she met a young ensign bound for duty in Guam. Romance rapidly flowered. The couple was married by the chaplain before the transport left Guam. Within two months she was back living with sister Gene once again. Her husband had died of some rare tropical ailment that ran a rapid, fatal course. Within six months Margaret Baker Clark had lost mother, father and husband.

Francis McComas, at the time of the Del Monte dance was a divorcée (his first wife was one of "the" Parrots of San Francisco), noted for more than his art. That evening at Del Monte I concluded that if the "intimate" manner of his dancing proved anything it proved that his bad reputation with the ladies was deserved. Gene Baker, who had been doing some feature writing for (naturally) the *Oakland Tribune*, decided that art was to be her field. She married Francis McComas, a Baker family friend of long-standing, who was many years her senior. She had hitched her wagon to a star and

Francis could give her some of the driving power. I think as such society-art marriages go that theirs was a success. Gene McComas achieved her goal as an artist in her own right, nationally recognized.

George Kocher, son of Jack and Lill, would have been one of the boys that 1918 summer. Because our mothers were friends, George (who in 1916 was taking work at Hopkins Marine Station) and I began to do things together with our families, then to some extent alone. George had been my chosen graduation dance partner. (I had loaned Leland and Baldwin to classmates that evening.) As far as I was concerned George could have had any amount of my dating time he desired. (In 1963 it was fascinating to hear Ray read from Carmen's college diary an equally enthusiastic response to George whom she had met and danced with the evening in 1917 that she made the entry.)

Actually I do not think George wanted any more of my time than he had. However, long years later, it was with quite a shock that I learned that the Kochers, warned by Irene's favorite remark that "though there is nothing organically wrong with Elizabeth she just is not strong," had counseled George not to get too involved, that they feared I might not be strong enough to bear his children. He married Lucile Wayland, daughter of Dr. Charles Wayland of San Jose. They had one son. Later divorced, George married again, but had no children. Quite late in life he found a talented Jewess who presented him with a son some time before the legality of his release from wife number two and his marriage to the Jewess were quite complete. Quite evidently he took no chance on his third wife not being able to bear him a child. George and I had been out of touch for long years when during my 1964 sojourn in San Jose, I phoned him. Telling him that I had thirteen grandchildren gave me a certain satisfaction. He seemed impressed—surprised, too, no doubt! Further it salved my ego to have him say, "I still have your picture—the one I took of you—I was looking at it just the other day!"

Baldwin and Gerry Rand would have been two of the boys to wait for me at the Pacific Grove Lab. By the fall of 1918 both George and Baldy would be in uniform on the Stanford campus but not Gerry Rand, who had entered the Chambers family fold as George Chambers Jr.'s close friend at Stanford and had become a family appendage. Gerry (who was killed in an auto accident in the early '20s) was a Canadian by birth but had been rejected for military service. He told me one day that he preferred the Canadian system to ours. In Canada when a man was refused for duty in the armed forces he was given a "T&R" arm band to wear so everyone knew he had been "Tried and Rejected." We were very patriotic in this war to end wars and tended to frown on all men sans uniform in 1918.

Arthur was no less patriotic than the younger men. War meant food was needed. Mr. Hoover was encouraging us to "Hooverite," i.e., eschew war-needed foods. Arthur would raise rice in Northern California. No matter that he had never raised so much as a rad-ish above ground or that his was, I believe, the very first of rice growing in the state. Up at Marysville Arthur went into the rice field endeavor so far that, this war over, though he refused to go through bankruptcy, he was $64,000 in the red. At the time of his mother's death in 1921 a large part of his inheritance was used to clear this debt.

Gerry Hand and Baldy that 1918 summer were in some way supporting the rice endeavor—at least, I am sure, getting some of that $64,000 for their support! Arthur gave them a furlough from the rice fields and they came chugging down to us at Pacific Grove in an old Model T of Arthur's. Result: more dancing! Most of the dances were at the beach pavilion at Pacific Grove. Quite refined it was, with a splendid Stanford student dance orchestra. We danced and danced! Irene must have cooked and cooked for all those lusty young men. I am sure she enjoyed them though as much as I did and was as happy doing that cooking as I was for the next generation twenty years later.

ALLEGRO
TEMPO
***

ACCEPTANCE AT STANFORD for a woman student was no mean accomplishment. The limit of 500 women was still in effect. Stanford, by 1918 a well-known and fine school, was the university choice of many college-minded girls. From these many applicants Stanford chose carefully the relatively few freshmen women that could be accepted. Miss Mira and Miss Body of the Merriman school were perhaps even happier than our 10 Monte household when I was accepted by Stanford—but no happier than Arthur!

By October 1918 Irene, Laura and I were living in a roomy two-storey duplex on the Stanford campus, sublet from Professor Percy Gray. (The Herbert Hoovers had been not too previous tenants of this same abode.) Fall term on campus meant, if possible, an increased amount of dancing and partying over that of the summer. First there was the president's reception and dance for the freshmen. Baldwin was my escort and introduced me to President Ray Lyman Wilbur as we arrived in the midstream of many arriving freshmen. There was dancing and more dancing. Finally Baldwin and I again went down the reception line to express our appreciation of the event and to say our adieus. I have never ceased to marvel at the fact that Dr. Wilbur shook hands warmly and unprompted said, "Miss Chambers, it is nice to have you here." How *could* anyone remember names that well!!

Baldwin, bless him, was always there saying, "Unless you are going with someone else I want to take you." I went to every social event there was to go to! Irene made a gracious hostess. There were suppers at the house for El Caminoans we knew—Herman Hubert (Jud) Hoss (then in law school and a friend of Ray's), Leonard (Barney) Barnard (subsequently an Oakland orthopedic surgeon), Baldwin and others. There were dances at El Camino. (Barney took me to the last one of those just a week before I was married. I had promised him a month or more before that I would go with him. Go I did!) George Kocher was on campus and a frequent caller. Chester Barker got away from his war job in San Francisco for a Sunday call or two. I missed little social life in my short college career, I can testify to that!

* * * * * *

Before long we added Mary and Ned Goddard to our campus ménage. Ned's war effort was in YMCA work. His assignment was the officers' Y at Camp Fremont, which joined the campus to the north. Some evenings we would drive Mary over to the Y and wait with her in Ned's semi-enclosed office to drive him home when he closed the building at ten-thirty. November eighth, one of our first evenings there, we noticed a first lieutenant wearing the sleeve chevrons that denoted overseas service. Some fellow officers crowded around him were avidly looking at the snapshots he was showing. Ned, too, was peering at them. Soon he brought Lt. Pilling, recently returned from France, into his office to introduce to us and to show us his late pictures of France. (They are still extant—a Roche plane shot down, the Vosges sawmill, etc.) As always Roy's vibrant magnetic personality had us all enthralled. He was so interested in the world around him, so vital. On the way home Mary said she thought he was handsome. I countered with some uncomplimentary remark about his prominent ears. My chatter was a cover-up! I had immediately been charmed by him, ears et al.!

One noon, not long after this meeting at the Y, still another ambulance load of flu victims passed our campus home. Mingled with the delirious cries of its occupants, hospital bound to win or lose their battle with Spanish influenza which was taking a greater death toll than the battlefields of France, we heard the blowing of whistles and clanging of bells. We knew then that the armistice had been signed. In the excitement of the moment I asked naively, "Does that mean that the troops will be sent home to Montana?" Showed where *my* thoughts were!

An officers' club for Camp Fremont had just been established in the old D. O. Mills home in Menlo Park. Roy was selected as the resident officer. He was assigned a full-time Japanese houseboy and allowed all the army personnel he might need. The historic stable had previously been equipped with the fine dance floor on which twice weekly danced the officers and their ladies. I would swoop up a group of my Gamma Phi sisters and off we would go, with Irene as chaperone.

Carmen Seemann, who loved to dance and danced beautifully, was always in these groups. Roy was entranced by her charm. I was thankful that Carmen was safely engaged (or nearly so, no one seemed to know which) to a Stanford law student then at Sacramento taking his bar examinations. The exams over, the young lawyer, Ray Lyon, materialized on the campus. I even met him as he looked on at a dance at the Gamma Phi house. Though he did not dance he and Carmen found other interests in common. Her Gamma Phi sisters tended to tease her about the wild flower walks she and Ray took, Carmen returning with lists of the different flowers they had found. (I saw nothing funny about that. Such rambles in the Pacific Grove woods had been a hobby of mine for years.) Freeman Burbank, who like his friend, Ray Lyon, had just finished his bar exam, saw me home from that dance at the Gamma Phi house. The next Sunday he brought the big Burbank family car from San Jose and organized a steak-fry, with me as his date. Never before in all his Stanford days had Freeman been known to date.

ROY AND ELIZABETH PILLING

My sorority sisters were agog, not only because he was dating but because, arriving at the Gamma Phi house, he shyly presented me with a single beautiful red rosebud from the Burbank's garden in San Jose. Ray Lyon was on that steak-fry picnic on the creek bank. I could not figure him out. I loved and admired Carmen so I felt sure he must be a fine young man to have won her. Ray Lyon was not easy to communicate with. He stood back, apart, almost ill at ease. (His passes at lasses were as yet an undeveloped art.)

One day Roy asked me for breakfast at the officers' club—quite swish it was, with the Japanese houseboy serving. Irene chose odd times *not* to chaperone. Breakfast in a house alone with one attractive officer and an unobtrusive houseboy was one of them. But Roy's intent was quite honorable. He had just wanted to think in terms of "Is this the woman I want to sit across the breakfast table from for the rest of my life?" Apparently it was! Neither of us, I believe, stopped to realize that this experience *could* be quite different in a palatial house with delectable breakfast unobtrusively served by an Oriental servant from breakfasts served while feeding the baby, wiping up the toddler's upset milk and getting the number one child presentable for school. It didn't really matter, for I think neither of us ever did notice the difference!

Ours was a short courtship, almost completely filled with dancing. One exception to that rule of dancing was an evening at the San Francisco Orpheum, which directly followed my Gamma Phi Beta initiation on November 17. I am vague indeed on the initiation rites though I do remember Carmen clearly-poised and beautiful in flowing white robe. She and others inducted one junior, Grace Jones (Bullie), and me. This initiation was not for the full pledge class. One quarter of satisfactory grades must precede initiation. My summer school A's paid off!

Irene, Jimmie Mann (Lt. James Buzell Mann of Honolulu) and Haynie (Lt. Hayne) completed the theater party. I still remember that Orpheum audience! The flu rampant, such gatherings were permitted only if everyone in the audience wore a flu mask, which was the usual white gauze rectangle worn in surgery by doctors and nurses now. The effect of an audience of white rectangles was bizarre to say the least! I was the one nonconformist for I wore a chic black "flu veil" which passed the entrance test. The upper half was large open veil mesh, the lower half, over nose and mouth, was heavy double crepe de chine.

*   *   *   *   *   *   *

Irene's hostility about the money spent on the Chambers-Barker wedding may have been in part due to a premonition that Madeline was getting more than I would ever get. If so, Irene was quite correct in her premise—wedding-wise. The fact remains, however, that Madeline had just the sort of wedding *she* wanted and I had just the kind of wedding *I* wanted. Only one thing marred the happiness of my wedding day for me—Laura was not present at the ceremony. Irene felt the long day would be too much of a strain for her. Laura stayed at our Stanford home on Saturday, December 14, 1918, when Irene, Baldwin, Roy and I drove to 155 Monte Cresta. On about twenty-four hours' notice Grandma Chambers had had her home modestly decorated with flowers and potted palms and was prepared to serve a simple "wedding breakfast." Roy and I were married at three in the afternoon by Charles L. Kless, the minister whose sermons I had enjoyed through the years at Plymouth Congregational Church. The necessary witness and signatures are Uncle George's and Uncle Raymond's. The wedding guest signatures read: Mrs. Elizabeth Chambers, Arthur L. Chambers, Irene L.

McColl, George R. Chambers, Madeline H. Chambers, Madeline Chambers Barker, M. E. Wright, Charlotte C. Wright, Muirson Wright, Elizabeth Wright, Genevieve C. Case, Elizabeth Case, Elwell Case, Joseph B. DeGolyer Jr., Gertrude Gee Knox, Morris B. Knox, Cora L. Hotchkiss, Mary Porte Goddard, Adelyn Porter Watrous, Mary Porter, Louise Sieferle.

After the wedding refreshments Roy and I left the little group of celebrants and went to the Hotel Oakland—THE Oakland hotel of 1918—before returning to Stanford the following afternoon. Wartime engagements, weddings and honeymoons are ever on the double-quick. Though his discharge from the army was assured, nevertheless Roy had to report at Camp Fremont on Monday morning.

BOOK

of

ROY

GEORGE CHAMBERS' RENOWNED CLERGYMAN FRIEND, Robert Collyer (1823-1912), gave him a history of England (published in the 1700s in two ponderous volumes) which has a map of Lancashire that shows Pilling Marsh and a town of Pilling. Pilling is an uncommon enough surname so that encountering an individual with that family name gives one pause. Upon being quizzed as to his antecedents invariably this new-found Pilling, though a bit vague about his ancestry, immediately declares that he is of English descent and that his forebears, he has been told, came from Lancashire. Just so is the version of Pilling family background in Roy's family.

In 1864 when Roy's branch of the Pilling family moved to Dodge County, Minnesota, Arnold Pilling, Roy's father, would have been six years of age, for he was born on February 24, 1858, in Huron, Wisconsin. The family in Dodge County was a big one because, from a previous marriage of his father's, Arnold had a half brother, William, and a half sister, Pauline, besides his full siblings, Alice, Safrona, George and the baby, Burt. The household must have been a lively one and may have engendered Arnold's quiet sense of humor and the beloved merry twinkle in his eye.

(In 1922 I met Burton and George, residents and esteemed citizens of Flandreau, South Dakota. Burt and Nellie Pilling's only child, Ethel Pilling Kipp, died childless about 1960. Ray Pilling, the lone son among George and Hattie's several children, was the only potential family member, save Roy, to carry on the Pilling name. Lola Pilling Paris, Ray's sister, a charming, capable and accomplished person, has held important state offices in various women's organizations.)

Ione Harwood, Roy's mother, born in Wisconsin on July 4, 1862, could trace her ancestry on her father's side back to William the Conqueror. After Ione's father's death her mother (whom I

ROY PILLING

knew in Pipestone, in her nineties as Da) had married Grandpa Hurlburt, Roy's boyhood idol. Grandpa had the ability to do things with his hands, a gift never bestowed on Roy's father. Grandpa Hurlburt let the boy help him hammer and saw and repair and build. Grandpa was no doubt the leavening influence that developed Roy's consummate manual skill, which found expression during his city-dwelling career years.

Ione Harwood was married to Arnold Pilling on July 2, 1881, at the tiny town of Wasioja in Dodge County, Minnesota. That same year the couple moved to Dakota Territory and homesteaded a tree claim a few miles northwest of what is now Flandreau in Moody County, South Dakota. In order to claim the land they had to plant and tend ten acres of trees. Ione taught in the rural school their first year or two on the homestead. It was on this tree claim that their first two children were born, Pearl on April 8, 1884, and Roy William on November 18, 1885.

Life must have been rugged on the little homestead and must often have tested the endurance of the young couple, yet only one incident has survived to come down through the years as a sort of family legend. In a blizzard in 1888 Arnold and Ione built up the fire of cow chips, their only fuel, and fast burning, and left Pearl and Roy snug in the warm cabin while they went together to the barn to care for the animals and do the necessary chores. But even they had not realized how disorienting a blizzard such as this one in 1888 could become. As they left the barn the wind buffeted them, blowing blinding snow to cut out their faces. Where was the *path* to the house? Where was the *house*? They groped about, finally found a fence and followed it. Would the fire last to keep the children warm enough? Frightened groping, clinging to one another,

they finally found the clothes line and followed it to the house, to the welcome fire, to their beloved babies, still snug and warm. And so down the years has come the story of Father and Mother Pilling lost in a blizzard between the barn and the house—the one cherished tale of their struggle to survive and to prosper in this new land that was often cruel and uncooperative.

In 1889 the little family moved into town and Arnold worked in a Flandreau lumberyard. Clara was born in Flandreau in 1890. Arnold was registrar of deeds in Moody County in the '90s. In 1896 the family moved to Fulda, Minnesota, where Arnold became manager of the Colman Lumber Company. Another move in 1899, when establishment of the A. Pilling Lumber Company took the family to Edgerton, Minnesota, where Beva was born in 1904.

Always Arnold and Ione Pilling were active in their community, ardent church workers and dedicated to the Masonic orders. Masonry had much more popular appeal then than now and the fact that Arnold held the high offices he did in his Masonic orders testifies to the esteem in which he was held. He was the first Master of the Edgerton Lodge, a Past Commander of both the Flandreau and Pipestone Commanderies of Knights Templar, a member of the Royal Arch Masons at Pipestone. He was a member and Past Worthy Patron of the Eastern Star and Ione was a Past Worthy Matron. The Ione Chapter of the Star at Edgerton was named in her honor.

Arnold was also affiliated with the Workman and Modern Woodmen in Edgerton. He served on the Edgerton school board and city council as well as on the Pipestone City Council in later years.

With all these memberships and all this community service Arnold had a host of friends who appreciated his civic participation. Probably, in his quiet way, he harbored further political aspirations. At all events he yielded to the entreaties of his friends and ran for a seat in the Minnesota state legislature. He was an ardent civic worker but not a born hand-shaking politician. He felt his record and his demonstrated desire for betterment of the area should be sufficient vote getters. His friends clustered round and told him how fine it was that he was going to represent them in state government. In fact everyone he talked to was voting for him and told him of the many others who were so grateful he was to be their representative.

But when election day ended it was apparent that his opponent had done a great deal of hand-shaking at each remote farm as well as on the streets of the towns. Arnold, to his utter bewilderment, was defeated. Such an outcome had not even occurred to him. His friends had been so convincing! In afteryears Roy never missed an opportunity to twit him about his political aspirations. Father's eyes would get the merry twinkle.

*   *   *   *   *   *

Roy had grown up with love and a jovial respect for his father but with a deeper love for his mother. It had been she who would be most likely to take him fishing on a stream. He felt closer to her and had appreciated her more dynamic character.

ROY PILLING

Arnold and Ione Pilling were devout Methodists. However Roy felt it was the overabundance of religion in his growing years—the family custom of daily Bible reading and kneeling for prayers at home—that had turned him from churchgoing later in life. He had "had it" in boyhood.

As Roy was budding into manhood in Edgerton, on leaving church one Sunday he walked down the block talking with one Kate Patterson, another member of the dispersed congregation. When he arrived home Father was waiting for his son. He explained that Kate was considered to be "fast" and that Roy was never, never to be seen speaking to her again. Roy in later years, looking back from the vantage point of years as a single man in the Northwest where he had made the passing acquaintance of various girls who had rightly earned the term fast, questioned the validity of its application to Edgerton's Kate. Probably, at times, picking her way between spring mud puddles as she crossed Main Street, Kate may have lifted her skirt an inch or two higher than necessary to display a shapely ankle. She may even have boldly rolled her eyes at a dapper traveling salesman in the drugstore as she purchased rice powder to prettify her face. Rice powder would have been "daring" but not downright "fast," as would have been a touch of peroxide to her hair, shadow to her eyes, rouge to her cheeks or lipstick to her mouth.

(Cosmetologists were unknown at the turn of the century and would have starved "aborning" in that era. Even in 1917 when I started to use lipstick I was the only girl in my small high school to use one and I am sure was considered "daring" by my schoolmates. That lipstick was no metal-cased bright-colored attraction but a Roger and Gallet Pomade of scarcely discernible pink, in a cardboard container covered with shiny pale pink paper bearing the

Roger and Gallet label in bold black type. It was little more than a chapstick!)

Kate Patterson eventually married the president of the Edgerton Bank, Frank Douty, but Time had intervened and Death had taken Frank's first wife. It was from this same Frank, a Pilling family friend, that their youngest child, Beva, had negotiated a loan. She had heard about bank loans for the A. Pilling Lumber Company. At about the age of five, finding herself in town one very hot day, she stopped in to ask Frank for a bank loan of a nickel to buy an ice cream cone. Frank felt it a worthy investment so Beva got her cone that hot afternoon plus endless years of family ribbing thereafter about her "bank loan."

HOMESTEADING
***

ROY FELT THE RESTRAINT OF HOME and was no doubt glad to be off to Hamlin, a Methodist University in St. Paul, where he became a member of the Beta Kappa fraternity (BOEE). However by 1907 the financial structure of the United States was in a precarious condition—a PANIC, in fact. (Even I remember talk of it in San Francisco, that fast rebuilding, busily spending city.) Roy had only a semester until graduation but he could not endure staying in the University considering the financial sacrifice it meant for his family. (Subsequently at the University of California, where he attended seminars on public administration under Professor Samuel C. May, Roy was awarded an Alpha Pi Zeta key, making him a member of that national political science honor fraternity.)

From Hamlin Roy went to the West Coast to learn the production end of the lumber industry. His sister, Pearl, had married Harry Francis, pharmacist son of old Dr. Francis, who had been the Edgerton M.D. By 1907 Harry and Pearl had a drugstore in Chehalis, Washington. Roy went to live with them and work in the local lumber mills, then later in nearby logging operations. Loggers worked and worked hard. They had but two annual holidays—July fourth and January first. The loggers made the most of those two days with wine, women—and song, too!

Roy may have gone from Washington directly to Montana or he may have worked for the Rogers Lumber Company interests in Minnesota first. The Rogers' head office was in Minneapolis. (As a bride in Great Falls I met Arthur Rogers, the senior brother of the company, who looked quite like an immaculate President Cleveland, and his like sartorially-perfect bachelor brother, George. A third brother, John, with his second wife, Cora, used to come to Carmel with Ruth and Herbert Templeton. John's two sons were charming young men—about Laurie's age.)

216

The Rogers' lumber interests spread to Montana, which was a Western homesteading frontier, a virgin land yielding bumper wheat crops from dry land farming. Here the Rogers' retail lumberyards were in partnership with Herbert Templeton. Rogers-Templeton yards pretty well covered the retail lumber trade in Montana. Roy, with his eye to homesteading, by about 1911 was manager of the Rogers-Templeton Lumber Company yard at Chester, Montana, on what was referred to as the High Line. Havre, Cutbank and other towns that pushed up near Glacier Park and the Canadian border were on the High Line. The Rogers-Templeton was not the only retail yard in Chester. St. Anthony and Dakota, a rival chain outfit, had its lumberyard just across Main Street in Chester. The manager was Alf Greenelsh—A. J. Greenelsh, whom his second wife, Margaret, my dear San Luis Obispo friend, calls Jimmie. I do, too, now!

Roy staked out his homestead claim, got his cabin built and began living the life of a single man in the Wild West, which included more straight whiskey than communion wine and Bible reading. Probably it was well that Clara, five years Roy's junior, the little sister who had always trailed after him in all his boyhood chores and play, decided that, now she had her teaching credential, she would go to Montana to teach and homestead next to Roy. Their carefree Montana years together were, in a way, the happiest years of their lives, for both Roy and Clara.

Even a decade later I saw Montana peppered with homestead shacks—crude dwellings of shed-like architecture. The homesteader, having filed on an available piece of government land through the local land agent, tossed up a homestead shack in which he had only to live for a certain prescribed period in order to "prove up" land and secure title. He then owned patented land which could be sold like any piece of privately owned real estate. Few homesteaded with the true intent of the Homestead Act. Homestead shacks, in their multiple numbers, used a great deal of lumber for their construction. Lumberyards in little towns like Chester did a big business—literally a land office business.

*   *   *   *   *   *   *

Their homesteads proved up, Clara and Roy stayed on in Montana but went their separate ways. Clara left Chester to teach home economics at Polson, west of the Rockies, on beautiful Flathead Lake. The coach and manual training teacher at Polson was an ex-army sergeant by the name of George Snyder. So Polson offered Clara more gay Montana years until suddenly World War I became an actuality. Quickly carefree gaiety gave way to more serious thoughts. Before George left for the service he and Clara were married. Overseas George not only did war service but quite a long stint with the Army of Occupation in Germany.

In 1919 the Arnold Pillings moved to Pipestone, Minnesota. George Snyder, finally honorably discharged from the service, became Arnold's partner in the International Harvester agency in Pipestone. (It-is-a-small-world item: some ten or fifteen years earlier that same agency was operated by Henry Seemann, Carmen Seemann Lyon's father.)

Arnold Pilling Snyder was born to Clara and George in the fall of 1920. Clara's labor and delivery were very difficult. Early in 1923 their "Jackie" died at birth and nearly cost Clara's life. Another baby of their own was out of the question but they wanted more than one child. In a year or so George and Clara were off to Omaha, Nebraska with their closest friends, Jack and Mabel Lambert. Each couple, having completed the necessary preliminary arrangements, was to select and adopt a baby from the orphanage at Omaha. The Snyders were very particular about heritage. They chose a baby of good German American stock. Both parents, it so happened, were known to orphanage personnel. The Snyders wanted to be very sure that the child would be sturdy and healthy.

The Lamberts picked the most beautiful baby boy in the orphanage and knew only that he had been brought there one day by his mother, a clean, neat but quite poorly dressed woman in her thirties who had desperately begged that they care for her eight-week-old baby while she rushed to her dying mother in Chicago. Thrusting the warmly wrapped infant into the matron's arms she had dashed back to the waiting taxi, saying she would return within the week. She did not return at all. When the orphanage started to check, not only could they find no one by the name she had given but they could find no such address, no such street even in all of Omaha. Immediately suspicion had wracked the orphanage staff for when his "mother's" taxi had driven off and the nurse had opened the inexpensive wrapping blanket the baby she saw was barely a day old and was dressed in the most exquisite of be-laced fine linen baby clothes. The educated guess the Lamberts got with their Jackie was that the young daughter of some wealthy and important Eastern family had become pregnant out of wedlock and been sent West with a trusted nurse who probably acted as midwife.

Returning to Pipestone together on the train the two couples unwrapped their blanket bundles to see just what they had! Jackie Lambert proved robust from babyhood. Mary Ruth Snyder's poor health is family legend! The Lamberts returned alone to the Omaha orphanage in a couple of years and came home with Billie—destined to become Arnold Pilling Snyder's first wife and mother of his two children, Barbara and George.

During his World War I service George Snyder had developed an ear infection which, neglected as he carried on his wartime duties, could never after be completely cured and subsequently spread to his brain to cause his untimely death. Mary Ruth was no more than a toddler when Clara was widowed.

Arnold Pilling, Roy's father, died in Pipestone on November 1, 1931. Roy, summoned from Berkeley by his serious illness, did not arrive till after his father's death. (One did not fly in 1931.) Almost harder on Roy than the loss of his father, who had been ailing for some time, was the Midwestern small town way of death. Much of the time before the funeral Mother Pilling sat desolate beside the open casket in the living room at home constantly patting Father's cold hand. Roy considered the viewing of the deceased at a funeral one of the less dignified forms of barbarity extant. Within him paged the conflict between respect for his parents' mores and those of the broader more modern social structure of which he had become so integral a part.

AFTER ROY'S HOMESTEAD IN MONTANA was proved up he acquired adjoining property—all to be leased on crop shares to a neighbor, Roy Walden, and his brother-in-law, Glenn Shepherd. Roy went to Great Falls, where the Rogers-Templeton head office was located, to become a field superintendent with a string of lumberyards to visit and supervise. Now, the boys Roy palled with were the other field men, Earle Shilton, Bob Graham, Jesse Odette, when they were in Great Falls for head office conferences. To Roy, like most of the others, home was a room in the Falls. For a time Roy roomed with Phil Pratt, who worked for another large lumber company. Harry Call, of Great Falls' Goodrich-Call Lumber Company, was another friend.

Earl Shilton's January 1937 letter gives the feeling of those Montana days.

> I hope Elizabeth that your children will know something of their Dad as he was in Montana. All men are fundamentally savage in a certain sense; they have a certain measure of values that seem to the dilettante rather crude and coarse but between men there is recognition of those elemental traits that cannot be effaced; And no one could know Roy without knowing something of the early environment at Chester and Havre and Fort Peek—then pioneer country with rough men and rough weather and rough times to live in. I have bunked with Roy many times along the "High Line" and by the hour he has told me of his boyish reactions to the strange situations that he encountered in those lonely days. That is a part of the saga—a part that his children are entitled to know about and while I expect that both you and Miriam would have wished that your husbands could

"H.A." AND MRS. TEMPLETON

***

221

have forsworn some of the history, it is in the book, and was and is a part of the men you both married. My adventures were tame enough compared to Roy's and perhaps for that reason, I rather clung to him in admiration and respect.

Roy was full of color and vitality and meat and was always a positive soul. But, with that certain almost forbidding exterior, he had a softness and poetry about him that very few knew.

Herbert A. Templeton (whom Roy called "H.A.") and his wife, Ruth Roberts Templeton, became Roy's personal friends. By February 29, 1916, the Templetons had four children, Jane arriving on that leap year date. Their eldest, Bess, and Bob had some only a year apart. Hall, who by 1916 must have been four or five, had followed Bob in a year and a half. By 1916 though, the days of strain, with so many little people to care for, were passed for Ruth Templeton. She and Herbert lived in a gracious roomy cube of a house in Great Falls. They had a driver for their big Winton car AND they had Celia.

(Dear Black Celia, born a slave, was horrified when I, not quite nineteen, wanted to help polish silver. "Why, Ah won't even let Mrs. Templeton hurt her hands with polishin' silver!" Around the Templeton household I began to absorb some precepts of housekeeping. Now that I was married, I noticed the mechanics of housekeeping for the very first time. For eighteen years I must have been in a trance in that department! I still do certain tasks the way I do them because Mrs. Templeton or Celia did them so.)

About 1916 Roy began to be plagued by stomach trouble, then came the diagnosis of ulcers. The Templeton ménage took him under its protective wing and, when he was in town, catered to his needed diet. In partial payment for the Templeton's kind hospitality Roy took a beating from their clambering children, keen for a romp. (About 1931 Bob Templeton, on a business trip visited us in Berkeley. As I was preparing dinner I glimpsed Arnold and Beva working Bob over as he sat in an easy chair in the living room. Roy walked through the kitchen. I asked him to rescue Bob. His response was, "Leave 'em alone. What I've taken from those Templeton kids as *they* grew up! Bob has this coming!")

Another factor of repayment for hospitality was Roy's own personality. He drew people to him so that he could count dedicated friends by the score wherever he lived. I often wonder if even Charles Russell, so noted for his storytelling, could spin any more interesting tales than Roy of incidents of the West, of the out-of-doors, of fishing, of hunting. Roy always held a group spellbound yet he did not seem to monopolize the conversation; it was just that people so enjoyed hearing him talk. His speech was peppered with delightful colloquialisms. These frequently used phrases of Roy's which were a part of him and of him alone, have become a lost language. Only two or three can I so much as recall—"not sense enough to pound sand in a rat-hole"; "roped and hog-tied," which equated "in the bag"; "crazier than a wooden watch."

Herbert and Ruth (or as Roy would have said, "H.A. and Mrs. Templeton," for to his dying day he continued to call Ruth Mrs. Templeton) took church work quite seriously. Herbert taught a large Sunday School class of young-marrieds. He was a rather quiet, quite devout type. Roy introduced into the Templeton household the bit of fun and exuberance that Ruth specially craved. They had a like zest for living!

By early 1917 Herbert Templeton realized that Roy needed to get away from the tension and strain of business life. In March the

Rogers-Templeton Company sent him on a month's vacation, paying his passage to the Hawaiian Islands.

Roy always claimed it was from Mr. Templeton that he learned all the practices of good business administration. Roy would say, "Have your administration properly delegated and the function is merely to sit on the lid." ("Sit on the lid" was one of those phrases of Roy's that seemed especially his.) "Your organization," he used to say, "will run smoothly even in your absence if you are a good administrator." Roy was a *masterly* administrator; this was demonstrated in the Depression when, even in the chaos of the Relief Administration, he brought some semblance of sanity to the operation as Director of Relief in Los Angeles County. His worth MUST have been recognized for he may have been the only stubbornly registered Republican to have held such a high office in the nation in that Democratic Relief Administration.

BY THE SUMMER OF 1917 war was sobering even the exuberant. Earle Shilton's letter of January 1937 tells of Roy's enlistment.

All of us loved Roy because he was so much a man's man. I well recall an incident that happened in our bungalow in Great Falls about July 1917. Roy had come up to sample the cooking of the bride and during the evening on the front porch we got to talking about the war. Our talk was of course as to our relationship to the struggle, and became quite pointed, because Miriam was inveighing against the whole idea. Suddenly, Roy planked his feet down on the porch and said, 'Well, we aren't deciding anything sitting

LT. ROY PILLING

here chewing-the-fat, I'm going down an' enlist.' And that is what he did and next morning he was in the army.

Roy was accepted for the second Officers' Training Camp at the Presidio in San Francisco. He was there in Eighth Company of the Sixteenth Provisional Training Regiment from August 25 to October 5, 1917, on which date he was honorably discharged from the Camp in compliance with an order from the Adjutant General at Washington, D.C. Roy W. Pilling's commission as "first lieutenant in the Engineer Section Officers' Reserve Corps of the Army of the United States" was dated "October 2, 1917, the year of our Lord and in the 147th year of the Independence of the United States—the commission to continue in force during the pleasure of the President of the United States for the time being and for a period of five years from date."

On October 4, 1917, a telegram signed by "Black, Chief of Engineers" ordered Roy to report to Camp American University, Washington, D.C., "immediately period do not delay needed promptly period clothing and equipage will be arranged here in some manner." Three captains, four other first lieutenants beside Roy and five second lieutenants (shavetails, Roy would have called them!) were sent to Camp American University by this order of the Adjutant General's to join the Twentieth Engineers. Roy was assigned to the Second Battalion Company D under Captain Perry. The Twentieth was a "lumberman's regiment' and said to be the largest regiment in the whole United States Army—in fact the largest regiment in the world in 1918.

Roy had feared that his experience in the woods and lumber mills might stymie him in the United States, as indeed it did some of his conferees, in order to expedite production on the home front.

This war—World War I—was a patriotic, flag-waving, do-your-bit-for-your-country kind of war with ticker tape parades of glowing heroes to be marching off overseas to fight in the trenches. By late November of 1917 Roy, with the Second Battalion of the Twentieth, was in France.

I believe Roy served first in the St. Mihiel Sector where the action was plenty close. Though he was under fire, I think Roy never succeeded in getting into trench warfare. He was directing the operation of a sawmill. Like many he was restless to get into the real fighting but here was a job that needed doing and that he knew how to do. By April eighteenth Roy was in the Vosges Sector at Epinal. In July he was sent from Epinal to Vagney, also in the Vosges, to direct the construction of a lumber mill.

"Sunny France" had turned out to be a country of cold drizzly rain but Roy had found good companionship with fellow officers. Frank Prince of Shevlin-Hixon Lumber Company at Bend, Oregon had been a first lieutenant, likewise ordered by the Adjutant General to Camp American University. In France, he and Roy were special buddies. In January 1937 Frank wrote, "Roy was my best friend during the most trying of the army days and I think it was our combined sense of humor that put us both over. Roy was a fine officer, respected and liked by his men. You have much to be proud of in his war record."

France in 1918 was not solely sawmills and war. Roy met a French girl or two. He met sufficient girls, at any rate, to discover that dentistry in France in 1918 was in the dark ages. Even the young girls had miserably poor teeth. (A few feminine letters followed Roy to the U.S.A. I kept up a lingually uncertain correspondence with one gal for a while, though as I recall she wrote only a time or two after learning Roy was married.) Frank Prince and Roy "did"

Paris together on leave. (Whenever they met in later years, the memory of that leave was excuse enough to finish off some bottles of stronger content than the famed wines of sunny France.)

By mid-August of 1918 Roy's discontent at not being in the thick of fighting in this war to end all wars gained him an assignment supposedly to one of the new sapper regiments. By the end of September the beautifully tailored uniforms he had had custom-made in France were packed in his footlocker and he was awaiting transportation to the United States. Impatiently he waited ten full days at Brest, finally arriving at Hoboken, New Jersey, on October 10, 1918. (Roy's captaincy had been promised to him on arrival in the U.S. Bogged down in red tape it never did come through, however army communications indicate the intent.) He was assigned to the Fourth Engineer Training Regiment at Camp Humphries, Virginia, but was given a fortnight's leave before having to report there for duty. He visited his family in Edgerton and the girl there to whom he had been "almost engaged" before going overseas. By now Edgerton to Roy was not home, but the place where his parents lived. He had broadened from the small Midwestern town way of life. In 1918 he was calling Montana home.

By October 28, 1918, Roy was en route to Camp Fremont at Menlo Park, California, to await shipment to Siberia where action seemed imminent. William McCaskey Chapman, a West Point graduate, was actually sent there for service shortly before the November eleventh armistice.

In France on New Year's Day in 1918 Roy had wagered Captain Perry ten dollars that Company D, Second Battalion of the Twentieth Engineers would not be in or even on their way to the United States by December 31, 1918. I am not sure about Company

D but by that date Roy not only was in the United States but had his honorable discharge from the army and a WIFE to boot!

THE GREAT FALLS OF THE MISSOURI

***

OUR IMMEDIATE POST-NUPTIAL PACIFIC GROVE VISIT, complete with Irene and Laura, is memory-marked only by a walk Roy and I took alone to the dunes where we discovered the sheltering low branches of a wind-flattened pine that made a nest-rest retreat just big enough for two. After Pacific Grove we returned to the Bay Region, where the big Chambers family Christmas gathering, and allied partying and theater-ing filled the days and most the nights till New Year's. We saw the old year out at a huge dinner dance at the Claremont Country Club. This was a very special celebration, for with the old year we ushered out John Barleycorn and with the New Year, coldly greeted the prospect of Prohibition. The table seemed to stretch out endlessly—family members, the Dinsmores, many other friends. By this time Toodles Dinsmore had become Toots Chapman—Mrs. William McCaskey Chapman—and Bill had left for Siberia. Her escort that New Year's Eve was Stanford football star, Bobbie Pelouse, who had been a prime contender for her hand but had lost to Bill a few months before. Bobbie was a dear! He couldn't have been nicer to me. We certainly had a chance to get well acquainted that night! Roy was busy partying with peppy, pretty, pert Toodles!!

About noon on New Year's Day a large contingent of the Chambers clan saw the "newlyweds" off at the Berkeley station as we entrained for Montana. I had the rudiments of a head cold to start my New Year and trip. Grandma Chambers thoughtfully appeared at the station with a bundle for me—many clean soft old linen rags torn in squares. They were a boon! (Kleenex was a generation in the future.) That trip is a misty Pullman idyll in my mind, accentuated clearly by the breathtaking beauty of the Kootenai River which the railroad paralleled for some distance.

Arrived at Great Falls, Roy registered at the Rainbow Hotel. He was proud of the Rainbow and eager to show it to me. The Rainbow was one of the West's finest hotels of its size, perhaps Montana's finest, surely Great Falls' finest. Roy was a perfectionist and having the best was important to him, whether it be hotel service or the quality of the possessions he purchased.

Herbert Templeton had returned to Great Falls in July of 1918 after months as a YMCA executive in war torn France. (At a French convent he had purchased the beautiful drawnwork linen tablecloth and napkins that became the Templeton's wedding gift to us.) Our stay at the Rainbow was short-lived for Herbert and Ruth Templeton gathered us to their hearts for a trip to their delightful two-storey log country house in Neihart. They wanted to show me snow on tree-clad mountains and to give me a ride in a one-horse open sleigh (a wagon equipped with sled runners drawn by their accommodating old horse, looked after by their caretaker at Neihart). Then back to Great Falls we went to stay with the Templetons until our permanent move to Choteau.

Only once did I visit the great falls of the Missouri River from which the Montana city beside them takes its name. That one trip to the falls, made during this stay with the Templetons, was however a memorable one. The first day Roy went to H.A.'s office for business discussions, he stopped aghast, mid-sentence. His eye had come to rest on Herbert's new paperweight brought back as a souvenir from France. Roy had immediately recognized it as a live bomb. Herbert paled perceptibly. Roy was already pale! THE question was how to safely dispose of the "paperweight." That afternoon Ruth, Herbert, Roy and I in the Winton with the grenade (which had come over from France, bounced and jolted about in H.A.'s footlocker) tenderly cushioned as we drove very slowly, very carefully to the edge of the great Missouri where it deepens below the falls. There Herbert gently eased his "souvenir" to a watery grave.

BY 1919 ROY, Earle Shilton and other Rogers-Templeton supervisors were back from war service to resume the jobs that *really* had been held for them. But there were administrative changes. "The boys" were given strings of lumberyards in which they were to be part owners with Rogers-Templeton. Roy chose Choteau as Pilling Lumber Company headquarters with Bynum, Pendroy, Agawam and Depuyer for his outlying yards.

Choteau! Even today my first impression of it stands starkly, thrillingly clear. We had taken the Great Northern from Great Falls. As two branch lines went to Choteau the town had *two* daily trains, the Chicago, Milwaukee and St. Paul arriving in its orange and yellow grandeur about noon, the more sedately toned charcoal-gray Great Northern in late afternoon. We had come over the snow-covered plain from Great Falls without incident. Subsequently I rode that line when incidents did occur. Loose range animals necessitated that the engineer keep a sharp lookout to avoid using his cowcatcher for *just that*!

One day a more unique happening, when I was returning to Choteau from the Falls, resulted from tumbleweeds. In 1919 these plants were, I think, unknown in California. To Montana they were fairly new but very prevalent on its vast uncultivated range lands. They were referred to by the name that accurately places the blame for their introduction into the United States. Russian thistles they were usually called in Montana! On the range lands of windy northern Montana the great globes of dry, uprooted tumbleweeds seemed always to be performing bizarre ballets across the landscape. This particular day a railroad out south of Fairfield was so clogged by packed wind-driven dry tumbleweeds that the train could not proceed. We had to wait till the weeds could be burned out before continuing on our way.

CHOTEAU

* * *

ELIZABETH CHAMBERS,
CHOTEAU, MT | *1919*

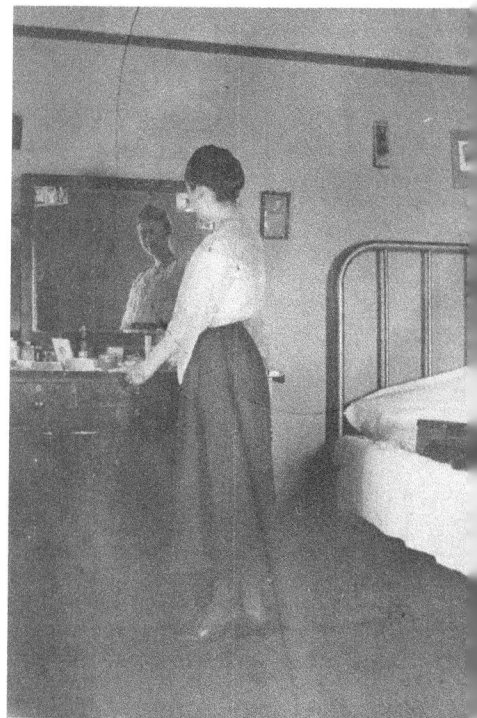

But that day in mid-January 1919 when I first rode the Great Northern to Choteau, the buttes, pushing dramatically up from the level of the plain were of themselves episodic to me. As we approached Choteau from the south, Rattlesnake Butte, massive, table-topped, then Priest Butte, smaller, were delicately sculptured in outline; they hit me with an emotional impact never to be lost whenever I looked upon them.

Then, in that northern latitude (so northern that the aurora borealis is a commonplace), in the early dusk of that late January afternoon, the train slid to a stop at the little, yellow-painted Choteau station. Even before we hurried to detrain I eagerly looked out the train window. I saw—even as I now can see before my closed eyes—across the alley from the station, two small weather-gray log buildings with SOD ROOFS. The sign above the door of one building still read Pioneer Saloon, though obviously both buildings were degraded by 1919 to warehouse use. Saloon or warehouse, this was the WEST! Though my youth, and the daze of newly-wed-dedness caused me to miss some important nuances, I intuitively responded to the West with the thrilled feeling of having been admitted, *as a spectator*, to a rare sort of closed society.

In truth the "society" was phasing out. Its very working tools had nearly gained the status of artifacts. I realize that now, I did not *then*. Roy was aware of it and cherished every vestige of the West that he found in Choteau life. There was much of it to be found! Cowboys from the ranches walked Choteau's streets en route to their favorite saloons. Shepherds came to town for perhaps their only week of human contact in the year. The whole flavor was the storybook West. I loved *observing* all this. I never sensed that living in it permanently would be a privilege. It might have, had I been properly oriented to it. I am not sure even now. At all events, by the time we left Choteau the business conditions were so unfavorable due to the many successive crop failures that Roy was as eager to leave as I. Eager to leave, that is, for better business opportunities. He never, never wanted to leave in the sense of getting away from Montana. Roy knew the precious values of the Old West and sensed their transitory quality in the early '20s. Already the homesteaders were fencing the open range. Already stockmen were enraged. The end was in sight. The West was a ghost, heading for the immortality of Hollywood and eventually of TV—even of ballet!

The post–World War I period in which I assessed Montana as a home state was not her best era. Beside the successive dry summers that brought crop failures, the specially severe winters took a murderous toll of range stock. All Montana was in a depression—not only economic but emotional.

By the time he was discharged from the army Roy should have been somewhat prepared for the Montana he was returning to. However his memories of past years, with one bumper wheat crop following another, obscured to a degree, his vision of the reality about which he had been forewarned. Guy Bulmer, assistant Rogers-Templeton manager, had written him on September 23, 1918, of the poor crop conditions that prevailed throughout northern Montana, adding, "Secretary of Agriculture Houston was out here about two weeks ago and looked over the situation and any farmers who need assistance can get help from the Federal Government next year." (Government aid to the farmers started THAT early??)

(Guy Bulmer, in his early 40s, lived in Great Falls with his rather delicate wife and small adopted daughter. In 1920 his death, as the result of a ruptured appendix in those pre-antibiotic days, was a blow to all the Rogers-Templeton staff. On the chance he might be of service to Mrs. Bulmer, or indirectly to Guy, Roy stood stalwart guard by Guy's door in the hospital corridor round the clock till the end came. But within himself, Guy's last difficult days tore Roy asunder with the unanswerable question of why so fine a man, so needed by his family, had to die.)

CHOTEAU WAS QUEEN of northern Montana's dry, bleak, treeless small towns. Choteau had cottonwoods along Spring Creek, which wandered through town east of the railroad tracks. Planted trees prospered in irregular patterns along the streets. The Teton River flowed west of Choteau through the plain which stretched toward the jagged blue cardboard silhouette of the Rockies, in which her mountains heightened to form one side of the box canyon that spawned the river.

Beside the railroad tracks rose the great-shouldered towers of the grain elevators. (Such elevators marked from afar every Montana town of the region.) Teton County's courthouse, of neat sandstone blocks from the womb of Rattlesnake Butte, stood at the south end of Main Street. At the far northern end of Main, on its east side was Choteau's proudest hostelry of 1919—the two-storey, frame-built Glenloyd Hotel. With no available rentals, a second-floor rear corner room became our first home. The lares and penates were improvised to meet our needs but the most essential need had already been met by running water in a small stationary wash basin to the right of the door. The room, though not small, certainly was not particularly large. Looking back I marvel at how much it held. Though one corner had to be sacrificed for the makeshift clothes closet (formed by a curtain) there were the double bed, dresser, three chairs, one small table, my big trunk, Roy's smaller footlocker, dining table, a Hoover cabinet (a hold-all movable kitchen fixture, popular at the time. A two-burner kerosene stove and a two-burner portable oven. When the bride's biscuits were not baking in the oven, that oven, on the flat roof of the first storey outside the back window, became our cat-proof refrigerator or deep-freeze—depending on the degree of cold. A minimum of three scrawny, prowling cats tested it each twenty-four hours. To serve the guests of its several second-floor hotel rooms, the Glenloyd offered just one bathroom—just one toilet, just one bathtub, that is. A hike down the long narrow dark hall to this necessary room often found it occupied. When, finally, one of us did gain access, armed with disinfectant for the communal bathroom fixtures, there inevitably ensued, beside the sterilizing process, a free-for-all battle in our never-ending war to gain supremacy over the many large healthy cockroaches that exercised their right of seniority to the area.

The view from our rear window, over the oven-cooler, the roof and the hotel's rubbish heap "out back," reached beyond the plain to the bench lands east of town and was gorgeous with its snowcover, reflecting the myriad moods of storm and sunlight. Montana winters played strange tricks. Unlike Iowa, Minnesota and such humid, cold, snow-all-winter states, though it claimed the lowest temperatures ever officially recorded within the continental United States up to 1919, Montana had its Chinooks. These gentle warm winds from the west, several times each winter, would melt away the snow. Twice I saw a strange phenomenon connected to the Chinook; the very force of the warm wind rolled loose snow into baseball size snowballs of its own making. Their trails showed a yard or two behind them as slight depressions in the level snow, as they rolled companionably across the plain. From time to time, very cold days brought sun dogs, pale pseudo suns which shone, one each side of the real sun. From that same rear window, we experienced zigzagging lightning, followed immediately by unimaginable booms of thunder that hammered at eardrums, then reverberated into the distance. All Montana's harsh strength of elements I found exciting, stimulating, thrilling. I did not do so well with its social structure. I could well have been less baffled, more understanding.

Our side window looked onto the neat backyard of the Weaver cottage, with its small outbuilding at the extreme rear of the lot. On several occasions I had seen a sad, wrinkled face staring from the little pane of glass in the door of the shed-like building. We soon learned the story, learned it because Choteau was a small town and everyone knew everything about everyone else. Having been raised in a city atmosphere devoid of gossip, this "knowing all" on the part of the townspeople struck me as an invasion of privacy. With time and depth analysis I came to realize that, on the whole, this was not scandal mongering, was not vicious, but was a living history or a kind of interested reporting of what went on in a community that otherwise afforded little entertainment for the womenfolk. Church work, an uncertain women's club, about completed the list of womens' away-from-housework activities. For the men there were vital recreations—fishing, hunting AND the Choteau Club. The Choteau Club was a basement room beneath the Citizens State Bank to which nightly, immediately after supper, every able-bodied male who rated in the community, repaired, frequently armed with a pint of Prohibition's best rotgut with which to enjoy the conviviality of the Old West. This Choteau Club, status symbol that it was to Choteau-ites, nearly proved to be my undoing. I simply could not understand this angle of local mores.

Now, back to Grandma Weaver's wizened old face blankly staring from the shed "out back." In 1919, most assuredly in Montana in 1919, one took care of one's own problems. Grandma Weaver was senile and tended to wander off. Therefore she was locked in the shed—year in, year out. The townspeople felt her son's wife, a sociable pleasant woman active in the Woman's Club and the work of her church, had quite a burden with Grandma. I would watch her take in a plate of food to Grandma each day and take out a slop jar. To that daily five-minute chore Mrs. Weaver Jr., who was noted for her neat housekeeping, added the weekly quarter hour it took her to sweep out and tidy up Grandma's quarters. In winter Mr. Weaver, Grandma's own son, daily carried in an armful or two of wood, deposited his burden and immediately came out relocking the door behind him. The thin wavering smoke of Grandma's fire climbed to the freedom of Montana's limitless blue skies. Grandma, trapped in her small world below, continued to gaze wistfully through the small pane of glass.

* * * * * * *

One of our first dinners in a private home in Choteau was at the banker's. Jim Ekhart was president-manager of the Citizens State Bank which was financed by several wealthy stockmen. The Ekhart home was a modest cottage but immaculate, indeed it was; housekeeping rivalry kept Choteau homes tidy and shining. In the long winters the womenfolk did a quantity of incredibly fine handwork. At Eckhart's I glimpsed through the archway a superb, embroidered linen tablecloth with filet crochet insets; matching napkins, fine china, shining crystal, gleaming silver. What a gracious atmosphere for our debut in Choteau home dining! Shortly, Jim motioned Roy to join him at the sideboard. He poured them each a heavy shot of straight bourbon from the cut glass decanter. They gulped their before-dinner drink. I was shocked! What lack of graciousness! The women had been utterly excluded! In truth I should have been prepared. Mrs. Ekhart, like most Choteau women, wore a tiny bowknot of quarter-inch white satin, pinned close over her heart— the badge of membership in the Women's Christian Temperance Union.

We saw still another interesting sight from our rear window when an accounting firm from Helena did an audit for the Citizens State Bank. The tall, well-endowed blonde and her two helpers roomed on our floor of the Glenloyd for the week or so the job took. It so happened Mrs. Ekhart was out of town during this period. Our window overlooked a makeshift outside stairway from second floor to ground, a sort of fire escape, never ordinarily used. During that week of the accounting, from our rear window, Jim Ekhart could be seen using this odd route of entrance and exit at the most unusual hours! Choteau's living history could be seen from our back window, too!

These were dancing years in the West. Everyone in Choteau went to the public dances. Each weekend there would be some dance. Occasionally one would be held at the high school but most frequently the dancing was in the second-storey Hotchkiss Hall on Main Street. A sizable cloakroom opening off this dance hall had benches along one wall. Half a dozen babies, and small children often slept along the length of these benches as young parents from outlying ranches tripped the light fantastic. Always the music was live. Mrs. Cohoe, a homely, pleasant little woman, would be at the piano. Not infrequently the drummer was Wallace Coffey, brother of attorney George Coffey. While we were still in residence, the Glenloyd pushed the tables out of prominence in the too-large dining room and a dance was held there, as dances were from time to time. At this dance appeared the unmarried son of a north county lumberman (whose name incidentally was not Smith). The previous week I had gone along on a business trip Roy made to confer with this lumber merchant. We had been introduced to the son. At this dance Sonny had a questionable blonde in tow. Roy whispered a bit of living history. They had registered at the hotel desk as Mr. and Mrs. Smith. About that time Sonny asked me to dance. Because of the business contact I did not feel I could refuse but dancing with him I felt defiled. No doubt several boys I had enjoyed dancing with at Stanford and elsewhere had at some time or other hopped into beds with willing blondes or brunettes or redheads but I had not known about it. A city shields those doings. Choteau blatantly showed life in the raw.

Alec Burrell, who was about thirty-five years old, managed the Glenloyd with the able assistance of his much more energetic wife—a redhead, full of pep and fire. Where Alec met her I would not know. One never asked such a question in that harsh Western land that provided few women. Men were glad to find a wife no matter what her former occupation. Alec's parents had "built what was then a palace yon side of the Teton" to quote A. B. Guthrie (Bud), who during my time in Choteau lived with his parents, younger brother, Charles (Chuck), and little sister, Jane, in that very house. By 1919 only the Burrell children, Alec and his siblings, survived.

Grace, the oldest, was the wife of Tom Givens, a wiry energetic little man, who was the owner of one of Teton County's big sheep ranches. Tom spent more time at the ranch than Grace, who enjoyed the social contacts of town. My recollection of the Givens ranch is of endless, low, shed-like buildings, beaten to a wonderful weathered gray by Montana's hot summer sun, rain, snow and the driving sandblasting force of the WIND. No doubt these were lambing sheds to combat Montana's WEATHER. Now it irks me that in those days I failed to voice intelligent, searching questions. Roy could have answered them all, but I posed few questions. To me *everything* was new and different. All I seemed able to do was absorb surface facts. "So that is what a sheep ranch looks like!"—lesson for that day, enough to assimilate. There it sat, that ranch, in the center of a brown and, to me, hopeless looking, bare-prairie-nowhere. Now I know there must have been wells, springs, potholes, some water, but how dry Montana *did* seem after lush California, with its hills and streams and moist foggy coast lands.

Grace had a warmth and quiet charm. I liked her from our first meeting. As I became better acquainted with Choteau's living history I found myself looking more and more carefully at her jowl each time we met. The report that she shaved daily seemed to have substance. I had an uneasy feeling that probably the rest of the story was true—that she *was* a hermaphrodite.

George Burrell, a spastic, had a little cigar stand on Main Street. Cecil Yeager, a local character who rated, used to mimic George rolling a cigarette. (No one in Montana, to my knowledge, ever smoked ready-mades.) George had a spastic reflex of forcefully exhaling, which invariably and frustratingly seemed always to occur when the Bull Durham was in the creased cigarette paper, but not yet protectively rolled. Cecil's imitation convulsed the men at the Chateau Club!

MORE LIVING HISTORY
***

JUST ACROSS FROM THE GLENLOYD lived Hoss and Alma Houck with their daughter, Mildred, only a few months my junior. Despite her youth Mildred had played a part in Choteau's living history. She had been young indeed to gain the physical status of womanhood—only ten, in fact. Thereafter, unfortunately, as the result of her "innocent child's play" with Johnny Weaver (son of Grandma Weaver's own son) several years her senior, an abortion had become necessary. Choteau accepted and digested such inevitabilities; they nourished its living history.

Alma Houck and her Choteau-dwelling sister, Stell Clelland, had grown up in Edgerton, Minnesota. We had a nucleus for friendship! I developed the closest tie to Alma, who tutored me on Choteau's living history (Omitting, of course, the part her own daughter had played in it!) Later, because the Clellands moved to Berkeley about the time we did, I had longer years to know and admire Stell, Erv and their daughters, Erma and Beth. These were all fine people. I seemed to sense their worth, though they were quite different from people I had known before. With a very few exceptions everyone in Choteau used noticeably poor grammar. They "run" when they should have "ran." They "drug" when they should have "dragged." They "done" when they should have "did" or "did" when they should have "done"! Such characteristic tics of speech seem to be set in early life and in general the language pattern appears to persist unchanged even through college education. Few college educations, however, graced Choteau in 1919!

Near the center of town, in a little gray-weathered log building, set back further than most on Main Street, Hoss Houck had his tin shop. He was an old-style tinsmith who could expertly fashion a teakettle. Factory-made products displaced such skilled craftsmanship. Hoss carried on the grosser phase of his trade—stove and furnace pipes, whatever was needed in tinsmithing in 1919.

In a little shop next door the justice of the peace, old Judge Haas (was his name Hass?), skillfully plied *his* trade as harness and saddle maker. Surprisingly, he had what was probably the largest private library in Choteau. Roy loved history and it was his probing questions about early days of the region that led the judge to loan his early unexpurgated edition of the Lewis and Clark journals. Roy and I read together of the many mighty grizzlies that they had found in the general vicinity and of the adventures some of their hunters had in fending off the attacks of these great animals when the bears became wounded. Frustrating book, it puritanically lapsed into Latin when describing the sex symbolism of Indian dances of the era. My high school Latin, though close behind me, did not suffice to translate *those* passages!

In Choteau I saw DEMOCRACY. No doubt I could have been in any small Western town and have seen it as clearly. Clarence Looney, the barber, and Johnny Moore, a drayman, were citizens held in high esteem, as indeed they should have been. Each was married, had children and was a fine, faithful husband and father. Jess Gleason, who owned a team and wagon and did hauling, was well thought of and prominent in Choteau. To be sure Jess was unmarried and his private life was his own—or almost his own! It is no coincidence that all these men were expert fishermen and hunters. They *all* rated.

One Choteau citizen loved and respected by everyone was our milkman, old Mr. Chapman. Almost seventy he must have been. How thankful I was to him! He had one specially healthy cow that gave fine rich milk. He kept that milk separate to assure Choteau's babies a good start. Mr. Chapman was well taken care of by his second wife, a good cook and housekeeper, a *very* generous woman at heart. Never did the poor or ill lack for good nourishing food and care when Mrs. Chapman knew of their plight. She was generous in other ways, too. In 1919 she was in her late thirties, I would guess. As there has never been another woman even remotely similar to Mrs. Chapman it is hard to gauge her. Dark hair and eyes, florid, not tall, most voluptuously equipped, she affected riveted denim skirts, boots and Stetson hat in a day when no *woman* "dressed Western." Back to her generosity—one early fall she went on a fortnight's hunting and camping trip in the Rockies. She was an excellent shot. (Even to look at her one *felt* she had a six-shooter in its holster strapped around her waist!) On this camping trip she was accompanied by Jess Gleason and a cowboy pal of his. As to generosity, all Choteau knew she had slept conveniently between the two men. That is how it comes about that Jess Gleason's private life was "almost his own"!

Though I have seen Mrs. Chapman, dressed in her customary uniform, sitting sedately in church, her various and many transgressions of the moral code of the church ladies (who did nothing at all about taking soup to the needy) left her devoid of feminine society, with one exception. Choteau, like many northern Montana towns, had its Chinese restaurant which served excellent American meals at unbelievably low prices. Usually these Chinese served the very best meals to be had in a northern Montana town. Soo Son (pronounced as in "on," not "sun") was no exception. Soo Son had a quiet, refined Chinese wife, whom the church ladies had seen no reason to clasp to their hearts. It was natural that these two outcasts of small town society found solace in one another's company. Though the Chinese woman seemed only a sweet nonentity to me,

I always entertained a healthy respect for Mrs. Chapman's vigor, independence and strength of her own convictions.

During our first year, another minority group was represented in Choteau by Cousin Charlie, the negro bootblack and handyman, who so liked fried chicken he insisted, "Ah eats 'em bones an' all!" Perhaps he thought on that particular dark night that dressed chickens might be stored in the basement beneath the meat market. As fate would have it, the outside entrance was by means of the familiar two great iron doors, flush with sidewalk when closed. Cousin Charlie must have raised those doors, that dark night, but not fastened them securely for, come dawn, he was found, head above sidewalk level, neatly hung by the neck in the nearly closed doors.

In Iowa the local drugstore was the hub of smalltown life. Not so in Choteau—too many saloons (we called them saloons, not bars in 1919), not to mention the Choteau Club. The Melon family— father, mother, son Russell and his wife—owned and operated the Choteau Drug Company. Old man Melon, to be sure, was not a licensed pharmacist but his registered pharmacist son looked lightly on the fact. When Father Melon felt inclined he busied himself with filling prescriptions. Choteau seemed to take it as an inevitable result of this cozy family arrangement that in one prescription for a small baby, Father's failing eyesight mistook "grains" for "grams." When the infant died there were a few hopeless wishes expressed that Father Melon would quit meddling with prescriptions, that Russell should tend to filling them himself. That was all—save the desolation of the babe's mother.

Certain others in Choteau stood eminently forth. The Hirshbergs, Ed and Arthur, Jews far displaced from synagogue and temple teaching, raised their families in this friendly Western town whose citizens looked up to them for the worth they showed in developing the area and in being good substantial members of the community. Choteau had a Hirshberg bank, the First National Bank of Choteau, and Joseph Hirshberg and Company, a general mercantile store. The rival Choteau Mercantile Company was in the MacDonald Block, a building on the southwest corner of Choteau's main intersection. Across that corner was the rival Citizens State Bank also largely owned by Charlie MacDonald. Mrs. Charles MacDonald, a refined New York woman, had come to Montana for her first teaching assignment and had been assiduously courted by the young Western rancher. After a New York wedding, out she came to live in the first house on the big MacDonald sheep ranch near Choteau. The bride had written East to her mother that she was happy, was pretty well settled, though to find a place for the extras—fine linens, dishes, glassware—that she would not presently be using on the ranch, was quite a problem. Her mother's answering letter advised, "My dear, just store them all in the attic." The ranch house was sod-roofed. That story, which Mrs. Mac told Roy's bride, came to symbolize for me the lack of understanding between the outside world and northern Montana.

Charlie Mac had a lecherous leer in his eye and plenty of money in his pocket. Mrs. Mac had her trials but long before my Choteau era she had learned to cope. In the mid-years of their marriage, in their second house on the ranch, one evening, although Charlie had not returned from town, Mrs. Mac retired fairly early. She fell asleep only to be awakened by a rhythmical thumping sound which seemed to come from the living room. Going to investigate she found that Charlie had indeed returned. He and the hired girl were on the floor. Mrs. Mac, in her sternest schoolmarm manner, told them to get up off the floor that instant and go to bed where they belonged. So Choteau's living history had the story by 1919, anyway!

HELEN MANNY AND I, in our warm relationship one to the other, have been less closely bound by common Remington ancestors than by a bond of like humor. It was for Helen, and to Helen, that I wrote the following bit of Choteau's living history in 1922.

THE BLIGHTED REDEMPTION OF A HUMAN SOUL

A True Story of Life in the Northwest in the Early '20s

By

My Husband's First

Wife

CHAPTER ONE

In the quiet little village of Choteau, nestling in the midst of the barren reaches of the northern Montana prairie in the glorious autumn of early October in 1922, the Episcopal Ladies' Guild planned a "Trip Around the World" at seventy-five cents for the round trip ticket. The purpose of the entertainment was to refill the depleted coffers of the church treasury. The plan was to guide several parties of "voyageurs" to the rectory where spaghetti with hot sauce, Italian flags and borrowed Caruso records gave the travelers a glimpse and taste of Italy; a block further, at Robinson's house, almond blossoms, tea and wafers, and girls in kimonos rendered Japanese atmosphere; four blocks further, at J. C. Taylor's, corn beef and cabbage, Irish handwork, creamed potatoes and greens made

249

one almost speak with a Tipperary brogue, then across the railroad to Norway at Crary's to eat rich numgratendam and runckuntertium wafers and see peasants in Norwegian costumes—then before returning to the good old U.S.A. at the Beaupre Hotel with coffee, doughnuts, confetti and a jazz orchestra to make the returning travelers feel at home, before this, they went to Mrs. MacDonald's apartment to China with a curio shop of Chinese things, chopsticks, bowls, rice and people in Chinese pantaloons.

CHAPTER TWO

When the ladies of the Episcopal Guild began to plan China, most intricately, they found a dearth of necessary Chinese curios and costumes. Mrs. MacDonald, herself, thought then of the charming young matron who is really the heroine of this tale—Eliza Ping. Eliza was known to possess four Chinese suits, which she used for negligee, and a great many Chinese ornaments. When appealed to by the guild ladies Mrs. Ping responded to the call. We must pause here to state that the charming young lady, in her twenties, had never before affiliated with any church work. It was like the redemption of a heathen soul when she consented to join in the work. However inheritance probably had a great deal to do with it, for Eliza's paternal grandmother had been an ardent church worker. Even in her endeavor to enrich her church when the real "grabs" gave out in the fish pond, this grandmother often just handed out wads of newspaper in exchange for the eager children's nickels. Also Eliza had a first cousin once removed, still living, who had all her life been an ardent Woman's Christian Temperance Union worker. Therefore the attractive young woman, who possessed a kind, sensitive nature, rose gladly to help in the noble task of a church entertainment, which she realized would not only benefit the church but give an evening of educational diversion to her fellow townspeople.

CHAPTER THREE

As a result for two days before the entertainment the attractive Eliza Ping busied herself with making Chinese characters on bright-colored papers for decorations, also an artistic dragon for a wall covering, and took all of her valuable possessions and "Chinese -isms" to the "curio shop." It was a hard task but Eliza rose to it gloriously, realizing how the whole affair would uplift the community.

The night of the "trip" Eliza elongated her beautiful dark eyes with gooey black marks, also changed the contour of her lovely eyebrows to slant them up and make them very black, put on sunken cheeks and shiny grease, a long thin moustache—collected from a goodly assortment of fake hair worn years ago by one of Choteau's social set—a tight old chink suit, a black skull cap and braided her beautiful, long oily hair into a Chinaman's pigtail, and for the good of her village became Wong Lee in "China." Through the long evening she ran about China serving rice to ardent voyageurs in her heelless chink slippers. The tall slender heroine did all this with great happiness, even willingly gave up the four following days to agony from lameness in the hind muscles of her lower extremities caused by the heelless slippers and the great amount of walking.

In the early evening, as Wong Lee, Eliza was practically a heathen redeemed. She felt her soul ennobled by being the tiny spoke that she was in the uplifting and beneficial entertainment that was in progress.

But it was not to be Eliza's fate to long maintain this noble attitude. In order to create atmosphere, the guild ladies had asked Mr. Shorty Joanis, the cash-and-carry grocer, to borrow Mr. A. Hirshberg's (the general mercantile man, whom Joanis' cash-and-carry business was ruining) dress suit and John Hall's (the city engineer) silk hat, which cost twenty-five dollars and was the gift of his beloved Masonic brethren, and represent Jiggs; while Mr. Myers, the butcher, in wig and evening gown, with cotton rolling pin, was Maggie, and Mr. Wyper, the dry goods clerk, was to represent an old maid. All atmosphere went as planned, and at about 10 p.m. Maggie and Jiggs on their tour, reached 'China'. They soon penetrated the tiny apartment kitchen and highly interfered with the serving of rice to travelers present in great numbers at three tables in other rooms. Wong Lee (the clever Eliza, still disguised) said to them four times, "Velly small kitchen, velly many people," but finally had to shove them a bit in order to clear the much-needed kitchen.

Poor Eliza, in her innocence, thought them only a bit thick headed and impolite. She even thought nothing of Maggie's having her (his) high-heeled shoes off and having her (his) dress low enough in front to show her (his) heart beating—though formerly, unorthodox Eliza's mind was not evil. It was not until Maggie at departure leaned heavily on Wong Lee and said, "Where—e'ugh—do we—e'ugh—go from here?" that Wong Lee noticed the intoxicating breath and answered, "Where have you been before?"

Poor Eliza was about to learn that a barber, a merchant, a doctor and a senator had passed out devilish intoxicating liquor during this eve of what she supposed to be moral uplift, and that when Maggie and Jiggs came to the jeweler's, whose wife was an ardent church worker, and received dandelion wine (receipt from the Methodist cookbook), that with the food from all the countries, and the stronger drinks, their stomachs became sadly upset.

At first Maggie just laid down to rest on Crary's lawn but soon moved on to lean over the rail of the bridge over beautiful Spring Creek which flows by the place of business of Eliza's husband. A few hours later Maggie, minus shoes and clothes above waist, was found there by Mr. Wyper, the old maid, and taken home, bathed and massaged back to life. Jiggs (Shorty) was taken home by Mrs. Shorty, not via the most direct route through the main streets, but up the railroad track and across lots. He said, "Thas it, dearie, take me home!" She said, "I'll take you to the Devil!" He said, "Dearie, I so sick—u—uu-uu—I think I'm going to throw up." She just slapped her hand over his mouth and said, "Don't you dare! You drank it, you keep it down! And don't you DARE get anything on Hirshberg's dress suit—you know perfectly well Maggie has already ruined John Hall's silk hat that the Mason's gave him. Stop now! Don't you dare let it come up!"

Mr. Wyper later returned to the U.S.A. (Beaupre Hotel) where he found others feeling the effects of getting outside the three-mile limit. Mr. L. E. Taylor, who thought Mr. Wyper didn't know that he knew that Mr. Wyper was Mr. Wyper and not an old maid, reached down and pinched Mr. Wyper's lower limb but created quite a sensation by an attempt to repeat this performance, his eyesight being impaired by imbibing strong liquids, he missed Mr. Wyper's and got a new middle-aged school marm's, who was making her debut in Choteau society. A lamentable circumstance! It was such occurrences that shook Eliza's faith in the evening's moral uplift and brought about the blighting of her soul's redemption.

Later Mr. L. E. Taylor, before an audience in front of the "U.S.A.," was proving his ability to ride a bicycle. He got it running nicely then missed the pedals and entangled his feet in the spokes so that nearly a dozen spokes had to be removed before Mr. L. E. Taylor and the bicycle were separated. Mr. Looney, the barber, greatly embarrassed his wife by attempting to don his hat in the U.S.A.; he made various wide and artistic circles but always missed his head. Shortly some kind hearted citizen carried him home.

Such horror that a soul so nearly redeemed may slip back into the old heathenish groove because of a few rather sad and boorish mishaps; but ever was it thus in the Northwest in the early twenties.

*　*　*　*　*　*　*

Author's Note—all these are actual statistics and facts.

THERE WERE A FEW PEOPLE WHO STOOD APART in the social structure that was Choteau—the DeYongs and the Guthries. Since 1919 A. B. Guthrie Jr. (Bud) had gained renown in the literary world—more specifically as a writer and authority on the Old West. He tells *his* version of the Choteau story in "The End of Their Wanderings, Choteau, Montana," a section of *A Vanishing America* edited by Thomas C. Wheeler and published in 1964, as well as in his autobiography, *The Blue Hen's Chick* published a year later.

Bud's parents were admired and highly respected in Choteau. In our day Mr. Guthrie, after having owned and edited Choteau's paper, *The Acantha*, was again principal of Choteau High School. I was very fond of Mrs. Guthrie. She was more the type of person I was used to. I think she sensed my feelings and surreptitiously mothered me a bit in our fleeting social contacts, thereby smoothing for my stumbling steps the path of adjustment in those early Choteau years. These were Bud's college years. Home on vacation he would dance with me, at the various and frequent public dances, and I would catch up on his school news.

One weekend in the summer of 1922 Roy took Laurie and me camping on Sun River, above Augusta. The Clellands had their camp nearby. Erma, fifteen, had brought along a school chum, Harriet Larson, daughter of the cattleman and state senator, Tom Larson. Bud had a job in the Sun River area. He came visiting at our camp one evening after having stopped at Clelland's. He allowed as how that little Harriet Larson was growing into a mighty cute girl. I truly think it was the first time he had looked at her to actually see her, certainly to size her up. He was pleased with what he saw for, nine years hence, they were married!

In 1924 Bud and Al Darby, with whom he had worked vacations on *The Acantha*, left poor drought-ridden Montana, like so many others, to try their luck in California. They came to Berkeley and for a while roomed at Clelland's. Bud worked for Westinghouse at Fortieth and San Pablo. Al got a job to paint white parking lines and the white lines down the center of the streets in Berkeley. It was a one man, one paint brush, one can of white paint operation, sans warning cones or signs to hold off traffic. One Sunday Al and Bud had us in hysterics planning a Rube Goldberg contrivance to accomplish the job in a more automated and safer manner. I think of the hearty laughter that Sunday whenever I see the much more complicated vehicular apparatus that stripes our highways today.

Bud had great affection for Roy. He would come for dinner in those Berkeley days. Once on an after-dinner ride Roy drove us to a lookout high in the Berkeley hills. Bud was grieving for Choteau. I was elated to be back in a city. I raved about the carpet of city lights spread before us. Bud allowed as how Montana plains would be his choice for a beautiful view. I told him that I found it a thrill even to pick up the big Bay Region phone book. He just looked at me. I sensed he was feeling sorry for me!

To be sure the thick and the thin telephone books typified the difference between city and small town. An even more revealing incident of telephone service brightens my Choteau memories.

Before the automation of the dial system, and more especially before World War II, operators (centrals, we used to call them) were puritanically restricted to about half a dozen phrases: Number, please?; The line is busy; They do not answer; The time is _____. And for the fresh guy or those with legitimate requests unanswerable by the set phrases, "I will connect you with my supervisor." It had never occurred to me that anything but formal telephone ritual *could* be used. On this memorable Choteau morning I was trying to call Miriam Shilton in Fairfield. I had been in Choteau long enough to know that it was not necessary to ask for long distance, as it would have been in Piedmont to place an out-of-town call. Through the day Choteau's entire small switchboard was operated by Dolly Graves. (On which side of the tracks Dolly belonged was problematic, but Choteau tended to give her the benefit of the doubt.) Three times I had failed to get Miriam when suddenly Dolly dropped all operator ritual of speech. Said she: "To give you the straight dope, Mrs. Pilling, that Fairfield line is on the blink."

Mary DeYong (born 1872), a trained librarian, refined, delightful, had spent her early years in Washington, D.C. Living in Choteau this wiry little woman was a cultural force in a town that knew little or no culture. Her husband ran a pool hall on Main Street. Their one child, Joe (born 1894), totally deaf as the result of some childhood disease, was his mother's build—small, well put together, wiry. He had her dark coloring and was quite unlike his big blonde father. We knew of Joe—Roy may even have met him—before we moved to Choteau. Joe was an artist protégé of Charlie Russell's.

COWBOY ARTIST
***

CHARLES MARION RUSSELL (1865-1926), son of an affluent St. Louis merchant family, came to Montana in 1880. His understanding family, after sending him for six months to a New Jersey military school, which he heartily disliked, let him enroll in a St. Louis art school, which he attended for just three days—his total formal art education. The boy's one engrossing desire was to go Out West. Though he was not yet sixteen his family arranged a job for him on a Montana ranch. No doubt they expected him to return within a few months. He never returned! He loved the West with a passion. In 1888 for six months he lived in Canada with the Bloods, a tribe of the Blackfeet Indians. He learned their sign language and legends. However it was in early 1887 that his boss wrote Charlie to ask how the herd he was wrangling had come through the winter. Charlie answered with a postcard-sized watercolor of one weak, half-starved steer, tail to storm. He wrote on it, *Waiting for the Chinook*. Later the name of this picture was changed to *Last of the 5000*. Telling so well the story of the effect of a hard Montana winter, it was his first picture to draw widespread attention.

For years before we were married Roy had known and admired Charlie Russell. To his friends Charlie's marvelous talent for spinning endless yarns of the West was as enjoyable as his artwork. Roy once wrote down the following story that Charlie had told him as he showed Roy a newly finished picture. Titling the story, *Artist with Brush and Tongue*, Roy wrote,

One of the famous characters of the old road agent days was "Big Nosed George" and Russell has painted him sticking up a stagecoach. The background is a thicket of buckbrush with a few large, wind-twisted cottonwoods and a prairie sky. The old Concord stage is at a halt and the tired ponies

258

are slouching in the harness, taking advantage of the sudden stop to blow. The driver is on his elevated seat, hands high in the air, and several passengers, typical of those good old days, have lined up alongside the coach, also doing homage to the forty-five. Among them is a sky pilot, with his Prince Albert coat and hungry look. The lone highwayman has just reached his end, in a quaking voice, the apostle speaks, "You wouldn't take money from a poor old minister of the Gospel, would you?"

Big Nosed George: "What church?"
Preacher: "Methodist."
George, as he shifts the objective of his gat (gun) to the next in line: "Put down your hands, that's my church."

The Russells lived a few blocks from the Templetons in Great Falls. The first piece of Mr. Russell's work that I saw was a bronze Indian smoking a peace pipe in the edge of a bronze ashtray at Templeton's. However it was Russell paintings that were famous. Even in 1919, David Windsor, then Prince of Wales, had bought one for ten thousand dollars. Charlie had murmured, "Dead men's prices," and truly, for that was a previously unknown selling price for the work of a living artist. Nancy Russell, fourteen years Charlie's junior, a school marm before their marriage, proved a good business manager for Charlie. She arranged one-man shows in New York, London and other large cities. One or two other ten thousand dollar sales resulted, as well as many lesser but still substantial amounts.

The Mint Saloon in Great Falls has the largest collection of Russell's works. These had been acquired in former days when

CHARLES MARION RUSSELL

Charlie paid his bar bills with a picture. Meanwhile Nancy and maturity had helped him to conquer John Barleycorn. A child of their own, who might have inherited Charlie's great talent, would have been the ideal but denied the ultimate they adopted Jackie. Early in 1919, when Roy took me to visit Mr. Russell's studio, which is now the Charles M. Russell Memorial, we stopped at their house first to meet Mrs. Russell. As we were leaving, Jackie, aged six or seven, ran up on the porch carrying a large doll, borrowed from some girl playmate, to show his mother the beauties of his temporary charge. He did seem, as Roy later remarked, a fairly large boy to be so utterly entranced by a doll but Nancy took it in stride. (Later when told Jack had been such a bitter disappointment to the Russells I often wondered just how. Except for the doll, all I ever heard, of all that he was enamored of were private theatricals and the designing of stage sets.)

We went on to the log studio next the house for me to meet Mr. Russell. Charlie was painting on a large canvas—a commission. (He heartily disliked commissions!) I was carried away by the lovely colors of a sunrise over the Montana plains so I have lost the subject and have no recollection of the precise figures involved, but I do remember the detail of one picture in the Mint because Roy had told me of the mechanism, operated by a button under the bar, that was wired to pull back the teepee flap of the picture. Roy discretely indicated this picture but of course there was no button pressing with a lady present. Out on the blank prairie stood a teepee. Outside it sat an old Indian Chief sucking on his pipe and holding a pouch bulging with tobacco. Beside the teepee, with reins thrown over his head, patiently waited a cowboy's horse. I am sure other pictures in the famous saloon showed greater skill of the cowboy artist, Russell, but none was quite so unique!!

Mary McDonald Collins, a San Luis neighbor, grew up in Great Falls. A young brother of Mary's, entranced with Russell's "Westerns," determined to own an original. Through the years he saved earnings from his paper route and odd jobs till in his latter teens he went to Mr. Russell, told Charlie how much money he had and said he wanted to buy a picture. This may have been slightly prior to the ten-thousand-a-picture sales which Nancy had engineered. As likely, it may not have been! This was a man-to-man business deal and Nancy was not invited in. Charlie helped young McDonald to make his selection and the boy left with his Russell original. Mary's father, owner of a shoe store near the Mint, took Mary as a child into the saloon to show her the Russell pictures. Too young to have been told about the wigwam flap, she knew nothing of the under-bar button wired to it.

From this era of innocence, though, Mary does remember frequently seeing a young man sitting and sketching in the back room of the shop, next the shoe store, where M. Russell had his pictures framed. The McDonald children knew this lad was a protégé of Charlie Russell's but as he never responded to their greetings they had thought him to be a deaf-mute. Not till early in the 1960s did Mary Collins learn, when visiting the Channing Peakes near Buellton, that Joe DeYong, a frequent house guest at Peake's, could talk.

Nearly forty years have passed since, shortly after Mr. DeYong's death, Joe and his mother moved to California. During that period Joe's principal work was as technical advisor on Western films. He knew the Old West and its trappings. Even as Charlie Russell could, so could Joe "talk" Indian Sign Language most competently. Though Joe has done nice sculptures of Western subjects, as well as paintings, his work is untouched by any glint of genius such as Russell's. Friendships of kindred spirits built in Montana were far from transitory. Joe, impressed by Beva's art work on our 1964 Christmas card, sent her a book he had found helpful on design and offered to share silk-screening techniques. Joe had not forgotten Roy!

February 11, 1966, Joe wrote Beva, "Your mention of your father calls to mind the fact that the first time I ever saw him was the day we came to Choteau, having—by chance—ridden up from Great Falls on the train with Charlie Russell and Ed Borein, who was to become well-known in later years in Santa Barbara. In any case your dad had an attractive personality and in addition was ALL MAN, in any company there was never any least doubt on that score."

*   *   *   *   *   *   *

Mr. Russell frequently came to Choteau to visit the DeYongs. Charlie's granite-like figure was as impressive on the streets of Choteau as in New York. No one else was at all like Charlie and not only because of his inevitable crimson wool sash which was as unusual in Montana, except on Charlie, as in New York. In Choteau of course his cowboy boots and broad brimmed Stetson melted into the landscape as they did not in New York. Mr. Russell had that stoic Indian Chief–like quality that would have placed him apart in any attire, in any locale.

In Montana in 1920 Roy had lately learned about a "pishkun" on the McDonald ranch. The Indians had various methods of controlling the direction of the stampede of a herd of buffalo that they had purposely alarmed so that the buffalo would rush head-long over a cliff predetermined by the Indian hunters. It was then easy enough to finish off the cripples which had not been killed outright by the fall. One method used on the narrowing v-route, from grazing herd to this pishkun, was the strategic placement of hunters armed with bows and with arrows tipped by tiny arrow heads. These weapons caused little or no physical harm but sufficed to confuse and stampede the herd *and* to help hold the stampede to the v-like course.

In 1920 nothing remained at the base of the cliff by the creek on the MacDonald ranch for the naked eye to perceive but a shovel and screen produced the most fascinating artifacts. It was here that we drove one day, taking with us Charlie Russell, who was visiting at DeYong's that week. Roy and I considered the real finds to be the tiny arrowheads—none more than three-quarters of an inch in length, and some wrought of Montana's beautiful native moss agate. We exclaimed delightedly over each newly found point. Roy was discerning enough to save some of the many buffalo teeth that screened out. (Later, through Ellis H. Thompson, D.D.S., many of them he gave to the dental museum of what is now the University of California Medical Center in San Francisco but which was known in my youth as the Affiliated Colleges and was in its same location at the edge of Sutro Forest.) But to Charlie, though he was interested in everything, it was the buffalo hair that most intrigued. Out came an empty Bull Durham tobacco sack and in it he tightly packed tuft on tuft of hair as it screened out. "Can't get over that hair—here it is off of those critters after all these years-Just look at that buffalo hair, will you, still here)" I think the hair made him feel closer to the days of the stone and bone. Of course he was so right! I was completely uninterested in buffalo hair at the time so I suppose I missed also some of the more subtle things about Mr. Russell but I well remember his scorn for the new Pasadena home of Nancy's parents—no doubt built from Charlie's brush strokes on canvas.

Montana was frankly cold in winter with forty-odd below recorded at Havre. Montana houses expected cold and therefore had adequate furnaces and were kept HOT. Used to California houses, less well heated in the early 1900s than they are today, I suffered. Even more so had Mr. Russell suffered in Pasadena but at the opposite extreme. He kept it no secret—"Just like meat houses, that's what all those California houses feel like. Nancy's folk's place, just like a meat house!"

In the fall of 1921 Charlie was with the group, including Roy, who camped in the Rockies west of Choteau for two weeks of October elk hunting. George Calvert, a Great Falls building contractor, and member of the Russell-Templeton social group, persuaded Charlie to go along. In those later years Charlie never hunted, wouldn't bring himself to kill one of the lovely creatures of the wild, but he loved the mountains and was a camp companion par excellence! Our Choteau next-door neighbor, George Coffey, was in the party as well as Elmer Genger, a Fairfield character. Elmer could pull his weight around camp all right but just how the sixth member of the group got there I am not at all sure. That he was an outlander I do remember. Seems a horse kicked him in the shin and he complained bitterly but on inspection there was no obvious maiming. Clearly he did not "belong" but had to be tolerated. (In retrospect I wonder if Nancy may have suggested that he be invited; he could have been a prospective customer for Charlie. He was either president or chairman of the board of Anaconda Copper.[5] I forget which.) Charlie was kind to all animal life and put up with him without complaint. They all did. Here they were packed in miles and miles of mountain trail. They were stuck with Mr. Anaconda Copper and they knew it and made the best of it.

5 Mr. Anaconda Copper, Jim Nobbins! Marcella Youlden, a fellow resident at Canterbury woods, who knew him in Butte, Montana, supplied the name in 1971!

The last Russell contact Roy and I made, accompanied by Jim Noe, was in 1936. We called on Nancy who was living in the Southern California home the Russells had built, in which to spend their latter years, only a short time before Charlie died. *Good Medicine* had been published after Charlie's death. Nancy autographed a copy for Roy. Her answers to our queries about Jack were vague.

After Charlie's death while the Montana state legislature stymied and haggled about the Mint's asking price of $80,000 for its Russell collection, the paintings were bought by a New York gallery for $125,000. This New York dealer immediately resold, without even unpacking the pictures, to Amon Carter, a Texas millionaire, for $250,000. Presently a bronze bust of Charles Russell, the self-taught cowboy artist, joined those of other great men of the nation in the Capitol rotunda at Washington, D.C., to honor Montana's most famous citizen.

After Roy's death I gave the framed Russell Christmas card, *Over the Great Divide*, that had hung in Roy's office to Jim Noe but first had a copy negative made. It is from this negative that Tom Baxter's picture was made. Actually Charlie whipped up this card for Christmas 1925 but when it was reproduced he disliked it and refused to send it to his friends. Nancy, however, must have used some for, interestingly enough, "Uncle Augie," Mrs. Seemann's brother, had one which had been given him by a Pasadena friend. Shortly before his death he gave it to Robert. Roy's came by almost as circuitous a route. Joe DeYong, visiting us in Berkeley shortly after Charlie's death, said to Roy, "Here's one of the cards Charlie didn't like well enough to send out—if you want it." Roy did!

*Here's hoping your trail is a long one
Plain and easy to ride.
May your dry camps be few.
And Health ride with you
To the pass on the Big Divide.*

OVER THE BIG DIVIDE

"Here's hoping your trail is a long one

Plain and easy to ride,

May your dry camps be few

And Health ride with you

To the pass on the Big Divide."

BESIDES SEEING CHARLIE RUSSELL in Choteau we would see other friends of Roy's Great Falls days from time to time on trips to the Falls. Always we would visit the Templetons. Occasionally we saw the Odettes and more rarely the Grahams. Once the Pratts came for a weekend with us in Choteau. But it was the Shiltons whom we saw most frequently, for Fairfield, a bleak, newly developed town some twenty miles southeast of Choteau, was headquarters of the Shilton Lumber Company. Earle and Miriam Shilton's parents were "very Chicago." They had not much approved of the young lawyer from the small town of Kawanee, Illinois, to begin with. They approved even less of Fairfield where Miriam landed after World War II. Miriam was as uncompromising as I was concerning plumbing. Roy's seniority and my aversion to outside facilities probably accounted for the fact that Roy chose Choteau, a town with water and sewer systems. Miriam was not so lucky but fared better as to housing. The Shiltons rented a new two-bedroom cottage but before she would come to Fairfield Miriam saw to it that a chemical toilet was purchased and ensconced in one of the bedrooms where it sat in solitary but functional grandeur.

It is little wonder that Miriam retreated to the Chicago Lying-In Hospital and the Baldwin ménage to have Virginia three months after Laurie was born at the Choteau Hospital. However Laurie's advent illustrated well that the miracle of birth is no less wonderful, though probably slightly more emotion-ridden, in a small town hospital in the West. All the essentials were met—the safe delivery of a beautiful baby girl. The incidents involved, to put it mildly, were a bit unusual to two of the principals implicated, the two mothers that is—for there were indeed *two* mothers.

The experience accounted for my conspicuous absence before the actual advent of my various grandchildren: "Tom excepted, for

THE ADVENT
***

267

Ned was still in the South Pacific on August 4, 1945. " Choteau 1919 convinced me that these should be hours that involve husband and wife alone through a poignant and thrilling, if slightly unnerving, experience. By the time of Arnold's birth I insisted it be so.—When I recall the profusion of floral tributes at the time of Arnold's and of Beva's arrivals in Berkeley, which was near all my family and most especially was where Roy was so well-known and so sincerely liked and admired, I marvel that Laurie made the grade with a single bouquet—six rather sorry looking carnations imported from Great Falls.

Irene had a bad time while her one and only beloved child was in labor. I had the first twinge of rhythmical labor pains about midnight Friday. Being no old hand at these goings-on I had been in a silly dither for quite some time about not reaching the hospital in time. The only method of transport these freezing nights was walking. I upped Roy and he walked me to the hospital, some four or five blocks, at 2 a.m. I arrived in plenty of time!! Nothing much happened all day Saturday, except the continuous, closely-timed pains, not too severe. My M.D., a hardy Montanan, had had enough of that by evening. He took himself off to a community dance. (He loved to dance.) Thoughtfully, he left instructions for the nurses not to call him till a reasonable breakfast hour on Sunday. So it was that Laurie was born at 8:30 a.m. Sunday, November 23, 1919.

When thoroughly awake that morning, Dr. Harmon Tolly Rhoades had ordered that I be given "a hurry-up shot." The normal, easy delivery took a minimum of his professional time and skill but he earned all his thirty-five-dollar fee, what with the battle waging in hospital between Irene and Roy. The furor was aided and abetted by my own upset confusion, it never having occurred to me in the nineteen years and eight months of my existence that my mother could be wrong about *anything*. The fact that it *was* my decision to have my first born in Choteau which was our home, rather than to return to California for the event as Irene had expected, proves that occasionally I did see a glimmer of connubial light. However I was poorly equipped to deal with the trivia surrounding the advent in the Wild West and it is the trivia that takes a toll on all concerned. I still feel that to plead I was only nineteen is no alibi. If I had faced the same situation ten years later I believe it would have seemed ten years harder. The only important thing is that the moment I saw her, I thought Laurie was the most beautiful baby I had ever seen or ever would see and my opinion has never changed. I knew Roy agreed. (He was always so gentle and loving and precious in handling each of our three tiny babies. With each of the three he would solemnly tell me that I must not expect him to care much about the tiny one; that he would have to wait till the small one grew up a bit and would go fishing and hunting with him. All the while his face would be glowing with joy as he cradled the baby in his arms.)

The Choteau Hospital which was in the center of town on the second floor of a business building, with the butcher shop fittingly situated below, had been built for room rentals. It was adequate enough with certain reservations. They had to make-do here and there. The nursery was a dark cubicle that served as a linen closet as well. The method of use was to wrap the babies in blankets and lay them on a shelf reserved for such small humans. It was cold in Montana that late November as a double wrap was used to give extra warmth—not two blankets to a baby but two babies to a blanket! Irene's reaction when she discovered the "nursery" and her first born grandchild bound to a tiny Indian breed baby was other than her son-in-law would have wished. As a matter of fact the arrangement *was* unusual. Most "breeds" tended to these matters in their village at the far edge of town. But the circumstance of the mother's high pre-delivery fever and general severe illness accounted for the cozy linen closet liaison. The mother, brought to the hospital, delivered Laurie's first little pal but remained desperately ill. However in a day or two the whole problem was solved. Both mother and babe were evicted. The Indian woman had done a double job at the hospital; she not only had had her baby, she had broken out with smallpox!!

In hospitals before World War II nurse's aides and licensed vocational nurses were unknown. Hospital care automatically meant care by a registered nurse. Not so in Choteau's hospital, which showed this one marked flair for future trends. There was always an RN on duty, to be sure, but was her word law? Ah, no! At Choteau in 1919 we had a very young, very pretty unlicensed vocational nurse aiding us when she happened to feel the urge, but always definitely lording it over the RNs. It was common knowledge that Dr. Rhoades was "sweet on Phoebe," as Choteau citizens phrased it. The fact that eventually the doctor divorced the mother of his four fine sons and married Phoebe (who by then had attained an RN of her own) in no way helped the strained working relations in the hospital nor improved service to the patients while the cold war waged in November of 1919.

One notable hospital skirmish, quite unconnected to the nurses' cold war, needs historical explanation. In 1919 and 1926 and 1928 and right through to World War II and 1942 a maternity case was hospitalized for two weeks, period. Everyone who was not a charity case, or verging on it, had a room to herself. BUT about my fifth day in the Choteau Hospital a woman—a really very nice woman from some remote ranch—was moved into my room. This was the END as far as Irene was concerned! I went right along with the revolt and became VERY upset. The woman was moved. Roy told me off in privacy for that one, suggesting I think more of the poor sick woman and less of myself. I had it coming! But back to my feeling about Mother always being right. I never did lose that feeling—what with Mama Indian's smallpox and the fact that I later learned my erstwhile roommate had a postoperative infection, one of those miserable pus deals that has no business rooming with a maternity case in ANY hospital.

CONSCIENTIOUS OBJECTOR
***

TO BACK TRACK: we had stayed at the Glenloyd about six months then rented the Houck's house while they were away during the summer of 1919. The Houck house was modern, else I would not have been interested. Modern in Choteau houses meant just one thing, INSIDE PLUMBING. The majority of Choteau homes were not modern, i.e., outside privy.

I was on the very nauseated, easily weepy side that summer. Leaving Laura in Carrie Kenny's care, Irene came to visit and get her daughter sewn into maternity clothes and equipped with properly pretty bassinet and first baby paraphernalia. Though thrilled with Irene's visit I was somewhat staggered by her insistence that she, being too lonely without me, was moving Laura and herself to Choteau; if I would not come home, they would come to me. Roy was not cheered by the prospect. He did not hesitate to voice his opinion that it was downright wicked to uproot an old lady past ninety and bring her to a six-thousand foot plateau of sheer cold. Knowing Laura I do not think she minded. Irene and Irene's child were her life entire.

By fall we were renting the four-room modern house of an elderly couple who were wintering in Long Beach. In that house a rather unusual incident of late pregnancy occurred—my attempt, dish towel in hand, on the upper step of the back porch, to shoo away a stray horse that was trying to feed on the clothes freezing dry on our back yard line. With my unbalanced figure, my urgent shoo-away gestures toppled me over. I fell from the top step to the ground below. The startled horse departed. I picked myself up unhurt. That evening when I told Roy the hilarious story of my awkwardness, far from being amused, he was deeply concerned. He need not have been; I was young and healthy.

272

Early in November down at the railroad station as the Great Northern slid to a stop, there on the platform, in a fine warm interlined coat that Irene had made for her for Montana's winter, stood Laura. Not till I actually saw her had I realized how desperately lonely I had been for my beloved Maltie—The emotion of that moment of reunion remains clearly etched today. Irene soon found quarters for Laura and herself—livingroom, bedroom and bathroom with kitchen privileges—in the Salmon house. Mrs. Salmon's mother, Mrs. Nat Collins, famous in her day as the Cattle Queen of Montana, lived with the Salmons. In 1919 the Queen was still quite a character!

Even before my confinement my dear Maltie suffered a severe stroke. She never walked again, seemed not too alert though she knew us always. She lived nearly six months. I cannot help but be glad she did. I hug close to my heart the day the sunlight shone brightly on Laurie, smiling and cooing in my arms, as I held her before Laura, who thrust aside the partial blindness of her years and SAW my lovely baby. She spoke of Laurie's bright blue eyes; she talked a bit of babytalk, even, to her happily responsive great-grandchild. Later Irene found a modern three-room cottage and moved with Laura there. Carrie Manny, always ready to travel, always ready for new experiences (how she thrilled at "a real Montana blizzard"!), always feeling the tie of Remington to Remington, came to help Irene with Laura's care.

Before the house Roy was having built for us was completed, even before Laura's death, that mighty battle of the wills of two strong characters, Irene and Roy, was waging. I stood inert between them feeling like a frail wall being battered from each side. Irene saw nothing in Montana to admire, nothing in my life there that was worthwhile. She chalked all this up against Roy. Meanwhile that miserable institution the Choteau Club (foolishly enough, I soon realized) had made me question whether Roy really wanted a wife and family. At this point I even took Laurie and went to California with Irene. I did not stay long! Roy came and fetched us home! From that time on I had a clear-cut idea of where a wife's duty lay—but I stumbled aplenty along the way.

Childhood observation had proved to me that unattached mothers lived with their married children, for this was still the custom during that period. When Roy and I were married I had simply taken for granted that eventually—and not too eventually—Irene would live with us. I soon realized this was an idle dream! Put aside living with us, Irene was *persona non grata* in Choteau as far as Roy was concerned. I felt I had failed Irene, that my home should have been her home. Yet I knew Roy was right! Our married life belonged to Roy and me to mold by ourselves—quite alone.

With all his fine qualities Roy was not always the easiest person to live with. Authoritarian and stubborn he was, but fair and just, too. He was subject to occasional black moods. Wishing I *could* help, I would sit quietly by till his depression lifted.

I loved Roy and I loved my mother. Roy and Irene each loved me dearly, that I know, yet through the years I continued to feel like a battered wall. Wall, though, is too strong a term, pane of glass might be more apt. Many times I felt on the verge of shattering; at other times I did crack a bit. Through these years I never would give up my close contacts with Irene by seeing her at times when Roy was not at home or, if separated, by letter (Irene would write daily letters and she expected and she received daily letters in return). I tried to be an adequate wife through those years, and I believe that Roy, forgiving my frailties, felt I was. Only I know the many small ways in which I failed. Herbert Templeton paid me a compliment which I cherish though I know it was not wholly deserved. Herbert said he felt my patient, passive persistence, that had resulted in the fine relationship between Roy and Irene during Roy's last few years, was one of the greatest human accomplishments of which he personally knew. Herbert was ever on the effusive side! Perhaps Herbert, too, preferred the role of conscientious objector to that of the soldier with courage to win or lose by fighting.

MONTANA MEMORIES
***

ESTABLISHED IN OUR OWN WELL-BUILT CHOTEAU HOUSE, in which Roy took such pride—despite the undercurrent of Roy and Irene's strained relations and despite my own feelings against Choteau as a *permanent* home—there was much joy in life. Our house was next the showplace of town, the George Coffey's two-storey brick residence. George, who called himself a college tramp, had spent some years at Harvard and had graduated from Stanford Law School. I enjoyed his good grammar and the stimulation of his reading tastes. My relation to Marie, his wife, deepened to close friendship. I stood with her through the numbing blow of being told that their twin sons, Jack and Jars, would be severely physically handicapped. Meanwhile Marie spoiled me outrageously. She was a marvelous cook in the Choteau sense—maker of superb pies and cakes. A richly frosted cake or a warm pie would appear on our kitchen table so often that I never myself learned to bake!

Roy had soon established himself in Choteau not only as a lumberman but as a community leader. Business in Choteau demanded a lot of idly making friends and getting acquainted, standing leisurely visiting on the street corner with other business men—all so strangely different from city business life.

Choteau claimed a population of one thousand but five hundred of those were Indian half-breeds living in the "breed camp" at the far edge of town. Except when a breed was contacted about taking in washing or tanning a hide, little was seen of them. By necessity, though, their children came into town to attend the grade school, housed in a typical old two-storey frame school building centered in a big playground area surrounded by trees. At recess time with the wind right, one could smell the school from the distance of more than a block! I became passionately dedicated to the premise that Laurie would not grow up in Choteau, would not go to that

276

SCHOOL. Roy could not understand my feeling. Now I know worse things could have happened to Laurie. I did not think so *then*.

*   *   *   *   *   *

I doted on taking Laurie and riding with Roy in the Dodge into the surrounding country. In 1920 most of Montana's roads were unpaved and frequently rutted and bumpy. Often as not Roy took off across the trackless prairie and to my amazement arrived at his predetermined destination. He seemed always to know just where he was in this vast outdoor land.

Roy invariably owned two or three horses, so sometimes our drives would be to 'see a man about a horse'—to me at times, it seemed he went to see 'a horse about a man'. Roy had an ability to know just where to find a certain horse he had turned loose on the range to graze, and the way he recognized each horse he had ever seen, as easily as I would a person I had met and visited with half an hour, fascinated and mystified me. Obviously more than the brands were involved, for he could identify a horse from afar even though it might be running with a strange bunch on the range. (There survives a bill of sale having to do with "all right, title and interest, in and to a five-year-old white gelding, named Tommy, and branded on the left shoulder.") Roy himself would draw up bills of sale, deeds, this or that legal paper as though Choteau were an attorney-less, do-it-yourself, pioneer land. This quick filling out of legal papers by a lay person I found not only confusing but almost frightening. If perchance Roy had gone to see a man (not a horse!) and if he had not previously known the man, there would be no crude getting directly to the business of the day. Roy always spent a relaxed interval with the man first. Indian-like he would lean against the side of the building or counter or fence near the man and say nothing—just silently lean or possibly lean and whittle a few silent moments. Then they would both be ready for business talk.

Roy carried his .22-caliber rifle in the car to have it handy for coyotes. Montanans *always* shot coyotes and jackrabbits, which were such a crop menace that occasionally rabbit drives were organized to exterminate as many as possible. Roy took great satisfaction in my taste for wild game. How many kinds we did have in Montana! In the fall, visiting his outlying lumberyards, Roy would take his shotgun along. Returning in the late afternoon he would sneak up on a pothole or two and come home with a brace of teal, or a mallard drake and hen, or some pintails. That evening by the furnace in our big basement together we would pick and dress the ducks. Occasionally there would be prairie chickens or grouse. Always with the October hunt in the Rockies there would be elk meat—or almost always. Once it turned out to be moose, which though legal over the Canadian line was taboo under Montana law. Nevertheless we had two huge, coarse-haired, Indian-tanned moose hide rugs after October 1920. The meat of antelope and mountain sheep, also illicit but donated by Jess Gleason, I found delicious, but Jess' gift of an illegal mountain goat roast proved too gamey even for me!

Montana offered a wild harvest for the making of jelly. Chokeberries, though the most scarce, made the most delectable jelly. The serviceberry (known to Choteau as the "sarvice" berry) was a good jelly maker. The buffalo berry (bullberry) was the most plentiful and the easiest to gather—spread a canvas under the bush, beat the branches with a stick, and you had gathered your jelly *and* your wine. This was during Prohibition; *everyone* made bullberry wine.

Our longest Montana trip, four September days in 1922, was camping through the east side of Glacier Park. It was on that trip that we had our mysterious hitchhiker. Anyone walking on a road anywhere in northern Montana was automatically picked up by the first car that passed. Montanans were usually riding horseback when not in cars. The occasional man, come upon walking, invariably wore cowboy ranch clothes and immediately told what errand or mischance had him afoot on the road. Our Glacier trip hitchhiker was completely devoid of a duffle and wore citified clothes—inexpensive blue serge suit and felt hat. He rode with us more than fifty slow bumpy miles in complete silence. Whither he came, whither he might be going, we never solved. Once more alone, we stopped at an old Indian cemetery between Browning and Badger Creek Agency. On a natural mound were a few burial houses (crude wood shelters), the bodies wrapped mummy-like in bright-colored quilts. Most of the burials were on the level, in shallow graves. Over the years, the elements and the gophers (ground squirrels to Californians) had brought bones and artifacts to the surface; a skull here, and there an arm bone, ringed by half a dozen corroded copper wire bracelets, a rusty spoon, beds, a small stoppered bottle. On we went to Glacier. We had idyllic campsites to ourselves at streamside and lake edge with massive glaciered mountains for a backdrop.

One other trip we took, though just the span of a day, to attend the Lewis County Fair at Augusta, stands clear in retrospect. After we had looked at the fine livestock exhibits, another feature of this September 1921 Fair intrigued Roy—an "aeroplane" ride. The tall young blonde pilot told us he would take the three of us aloft for ten dollars. Roy was eager for us to have the experience of a plane ride. I was not eager at all! I demurred on the premise that, though the young pilot was fine appearing, he seemed too young, too inexperienced, *too inadequate*. We did not go up. Sometimes I question my own flash judgment! Less than five years later, that pilot proved adequate enough to fly the ATLANTIC! No one had *ever* done that before! Had I shared Roy's enthusiasm, Laurie and I could say we had our first airplane ride with Charles Augustus Lindbergh. He was barnstorming that summer at fairs in the Northwest.

We sat in our car at the edge of the Fair's rodeo ground to watch the events, and were startled to hear them announced in loud tones for all to hear. "The Magnavox," they told us—our first inkling of a public address system. As we sat watching the rodeo, another Choteauite came to the Fair. Mr. Porter, Choteau's Great Northern and Western Union agent, handed us a telegram. Grandmother Elizabeth Chambers had died.

ALL OUR CHOTEAU YEARS were difficult years for Irene. Menopause dealt lightly with her, nevertheless it came during those years. For a time Irene had an apartment in Bend, Oregon, in the same building with Carrie and Helen Manny. Subsequently she took housekeeping rooms in Great Falls, sacrificing comfortable living among her friends in California just to be nearer Laurie and me. She was a desolate, wandering soul. Then quite suddenly came a turning point in Irene's life. In October 1921, word came to Irene in Great Falls that Flora Gladding had died. Immediately followed the news that Flora's will named Irene an equal beneficiary with Mrs. MacAdam in the estate. Irene returned to California. Ten Monte was conveniently free of tenants but Irene was barely started in the legal intricacies of the equal distribution of Gladding property when she went into surgery. The breast tumor was indeed malignant and far advanced. Dr. Charles ("Gus") Levison was one of San Francisco's finest surgeons. The subsequent, newly instituted postoperative course of X-ray treatments proved entirely successful. Arthur had summoned me when Irene was hospitalized. Laurie and I were present therefore, when on November 10, 1921, Irene, back at 10 Monte and convalescent, was married to Arthur for the second time. Roy was heartened by the turn of events—substantial inheritances for Arthur and for Irene, then their remarriage.

Year after dry year the drought continued. Northern Montana was a near disaster area. Consequently retail lumberyards were not making money. Arthur, after the rice fiasco, had resumed his lucrative contracting business in California. He urged Roy to come and take over his share of the business, into which he had already inducted George DeGolyer. By late December 1922 our household effects were en route to Oakland. Roy, Laurie and I spent a pleasant leisurely yuletide in Pipestone and Minneapolis with Roy's family.

Moved to California, nothing seemed to work out right—quite like the majority of all business ventures in which relatives are involved. There were certainly two sides to THIS story. As usual, both sides battered at my weak and passive resistance to ensure complete family chaos. Surely Arthur and Irene did everything they knew how to do for us, and meant well by it. Not surprisingly, to Roy everything about the business, the Bay Region and cities in general was hateful. He had loved and DID LOVE Montana. When matters were at a low, low ebb Berkeley, having just adopted the city manager form of government, selected Montana's Chief Highway Engineer, John North Edy, as its first city manager. John came to a strange city where he knew no one. He had to reorganize a large city government. He had to have at least one man he knew to be absolutely faithful to him and devoid of local prejudices. In Montana, his good friend, Herbert Templeton, had told him to contact Roy Pilling which he did at this psychologically low moment. Roy became purchasing agent for the City of Berkeley and subsequently assistant city manager. Harry Jamison, a graduate student in public administration at the University of California, had some assignments at city hall. Instantly Roy and Jamie became fast friends.

Settled in Berkeley but still lonesome for Montana, thoughts of Charlie Russell and Joe DeYong stimulated Roy to try sculpting. First his deft fingers shaped in clay over a crude armature a starving, winter-worn prairie horse, *April 1920*, the prototype of the hundreds of horses and cattle on the Montana plains that met death in that too-late spring and whose carcasses were collected and shipped East to glue factories by the *trainload*. Next Roy began using plasticine. Together we learned about making molds and casting his pieces in plaster. Starting with bas-reliefs, like the one which indicates, by the strong clear-cut lines of the steer and the misty bison, that the plains buffalo were being supplanted by domestic herds, he went on to do a bust of the Indian Chief, Red Cloud.

Through reporters at City Hall, the word of Roy's sculptured Western subjects got about. *The Oakland Post-Enquirer* in September 1923 sent a photographer and reporter for a home interview. A full-page feature was devoted to Roy's hobby of preserving the story of the vanishing Old West in sculpture. It made a most interesting page, and was due recognition of which to be proud.

In 1965, in one of his *Chronicle* columns, Herb Caen defines "the Victorian pinnacle of respectability" as "getting their names in the paper only twice—birth and death." I seemed to have absorbed from Laura the feeling that the better people never had their names in newspapers, that it was only the objectionable social climbers who sought publicity. I nearly perished with shame about Roy's *Enquirer* page: actually it took me till Roy's death to view personal publicity rationally—and even gratefully. At that period of the '30s, radio news automatically meant the 10 p.m. Richfield Oil Company's news broadcast, which was listened to throughout most of the Western states. One item of the *Richfield Reporter*'s news on January 6, 1937, was the quite sudden death of the Director of Relief for Los Angeles County, Roy. W. Pilling. By morning came wires and phone calls from as far as Montana, as well as from far-flung friends and relatives along the Pacific seaboard—Marie Coffey, Ralph Walt, Genevieve Chambers Case, Harry Jamison, the Bill Milners, the Gilman Smiths. Everyone knew. I did not have to tell people: *that* hurdle was conquered for me by publicity; by the "news" which ever before I had been contemptuous of. It is well I learned my lesson then, for it seems that one way or another, each of those nearest and dearest to me has had a picture in one paper or another, because of one thing or another, at one time or another ever since. Thankfully I have reacted to this legitimate publicity with normal pride!

Roy took a few lessons in the techniques of sculpting from a strange, quiet professional sculptor, Bill Manatt, who starved happily along in a dank tankhouse on Dwight Way below College Avenue. He invited Bill for dinner a time or two; after that Bill automatically dropped by occasionally for a good warm home-cooked meal and a long evening conversation of silence. He never knew when to go home. We both enjoyed his coming and dreaded his not leaving. In 1925 Roy did a very good portrait head of Jack Edy, teenage son of John and Polly Edy. (Before that Roy had created a head of Laurie, with her neat Dutch cut hair but, because he used the blank eyes of Grecian sculpture, as a portrait the work seemed unconvincing. A high relief profile head of Laurie which he made seemed much more pleasing.) Bill Manatt, as he stopped by to gorge, offered a suggestion or two on Jack Edy's eyes. The finished plaster head was a good likeness and a quite delightful work of art.

In later Berkeley years Roy added to his sculpturing the hobbies of trout–fly tying and the complicated manufacture of finely callipered split Tonkin Bamboo fly-rods. (Beva's talent in art and in craftsmanship surely marks the truth of inheritance. How Roy would have thrilled at her perfection of rendition!) Roy's vacations were spent deer hunting with his pharmacist friend, Ralph Walt, and Jamie. Sometimes their hunting camp would be on Walter Schwan's family ranch in Mendocino County, other times in Modoc County where they hunted mule deer.

Roy had an ardent interest in history and archeology. In Berkeley when Arnold was little more than a toddler Roy was entranced by every scrap of news concerning the archeological finds, in the Holy

Land, of Dr. Bade, who had led a most successful expedition there under the sponsorship of Berkeley's Pacific School of Religion. Bade made headlines. Local papers carried full pages picturing his expedition and the artifacts found. I like to feel that Roy's zeal was communicated to his son. I know he would have been pleased with Arnold's choice of career. He felt keenly that he wanted to have his children pick one subject to specialize in, rather than spread their educational and career interests too thinly.

Roy was tremendously active in Berkeley community affairs. He worked closely on projects with University of California's Robert Gordon Sproul, Monroe Deutsch, various faculty members and numerous other of Berkeley's professional people and business executives. Roy seemed to know everyone and, with his propensity for drawing people to him in friendship, everyone seemed to like and admire him. He transferred his American Legion membership to Berkeley's Post 7. He was invited to membership in an exclusive Berkeley luncheon club, sort of a local Rotary, the Twenty-One Club. Later he became club president.

In 1926 in California an attempt was made to curb the octopus-like growth of the Bank of Italy by denying further charters. Various subterfuges were used to secure national charters for new branches. In December 1926 a national charter from Washington was granted the Commercial National Bank of Berkeley, which opened on the southwest corner of Shattuck and University Avenues. After three and a half years in public administration, an offer from private business sounded attractive to Roy. His wide acquaintance in Berkeley had already sounded attractive to Bank of Italy officials, who were dictating moves from behind the scenes. When the new bank opened, Roy was vice president. Gilman Smith's father, who had been instrumental in pulling Washington strings for the charter, was named president. Roy and Gilman's friendship began.

Before long, the bank became a branch of the Bank of Italy even in name. In October 1930, after the Bank of Italy had absorbed the Bank of America and preempted its name, the Berkeley branches of the two banks merged. Roy became a vice president at the Bank of America at Shattuck and Addison where Bill Milner was also a vice president. Soon Bill and Daisy Milner were coming to us for evenings of bridge, even more than Gilman and Helen Smith.

ROY TENDED TO BE DISCONTENTED in whatever position he held. Always he was looking beyond, with high hopes of a more satisfactory situation. Whether this was simple ambition or an emotional quirk, or the urge of the true ability he did possess to administer from the top, I never could quite decide. At all events Roy did not find the Bank of America, with its original officers so firmly entrenched, a likely opportunity for advancement. In 1932 he became Chief Collector of the Federal Land Bank, with headquarters in Berkeley. This job did not develop as he had anticipated. Further, there was a personality conflict with his immediate superior. Right BANG in the midst of the full-flowering Depression Roy resigned. Thanks to a lead from Jamie, before long in 1933, Roy was working for the State Emergency Relief Administration (SERA) with offices in San Francisco. He rose to Assistant State Relief Administrator. While he was Acting State Relief Administrator, in January 1935, the Los Angeles County Citizens' Relief Committee, convinced that he was the man to reorganize an administration that was rife with "chiseling," that was dispensing relief funds to 400,000 people, offered Roy a thousand dollars a month to come to Los Angeles, which was at the time "conceded to be the darkest spot on America's 'relief' map."

Roy had not wanted to leave Berkeley, where we were comfortably settled, where the children were in good schools, where he had so many friends, but once moved and somewhat accustomed to the manifold problems of one of the biggest relief jobs in the United States, Roy found satisfaction in the home he bought for us in Glendale. He had nearly completed a studio-workshop in the rear garden and was having a little more time to relax. The old stomach trouble, which had begun to bother him again in Berkeley banking days, still pestered him, but Roy had become somewhat

THE END
* * *

287

adjusted to the discomfort, which *seemed* to be no worse. He was at his office as usual six days before his death.

With the rapid and far-flung spread of the news of Roy's death came not just conventional notes of sympathy but scores of long letters, each detailing the writer's feeling for Roy, and appraisal of him. Resolutions in memoriam were passed by various and many organizations. Chairman A. E. Young of the Los Angeles County Citizens' Relief Committee released a statement to the press saying in part, "The loss of Mr. Pilling is a calamity to the community." The *Berkeley Daily Gazette* of January 8, 1939, told that the following Sunday a redwood tree in the East Bay Regional Park would be dedicated as a living memorial to Roy W. Pilling, and credited him with a key part in bringing about the successful consummation of the East Bay Regional Park project. Speaking at the dedication, Charles Davis said, "(He) threw his influence toward development of this area at a time when it was needed most and will be of lasting benefit to the people of the East Bay."

Ralph Walt wrote, "His death was an awful shock to everybody, as he was the most loved man in the East Bay. The day the report came here, the phone rang constantly."

A letter from Jamie told us, "The last letter I received from him was full of contentment with his life. He spoke about enjoying the work around the house and his checker playing with the Boy."

Herbert Templeton's long brotherly letter said in part, "His sense of humor was one of the finest and staunchest things I have ever known in human character. Have you read Hutchinson's *If Winter Comes?* The author makes one high point in his story—viz., that a thing is right or it is wrong, there is no middle ground— no room for argument or shifting position. That was Roy most thoroughly—even to the point of stubbornness it sometimes seemed to me—for he was terribly stubborn."

Carmen Seemann Lyon's letter warmed me with its reference to the Stanford Camp Fremont days. Now it seems to have had a prophetic note. "Seems such a short time ago that we were all carefree college youngsters with our decisions to make and our destinies to fulfill. How soon some of them are to be completed."

Quotes from many different letters outline character traits in an accord of summation of Roy's fine qualities.

the most magnificent human being I have ever known

his ability and courage

the almost unfailing accuracies of his judgment

his ability and keen sense of equity

his unswerving loyalty to ideals and standards leaves a strong permanent influence that is monumental

under fire, under praise, under pressure he was at all times Roy Pilling—the simple essence of personal honesty and sincerity

here walked a man who lived in honesty and justice, kindness and strength and again and again in honesty

public service can ill afford to lose men like Roy Pilling

a forceful administrator [with a] cooperative way of working with others

[few] who inspire such an intense feeling of loyalty and affection in the hearts of their associates

what a help and source of strength Roy was to me in my work

so strong, so thoroughly masculine as to appear rough at times yet sensitive as a child

To the following and final excerpt from letters of condolence I humbly add, Amen: "I don't think any man loved his family more than he did."

The *Los Angeles Daily News* of January 6, 1937, mentioned Roy's "colorful career" and credited him with having "played a dominant role in the affairs of three Western states as a soldier, lumberjack, merchant, bank executive and public administrator." The same article quoted Roy as having recently said, "I was never cut out for desk work, and I am convinced I was born fifty years too late—If I had my life to live over again I'd never come within a hundred miles of a city."

AFTER ROY'S DEATH, Elizabeth moved her children to Carmel, California, not far from her parents. Her mother, Irene, had designed, and she and Arthur had built, another house, this one at 1015 Vaquero Road in Pebble Beach. Here she and Arthur spent their final days.

In Carmel Elizabeth raised her children on her own, as a single mother. After they had all gone off to college at Cal, Berkeley, she married Ray Lyon, the widower of her college friend, Carmen, mentioned in this memoir. Ray was a superior court judge in San Luis Obispo, California. After Ray's death, Elizabeth vacated their home in San Luis Obispo (now an Alpha Phi sorority house at Cal Poly), so his children could inherit it, and moved into Canterbury Woods, a retirement community in Pacific Grove, near where she had spent her early summers. After a decade of 'retirement', full of volunteer work, travel, and time with friends and family, capped by a period of convalescence following a major stroke, she died in 1978.

www.ingramcontent.com/pod-product-compliance
Lightning Source LLC
Chambersburg PA
CBHW061959090426
42811CB00006B/986